SEPARATION AND THE VERY YOUNG

This is the first history of the work of a uniquely influential couple in the field of child health. In the 1950s James Robertson, a young psychoanalyst, pioneered research into the psychological effects of separation from Mother when a young child went into hospital. His results, captured in two internationally renowed films, gradually transformed hospital practice in the 1960s. Visiting and staying with the child became freely encouraged, a practice now sufficiently widespread for its novelty to be too easily taken for granted.

Separation and the Very Young describes the work of James and Joyce Robertson, initially on hospital practice, and later on fostering and the problems of childcare services. It is a lively text, full of reminiscences and hard-hitting polemic, combined with many unforgettable film stills.

James Robertson was a psychiatric social worker and psychoanalyst based at the Tavistock Clinic and Institute, London, from 19848 until 1976. He died in 1988. **Joyce Robertson** was a student at the Anna Freud Wartime Nurseries, and worked at the Anna Freud centre from 1956 until joining her husband to work at the Tavistock Institute.

James and Joyce Robertson, 1979

SEPARATION
AND THE
VERY YOUNG

James and Joyce Robertson

'an association in which the free development of each
is the condition of the free development of all'

Free Association Books / London / 1989

First published in Great Britain 1989 by
Free Association Books
26 Freegrove Road
London N7 9RQ

British Library Cataloguing in Publication Data
    Robertson, James
    Separation and the very young.
    1. Hospitals. Patients: children. Care.
    Psychological aspects
    I. Title   II. Robertson, Joyce
    362.1'9892

    ISBN 1-85343-097-8
    ISBN 1-85343-096-X pbk

Typeset by MC Typeset, Gillingham
Printed and bound in Great Britain by
Billing & Sons Ltd, Worcester

Contents

List of Illustrations

Acknowledgements

During the writing of this book we have looked back over 50 years and memories of people we wanted to acknowledge came flooding back.

This is our opportunity to say thank you: to John Bowlby and Anna Freud, who recognized the potential in James before he did himself and who opened doors that set him on his way. To Pat Willard, James's secretary from 1950 until 1973, who weathered the early ups and downs with him and who became fully identified with the hospital cause; who then took me under her wing when I joined the Tavistock in 1965. To Jack Chambers, who helped edit the two hospital films in the 1950's coping admirably with the technical problems which James's enthusiastic innocence presented. To Arnold and Ina Shalon Behr who worked with us on the editing of the five films in the *Young Children in Brief Separation* series. They showed enormous sensitivity to the subject and great patience with our amateur struggles in the film world. To the children, Jane, Lucy, Thomas and Kate, who taught us so much, and to their parents for entrusting them to our care; to John, Laura and Sally's parents for their co-operation at a time of stress. To the many doctors and nurses all over the world who welcomed us into their wards and to the matrons of day nurseries and residential nurseries who allowed us to observe, and who gave time to discussing our observations. To the Tavistock Institute of Human Relations and the Irving B. Harris Foundation, Chicago, who supported the setting up of the Robertson Centre. To the Grant Foundation, New York, who funded our research for eleven years in a generous and insightful way. To Ann Scott of Free Association Books for commissioning the book and for her creative suggestions for its final form. To our daughters Katherine and Jean and their families who lovingly supported me during the months after James's death and without whose practical help the book would never have been completed.

The publishers would like to thank Margaret Walker, Tavistock Joint Librarian, for making the Robertsons' films available to them and for providing bibliographical assistance.

Preface

It is with mixed feelings that I write this preface – sadness that James is not here to write it himself and great pride that I was his colleague and life partner for nearly 50 years. What has become Parts 1 and 2 of this book was written during his last two years, and our joint work on the whole manuscript finished just three weeks before his death in December 1988. During the spring of 1989 some changes were made and some ideas amplified or clarified when the manuscript was edited.

This was a difficult time, but I was helped by our family and encouraged by the many obituaries and letters of affection and appreciation that came from all over the world. 'Children throughout the world have reason to be grateful to him', wrote Jean Lovell-Davies in the *Guardian*, while from Australia Dr Dennis Merrington, the founding president of the Association of the Welfare of Children in Hospital, paid this heartfelt tribute: 'It is difficult to recall others during this century whose work has similarly combined compassion and steadfast application and has so successfully catalysed a total reappraisal of child care.'

Our two daughters and I had felt for a long time that a book tracing some of the changes in the lives of children that (our, but especially) James's work had influenced, ought to be written, because much of it was known only to him. We argued that it was a bit of social history that should not be lost. He was reluctant because the very nature of the single-minded battle that he fought on behalf of parents and children in hospital, and the eventual success of his endeavours, could make such a book sound like a self-congratulatory exercise, and an unavoidable streak of criticism of fellow professionals and lay people might irritate readers.

While walking on Hampstead Heath – an activity we enjoyed in our eventual retirement – I often tried to talk him into this writing but he continued to resist, until I suggested in 1986, that he write it for his grandchildren who were becoming interested in knowing about our lives. That was the trigger. However, there was a problem – his sight was failing. A word processor with a large screen and tutoring from a patient and knowledgeable grandson solved the problem.

Once started he could admit the real purpose of the writing. This generation of parents, doctors, nurses and social workers needed to know that some of the improvements in child care and in hospitals were hard won, and called for a continuing awareness if the improvements were to be held and built upon. He knew only too well that defences could come into play and erode the improvements.

It was therefore a happy coincidence when Ann Scott from Free Association Books approached us with a view to publishing a history of our work. We were able to offer her an almost completed historical account, and our selection of photographs from the films, and a collection of other papers from which Parts 3 and 4 of the book were compiled.

Although this book traces our work chronologically, it is introduced by a paper written in 1970, more than 20 years after James began observing in children's wards, and almost at the end of his study of young children in brief separation. It begins the book because it provides a context for all that follows. The core of the problem, as we gradually understood it, was professional anxiety, the defences against it and the blindness that could ensue. Whatever criticisms of professionals we have made should be seen in this theoretical light. More importantly still, it was James's conviction that film could pierce those defences and open professional eyes as the written word could not do, which gave direction to our professional lives.

Part 1, A Phase in Paediatric History, traces James's work in this area from 1948, including the making of the two hospital films and the reaction of the medical and nursing professions to them.

Our research and the films that resulted are different from most others. Statistical research, that dips in and observes many children for a period of time each day or each week, did not satisfy our curiosity about child behaviour. We wanted to know not only what a child did, but also what led up to that behaviour and what followed it. All of our film studies were backed by written observations which covered the child's waking hours, and with the fostered children discussed in Part 2, covered the nights also. The time spent on the actual filming was no more than 30 to

40 minutes a day. In Part 2 therefore, 'Young Children in Brief Separation: A Fresh Look', the children's case notes are given fairly fully. This is especially true of Kate: because she was able to express herself well and because she stayed for a month she taught us a lot. We hope the reader too will agree that the detail is worth while and of a kind not to be found elsewhere.

Such a level of observation was strenuous in the extreme. To act as a foster-mother to a young, separated child was something I anticipated with fear and trembling; add to that the role of observer under the eye of a camera and you have some idea of the task.

The camera man had his own problems: a foster-mother who saw her main task as caring for the child, who would not have bright lights which might disturb the child, had no eye for camera angles, and was unaware of the wonderful shots that got away. It was, as I say, strenuous, but for us the only way to get at the truth about separation behaviour; we were not surprised that others did not copy us. Perhaps only a husband–wife team could have done it. We had absolute trust in the ability of the other, knew that each would keep to his side of the fence, and each of us respected the decisions of the other – I on the care and well-being of the child and James on the filming.

Here let me say something about ourselves. Our backgrounds were similar and we developed together along a psychoanalytical path.

James in Glasgow and I in London, had grown up in closely knit working-class families, where babies were cuddled, fed on demand, and picked up when they cried. Toddlers were always under the eye of Mother, Father, or Grandma, who were ready to comfort, protect or chastise. We grew up knowing that young children needed their mothers or someone else who loved them, and were sensitive to the pain that separation could cause.

James had become a Quaker in his late teens and when the war broke out he registered as a conscientious objector. He joined the Pacifist Service Unit in the East End of London in 1940, working with the victims of the bombing.

We joined Anna Freud in the Hampstead Wartime Nurseries in 1941, at the time of our marriage, I as a student caring for infants and very young children who had lost family life through the bombing of London, and he to organize the maintenance and fire-watching services. He eventually became the social worker. The teaching we got from Anna Freud on the psychological development of young children fell on fertile soil, and from her we gained the theoretical basis for what we knew in our bones. A wartime Social Science Diploma led James into the Psychiatric Social Worker course at the London School of Economics in 1947.

It was then a logical step for James to join John Bowlby at the Tavistock Clinic in 1948, to make observations on the behaviour of separated young children to be used in Dr Bowlby's theoretical writings. James was by then a young father, and I was at home caring for the children. Both of us were fully in sympathy with Dr Bowlby's concern about the child's need for continuity of mothering care – a concern which is still shared without reservation, though we parted company on other issues later. During this period James trained as a psychoanalyst sponsored by Anna Freud.

In 1957 I, having stayed at home until both daughters were settled at school, returned to work at the Anna Freud Centre, observing mothers and babies in the Well Baby Clinic, and later in a residential nursery; the papers in Part 3 were written during this period. I joined James at the Tavistock Clinic in 1965, to do the Young Children in Brief Separation research.

In 1975 we retired from the Tavistock Clinic and formed the Robertson Centre, and Part 4 reports on that final phase of our work. It was a particularly enjoyable phase because we were surrounded by long-term colleagues and friends, and joined by our daughter Katherine, who had sensitized her parents to separation when she was taken into Great Ormond Street Hospital as a baby, when parents were allowed only to see their children through a glass panel.

By this time we were accepted as specialists on the emotional needs of infants and very young children, but on our travels around the world we never quite got used to the V.I.P. treatment. We had spent so many years learning about the under-three-years-olds that we were sure we knew more than any one else that we had met, but we did wonder aloud whether we were in danger of seeming arrogant.

After each trip to Australia and New Zealand we would spend some days in Honolulu, in a hotel overlooking Waikiki Beach. I recall the last time, in 1979, with nostalgia. We stood on the balcony on a warm evening, listening to the doves in the palm trees, watching the surf as it broke on the beach, and we took stock. We decided that we were not arrogant, but that together we were unshakeable in what we knew about the emotional needs of infants and young children. This knowledge we had gained over 50 years of close contact with infants and very young children in a variety of settings – hospitals, day nurseries, residential nurseries, baby clinics, mother–toddler groups, foster care and families.

General Introduction:
The Problem of
Professional Anxiety*

James and Joyce Robertson

IT IS COMMON KNOWLEDGE that experiences in the first years of life have a profound influence upon later mental health. In particular, it is known that to ensure good social and emotional development the young child needs a stable relationship with a responsive mother figure (Bowlby, 1951). This is an experience that most young children find within the security of their families.

An implication of this knowledge is that if a young child has for any reason to lose the care of his mother, it is essential that his experience of responsive mothering be maintained. But at the present time, if a young child goes into hospital without his mother, he will be handled by a succession of nurses, and if he goes into residential care he will rarely find there a stable mother substitute.

Why does this happen? Why is it that although the importance of meeting the emotional needs of young children is well established by research, and is taught in many trainings, this requirement of mental health is not well attended to in our child-care practice? Why is it that although we know it to be imperative that young children have stable relationships, we still fragment their care among many people when they come into hospital or other residential settings?

If the relevant professions had a serious concern to meet the mothering needs of young children in their care, practical difficulties arising from staff shortages and the short working week might be found to be hard to overcome. But scanning the journals of the paediatric, nursing and other caretaking professions reveals that, although there is an

* This was originally given as an unpublished lecture in 1970.

1

endeavour to provide play and education, there is little or no reference to the much greater need for mothering-type care.

Systems of care that disastrously fragment relationships can operate in institutions busy with 'child-oriented' activities, and are more likely to result from planning for work efficiency than from staff shortage. It is well known, for instance, that even in large teaching hospitals where there is no staff shortage, nursing is commonly organized on a 'job-assignment' basis in disregard of the emotional needs of the young patients, even though in the same hospitals the nurses are likely to be taught the importance of stable relationships.

The major obstacle to suitable care is neither practical difficulty nor lack of knowledge. It is that, whatever level of intellectual understanding may obtain throughout the professions, the appropriate sense of urgency and alarm is missing, or is dampened down. There is a tendency for even the best-educated and the best-motivated of people working with young children to become to some extent habituated to the states of distress and deviant behaviour that are commonly found in young children in hospitals and other residential settings.

Thus the medical or nursing student, who in the beginning may be seriously affected by the distress of the young patients separated from home, will in time develop a 'second skin' against being upset by these painful sights and sounds. Later encounters with similar distress make less and less impact than did the first, and to some extent sensitivity is blunted.

Similarly, at more senior levels those who are all the time associated with situations of stress for young children – the executive officer with absorbing administrative responsibilities, the child-care officer with a heavy case load – may become distanced from the problem and lose the sense of urgency which goes with full awareness.

Intellectually there may be good understanding of the typical distress responses in newly separated toddlers and of the personality impoverishment that results from lengthy experience of discontinuous relationships common in residential care and in long-stay hospitals; but because concern is blunted the reality situation has a certain psychological distance even for those working within it.

Paediatricians, child-care officers, policy-makers and administrators may understand very well that the behaviour of bright and disarming, deprived young children is unsatisfactory development, yet take comfort from the bland behaviour just because it is superficially reassuring and fits into the need for peace of mind.

The worker's defence against pain may cause him unwittingly to avert from the newly admitted child whose extreme distress is painful to see, accepting with resignation that this is inevitable and that in time this child, too, will merge with the others who are bright and unattached. Young children tend to be seen *en masse* or only fleetingly as people, with little awareness of their individuality and less of their extended individual experience. Although this may be imposed by the nature of the job, the fleeting contact or the view *en masse* can only be a way of defending against the hurt of coming close to the plight of the individual in distress.

It has to be acknowledged that this defence against hurt is not confined to the professions. It is used by all human beings as a way of dealing with persistent threats to comfort, becoming deaf or blinkered as the situation requires. But when it becomes insidiously effective in the caretaking professions, a consequence is not only reduced stress for the worker but the sense that the problem itself seems less pressing.

Even the literature comes to have less meaning than in student days when it was first learned that early separation from the mother into hospitals and residential institutions commonly results in overwhelming distress – in protest and despair. These phrases, so evocative when first encountered during training, come in time to be barriers against the empathic pain they once aroused. Familiarity gives a palatable gloss to case material.

A degree of fatalism enters in. The problems may seem too immense, and the detriments inevitable and unavoidable. Without putting the reservation into words, or even into clear thought, the consoling notion may be harboured that young children in long-stay wards or residential institutions are in some way different from our own more fortunate children – not to be compared to them. So, with these elements of defensiveness and rationalization, many within the services acquiesce more or less in child-care practices that are an affront to their under-standing and training and that endanger the well-being of the young child.

In this situation it is not only that the children are cared for in ways which are detrimental to their good social and emotional development. Their caretakers, mostly young girls with little intellectual understanding of the problem but with affection for children, are also denied the conditions of work that would fully utilize their potential to be good substitute mothers. They in turn tend to become defended against disappointing relationships with the children and frustrated in the expression of their mothering concerns. Their natural empathy becomes

3

blunted and they grow less perceptive of the needs of the young children whose care they share with others. Their ability to help and support the younger children is thereby diminished.

Thus, in the everyday handling of young children in hospital and other institutions the rank and file develop defensive attitudes to distress and deterioration similar to those in the higher levels of the professions, pressed upon them by work situations that deny them adequate involvement with the children.

Although there is everywhere goodwill and good intention towards young children in care, with great resources of knowledge and understanding of their needs, and although statements of principle issue from the Ministry of Health and the Home Office, the field situation stagnates because the common defence against pain allows the acuteness of the problem to be dulled as by a tranquillizer.

Without a sufficient degree of anxiety in the professions there can be little improvement, no matter how much knowledge is available. The problem is how to bring pain and anxiety back into the experience of professional workers, but in such a way that these are put to constructive use instead of being defensively sealed off by the constant pressure in all of us to escape hurt.

Our way of focusing attention on the problem was to turn to narrative film. The advantages of a narrative film record are twofold: first, presentation on film gives the nearest approximation to actuality and the visual medium is much more effective than the spoken or printed word in piercing resistance in the field of child-care. Secondly, by focusing on one child it is possible to show the sequence of events from first day to last, noting shifts and changes in significant areas of behaviour, and to condense the related factors within a relatively short presentation. This allows the child's experience and behaviour to be perceived in a longitudinal way that is not possible for staff caught up in multiple duties and diversions or for the occasional visitor open to impressions from the entire child group.

PART 1

A Phase in Paediatric History

James Robertson

Introduction

IN THE FIRST HALF of the twentieth century the wider community had conflicting views on its hospitals. On the one hand, hospitals were held in awe and respect as places that dispensed treatment for the community's illnesses and were endowed with almost magical expectations of skills leading to recovery. But hospitals also evoked feelings of anxiety and fear. When child patients were admitted, they were immediately shut off from contact with their parents, absorbed into a highly authoritarian structure in which doctors and nurses knew best what was good for patients. Relatives were excluded as likely carriers of infection and as potential disturbers of the smoothness of long-established ward routines.

The visiting of children was severely restricted. In 1951 a Ministry of Health inquiry revealed that out of the 1,300 hospitals in Britain which admitted children only 300 allowed daily visiting (usually limited to thirty minutes) and 150 prohibited visiting altogether (*Nursing Times*, 1952a). This caused great distress to young patients and it was common knowledge in the community that young children could be 'changed' by a stay in hospital. But little of this community disquiet reached the hospitals. Parents were intimidated from expressing concern by the calmly authoritarian demeanour of the white-coated doctors and nurses, confident about the rightness of traditional practice and inaccessible to discussion. Doctors and nurses were not trained in the psychological development of children, but the community's belief in the magic of medicine endowed them with an aura of omniscience that extended beyond control of life and death to views on child behaviour which could not be challenged.

The topic of frequency of visiting recurred occasionally in the medical and nursing press, but although editorials commended authoritative articles on the hazards of hospitalization for young children these made a negligible impact on the attitudes of most doctors and nurses. In 1943, for example, Dr Harry Edelston, a psychiatrist in Leeds, published the first known series of case histories of psychological damage to children caused by a stay in hospital (Edelston, 1943). Little attention was paid to it and, as Dr Edelston commented in a letter to the *Lancet* ten years later, 'Resistance appeared from one's general medical colleagues, some of whom even today "do not believe in" the hospitalization trauma' (Edelston, 1953).

In 1947, L.A. Parry, consultant surgeon at the Royal Alexandra Hospital in Brighton, contributed to the *Lancet* an insightful article, 'The Urgent Need for Reforms in Hospitals', in which he wrote scathingly about the restrictions imposed on contact between children and their parents (Parry, 1947). The theme was taken up in a strongly supportive editorial in *Nursing Times* (1948). But in a survey published a year later (Munro-Davies, 1949) the following were the visiting times in principal London hospitals in 1949:

Guy's Hospital, Sundays, 2–4 p.m.;
St Bartholomew's, Wednesdays, 2–3.30 p.m.;
St Thomas's Hospital, first month no visits, but parents could see children asleep between 7 and 8 p.m.;
Westminster Hospital, Wednesdays, 2–3 p.m., Sundays, 2–3 p.m.;
West London Hospital, no visiting;
Charing Cross Hospital, Sundays, 3–4 p.m.;
London Hospital, under three years old, no visits, but parents could see children through partitions. Over three years old, twice weekly.

The Ministry of Health wrote on two occasions to hospital management committees recommending an increase in visiting facilities, but to little effect. Under the new National Health Service of 1948, these hospital management committees had been established to represent community interests; but in the matter of child patients they singularly failed to do so. In justifying non-acceptance of the Ministry's recommendations, several committees explicitly acknowledged having deferred to medical advice that visitors upset children, introduced infection and generally were nuisances.

Helpless though parents felt to challenge the restrictions imposed on them, there were occasional eruptions of complaint in newspapers and a few MPs raised the matter in Parliament. Undoutedly this influenced the Ministry of Health to issue mildly worded recommendations to hospitals.

But most hospitals were unresponsive and continued with the severely restrictive practices that had served generations.

In March 1952 a survey by *Nursing Times* (1952b) of eight well-known English hospitals elicited statements on visiting arrangements in which ten senior nursing staff, supported by their medical colleagues, reflected the restrictions that persisted, the trivial nature of improvements and the poor understanding of child development and family relationships that was typical of the times.

Viewed with hindsight, some forty years later, it is obvious that doctors and nurses before 1950 cared for young patients conscientiously but without the tenderness and empathy they would have given to children of their own. They had inherited a system of care that was geared to ensuring that the system functioned smoothly with the focus of attention on physical illness, and were defended against recognizing the distress and danger for mental health this caused. The relationships of child patients and their parents were not understood to require special consideration. Thus the fact that the under-fives cried on being visited was noted as 'trouble', not as a danger sign: there was no insight into a concept of distress and psychological damage. Moves from wholly restricted visiting to thirty minutes per day, when parents were 'allowed' to see their children, were no more than token concessions to Ministry recommendations.

Press attention was occasional and short-lived. The plight of young patients was of concern to parents but was not a public issue. It was within this context of complacency by the hospital professions – the assumption that all was well in their strictly controlled wards – and of simmering unease in the community, that in 1948 I began research on young children in hospital.

1
Young Children in Hospital

IN 1948 I joined Dr John Bowlby at the Tavistock Clinic to study the reactions of young children to separation from the mother. In psychiatric clinics around the world it was believed that certain forms of psychological disorder had their origin in early separation; but these theories were largely based on reconstructions from the psychotherapy of disturbed children and adults. There were virtually no direct observational data on the behaviour of young children during separation from the mother.

In 1944 Dr Bowlby had published 'Forty-four Juvenile Thieves', a paper that attributed the affectionless character to extreme deprivation of maternal care during prolonged separation (Bowlby, 1946). As with other authors, however, this was based on inferences from his therapeutic work; there were no first-hand observations on the processes of separation/deprivation. I was therefore employed as a field worker to observe and describe the behaviour of young children during and after separation from the mother and thus to help fill the gaps in first-hand observational data.

The task seemed simple enough. First thought was to observe children who were at home while the mother was in hospital; but to locate and gain access to numbers of individual children would have been difficult and time-consuming, so in order to get a first impression I went to a place where there was easy access to numbers of young children separated from the mother – to the children's wards in local hospitals.

On 11 February 1948 I went in all innocence to the short-stay children's ward at the Central Middlesex Hospital, the parent hospital of the Tavistock Clinic. This was solely for the convenience of observing a batch of children in one location, and not because of any awareness on my part that young children in hospital presented a special problem. The consultant paediatrician and his ward sister, for their part, welcomed me into their bright and tidy ward. The nurses who moved briskly about smiled at the young man in an ordinary suit who had come among them. The atmosphere was of orderliness and of everything being under control. I was told that this was a happy children's ward. But within a few hours I grasped the essentials of a problem of distress that was not being acknowledged in the hospital professions. It determined the direction of my professional life for many years to come.

Let me give some background. In 1948, when children went into hospital they were separated from their parents, whom they might then see once a week or once a month, or not at all. I recognized that older children, certainly the ten-year-olds and upwards, could in a sense be 'happy', as was said. By that age they were accustomed to being out of the home for hours of the day at school, to managing much of their lives by themselves. With that degree of maturity they could relate to each other and to the nurses in the ward. They had a sense of time and could understand explanations. They knew that their parents would visit in a few days; to some extent they understood that the doctors and nurses were making them better. Because of their relative maturity, then, they could make an adjustment to separation from home and to life in the hospital ward, could co-operate in their treatment and knew they would return home one day.

But I was stricken by the quite different situation of the very young patients, those under about five years and, most of all, those under three years. In a ward that was busy with the movement of nurses, and with the activities of the older children, these younger ones sat in their cots desolate and tearful or deeply silent. They did not understand why the parents who had cared for them were not there; their needs were immediate and they had no time sense to help them understand that their parents would come tomorrow or the next day. They were overwhelmed. If a nurse stopped beside a silent toddler, he would usually burst into tears at the human contact and the nurse would be rebuked for 'making him unhappy'. A quiet ward was prized above all, so nurses kept away from recently admitted young patients except to feed and clean them.

Nursing was on a 'job-assignment' basis. Except in special circumstances, nurses were not assigned to individual children. It might, for instance, take seven nurses to give a child breakfast – one to deliver a plate, another to place food on it, another to bring a drink, another to clear away afterwards, another to wipe the child's face and two others to shake the bedsheets free of crumbs. The mute young child would sit bewildered amidst the activity, with meagre exchanges between him and any of the nurses, who were intent on avoiding provoking tears. So great was the fear of emotional involvement that I found a dangerously ill two-year-old being 'specialled' (that is, a single nurse was assigned to him) in a side room by a nurse who sat behind the cot out of sight of the child. That was usual practice, the escorting matron told me, because if the child saw the nurse he would 'make demands'.

During the next few weeks, as I sought to understand the situation, I pointed to the unhappy little ones who were cleaned and fed but got no other attention than was needed for medical reasons. The staff thought me naive in my concern. I was told that the distress I was seeing was usual and inevitable and that because it was commonplace there was no cause for concern. Every young child admitted to hospital began by crying for the mother, perhaps rattling his cot. But, I was told, within a few hours or a few days he would 'settle down' – he would 'forget' his mother. Every crying child 'settled' in time and became quiet and uncomplaining.

Parents who were anxious about their child being in hospital and telephoned would be told 'he cried at first, but now he has settled'. Parents were not allowed to visit more than once a week, because, it was said, visits 'upset' children – as seemed to be proved each Sunday, when anxious parents crowded into the precious two-hour visiting period and the ward rang with the cries of young patients who had been quiet until their parents appeared. I came to understand that these visits did not so much cause upset as reveal the distress hidden by the quiet exterior of 'settled' children; likewise, when a young patient cried to a friendly nurse she was not causing the distress but discovering it.

In every children's ward I visited in London teaching hospitals I found this same situation: staff inattention to distress in young patients because it was thought unimportant and would soon pass. But I understood it differently, in the context of the young child's intense attachment to his parents and dependence upon them for comfort and security. When admitted to the unfamiliar setting of the hospital he was shut off from their care and comfort just when he needed them most, when he was ill and perhaps in pain. He became very distressed and cried bitterly for his absent mother; but he could not cry for ever. After a few hours or a few days he would become quiet, with occasional outbursts of sobbing.

This was the usual sequence of adaptation to short-term hospitalization with which the paediatricians and nurses were familiar and about which it appeared they were not troubled. In their view the child had been upset, as new young patients always were, but now he was all right. In the hospital language of the time, the child had 'settled'. Doubts I expressed were smilingly put aside as those of a sentimental psychologist. But I followed some of the children back home and found invariably that the 'settled' state in the hospital ward had given way to difficult behaviour – clinging to the mother, temper tantrums, disturbed sleep, bedwetting, regression and aggression particularly against the mother as if blaming her.

When I sought to influence ward staff with my anecdotal material about the after-effects of a stay in hospital, I was told that, since the children had 'settled' in the ward and been easy to manage, any difficult behaviour afterwards simply meant that mothers were less competent than nurses in handling children. I gradually realized that there was a tremendous resistance in paediatrics to recognizing the painful problem, a resistance that sheltered behind the myth of the 'happy children's ward' that had sustained generations of paediatricians and nurses. (For example, for years Christmas Day on BBC television included a party in a children's ward. A jolly man went from bed to bed inviting patients to say 'Happy Christmas, Mummy' into a microphone. Older children responded and helped sustain the myth. But when the microphone was offered to little ones they usually burst into tears at the mention of 'Mummy' and the microphone was hurriedly pulled away. In due course the little ones were avoided.)

During the next few years, then, I conscientiously made the objective observations for which I had been engaged and passed them to Dr Bowlby for inclusion in his theoretical studies; in Volume 1 of *Attachment and Loss* Dr Bowlby acknowledges, 'The main data on which I have drawn are those of James Robertson' (1969). Those working with Dr Bowlby had latitude to develop their own interests and quite soon much of my time and effort became diverted to the painful problem of avoidable distress in young patients and to my wish to influence paediatric practice. My colleagues were interested in my reports but none were involved in the fieldwork as I was. None was confronted daily by the inhumanity of the paediatric situation; they were preoccupied with their own projects. My urgent concern to help humanize paediatrics therefore became a solitary campaign, supported by the interest of my colleagues, but not a shared project.

Alongside my observations in short-stay wards I spent two years observing in a long-stay ward at Harefield Hospital in Middlesex. This had sixty beds for children with pulmonary tuberculosis, which in 1948 was still rife. Before the days of modern medicines, stays of three and four bed-ridden years were common; the children were in a single-story building, with glass-fronted cubicles which opened on to a lawn where rabbits scampered.

At first glance it was an idyllic setting, but for the children the caring context was as impoverishing as in any other ward I had seen. The sister was a kindly person, but, in the few hours of each day that were free of administration and store-keeping, her attention could only spread thinly over the sixty children in her care. The nursing was done by students on brief placement from a London teaching hospital, untrained in child-care; these, too, were instructed not to get close to the younger children. Every six weeks they were replaced by the next batch of students. There was no concept of relationships and continuity of care.

The only intimacy was in the nursery school attached to the ward. Young patients who were well enough went there in the mornings to play with toys, sand and Plasticine. The nursery nurses had a different training from the hospital nurses. They knew the importance of relationships, took a personal interest in the young patients and interacted warmly with them. But the hospital nursing system reached out to spoil that. While I was there it was decreed by the ward sister that if a child needed potting or cleaning, or any other bodily attention while in the nursery school, a nurse must be summoned from the ward; toileting was in the hospital nurses' domain and nursery nurses must not intrude.

The nursery nurses, who knew the importance of body care in deepening relationships, felt this demarcation to be an interference with their work and against the interests of the children. The matter was referred to the medical superintendent, who ruled in favour of the hospital nurses. The nursery nurses were instructed to confine themselves to play and the quality of their work was therefore diminished. The children were victims of inadequate hospital nurse training. Moreover, the senior nursery nurse resigned.

Visiting by parents was for two hours on Sunday afternoons, when special buses brought them from various parts of London. Recently admitted younger children reacted to their parents in the same way as the short-stay patients. They went through the phases of Protest (they cried, clung, turned away, screamed when parents left after visiting) and Despair (with occasional sobs but few tears until parents came; between visits they were quiet, uncomplaining and 'settled') (James Robertson, 1953a). See below, pp. 17–18.

Those who had been in the hospital for some months had moved from Protest and Despair into the third phase which I called Denial/ Detachment (denying the wish for relationships). They had no attachments to nurses who changed so often. During the week they presented a superficially disarming picture. It did not seem to matter to them which nurses were on duty. They no longer sought attention or cried when approached by strangers. They smiled at anyone who came into their cubicles, lacking the reserve appropriate to their age. Visiting groups from medical conferences enjoyed their 'friendliness'.

On Sundays these 'detached' young children seemed indifferent to the arrival of their parents. There was no crying, no clinging, no turning away. They were more interested in what their parents had brought than in the parents themselves. They searched bags and stuffed chocolate into their mouths. My impression was that feeling for their parents had died because of the passage of time and repeated disappointment of the wish to be taken home and had been replaced by hunger for sweet things which did not disappoint. 'Don't be greedy,' perplexed parents would say.

Parents brought extravagant presents to assuage their helplessness in face of the children's plight and would try pathetically and unsuccessfully to get a 'Thank you' response. When it was time to leave, their children appeared unconcerned and could hardly be induced to give a parting wave. They no longer had expectations of parents who came and went. Parents were hurt and confused by each unsatisfactory visit, and dreaded the next.

Mary was a child of two years whom I saw through a twelve-month stay at Harefield. The youngest child of a sound working-class family, she began with the overt upsets of Protest and Despair. Her parents were miserable about her unhappiness and felt relieved when she no longer cried. But after some months they were equally worried that she did not cry when they came or went. One day Mary's mother got off the bus just before it left the hospital and came back to the ward in hope of eliciting a loving wave from her little daughter. She looked in through a window. I saw Mary glance up for a moment with a sombre expression, then turn away. A few days later the mother told me the incident haunted her. Mary had moved into Detachment.

Some young patients, although giving no sign of affection while parents were there, held firmly on to the toys that had been brought and shielded them from the interest of other children. But when the parents had gone the toys were thrown from cots on to the floor or vigorously destroyed despite the protests of staff. (In these children, attachment and expectation had not entirely gone but lay deeply submerged, to manifest themselves in silent destruction of tokens of love that was disturbing to see. As separation became further extended, even that oblique expression of feeling would disappear.)

At the end of visiting time the orderlies swept up the remains of playthings that had been tokens of parental love and had cost a lot of money. Each week parents complained that their children no longer had the toys that had been brought the previous Sunday and wanted to know where they had gone. The nurses had no answer except to say that the toys had not been stolen but broken. I could not bear to say to parents that the toys had been destroyed in anger against them.

Mary's mother brought an expensive 'indestructible' doll. After the visit, Mary, using hands and teeth, rent it apart. The kindly sister did not have insight into what was happening and over several weeks she repaired the doll many times with sticking plaster for the sake of the mother. But in the end she was defeated by the two-year-old's fierce determination and strong teeth. The destruction was done in silence.

I was of the opinion that 'short-stay' hospital separations could leave a scar that might be known only to the individual as a nub of anxiety which could be activated by trivial happenings. This view was difficult to sustain in face of sceptics' claims to know people who had been unaffected by childhood hospitalization, and for lack of immediate proofs. But there was no disputing the damage that lengthy hospitalization caused to the very young children I observed at Harefield Hospital. The deprivations had been too severe and too formative for the consequences to fade away. During my two years at Harefield I got to know Mary, Richard, Valerie, Susan and Julia, and followed them for several years afterwards. All were seriously affected in their relationships within the family and elsewhere.

For instance, when Mary was discharged home at three and a half she was a sturdy, good-looking child. But she was no longer the cuddly little girl of a year earlier. She squirmed out of her mother's embrace, then stood as if not knowing what affection was about. She did not fit into the reciprocity of family life. She was self-centred, not selfish but intent on looking after herself; for more than a year her needs had not been met by others, and now she had no expectation of being looked after by her parents or having fair shares within the family. In competition with her older brothers she always defeated them by ruthlessness in which she used just enough force to get what she wanted; she was unable to give and take as brothers and sisters usually do in a family.

Mary's mother was unhappy that her little daughter did not seem to need her but noticed that if she put an arm round another child Mary would push it away. It was as if jealous longing stirred in her but could not come into consciousness and positive behaviour. Towards me she was ambivalent, welcoming my visits to the home yet avoiding me as if perhaps fearful of my connection with the hospital and the separation. A deep and probably dangerous complex of feelings was there in this three-year-old.

Mary achieved well at school, a handsome and competent child, yet solitary. The attachment I had to her as the first long-stay child I had got to know competed with my professional objectivity. I was offended when at twelve years of age her school teachers confirmed my worst expectations. Mary was an athlete, school champion high diver; but she was unpopular. She always got her own way. For instance, if the class were short of books Mary would forcefully get one or protest strongly if she did not, in a way similar to her self-assertion at home.

I was taken aback by the unanimity of negative feeling in the headmaster and teachers and tried to enlist their compassion by outlining the causes in Mary's lengthy hospitalization. But this elicited no sympathy. They were irritated that the handsome and intelligent girl should be so 'selfish'. Disappointed though I was, I admitted to myself that I would not wish a son of mine to marry Mary.

Visiting isolation wards for infectious illnesses was generally forbidden. There was the apparently irrefutable obstacle that parents would carry infections back into the community. But solid although this claim appeared to be, I found that it was largely a rationalization behind which lurked familiar resistances.

Valerie, whom I had got to know in the long-stay hospital, developed an infectious illness a few weeks after her return home and was taken into Coppetts' Wood Isolation Hospital in north London. I conveyed her mother there on the first Sunday afternoon in expectation that she could visit. To our dismay we discovered that visiting was not allowed and that she had to inquire about Valerie from the gate porter. But I, although myself a parent, was apparently, as a research worker, immune to infections. There was no objection to my going into the wards. The medical superintendent took me on a tour of the hospital accompanied by his shaggy dog. This emphasized the absurdity of the restrictions.

I knew that ward staff and ancillary workers moved freely to and from the community, travelled on buses and were as likely to convey infection as any visiting parent. No restrictions were imposed on their movements. This showed the irrationality of the reasons given for preventing parental visiting. Poor Valerie caught a secondary infection in the ward and had a second extended separation.

PHASES OF RESPONSE TO HOSPITALIZATION

Having observed young children in short- and long-stay wards, in accident, general and isolation wards, in the early 1950s I formulated with confidence the phases of response of the under-threes to a stay in hospital without the mother: Protest, Despair and Denial (later called Detachment) (James Robertson, 1953a).

In the initial phase of Protest, which may last from a few hours to several days, the young patient has a strong conscious need of his mother and the expectation, based on previous experience, that she will respond to his cries. He is extremely upset to have lost her, is confused and frightened by unfamiliar surroundings and is distraught with fright and urgent desire to find her. He will often cry loudly, shake the cot, throw himself about and look eagerly towards any sight or sound that might prove to be his missing mother.

Despair, which gradually succeeds Protest, is characterized by a continuing conscious need of his mother coupled with an increasing hopelessness. He is less active and may cry monotonously and intermittently. He is withdrawn and apathetic, makes no demands on the environment. This is the quiet stage which is sometimes mistakenly presumed to mean that distress has lessened, that he is 'settling in'.

Some children who are in hospital for a short time only will reach the stage of Despair, though others will go home in the initial stage of Protest. But if the young child stays longer in the typical conditions in which he is looked after by a changing sequence of nurses he will enter the next stage, of Denial.

In the stage of Denial, the patient shows more interest in his surroundings and this may be welcomed by staff as a sign that he is becoming 'happy'. It is, however, a danger signal. Because the child cannot tolerate the intensity of distress, he begins to make the best of his situation by repressing his longing for the mother who has failed to meet his needs, particularly his need of her as a person to love and be loved by. Then he is free to take such satisfactions, food and attention, as the ward can offer. It may be thought that because he smiles and responds to play he has 'settled' in the sense that all is well. But it will often be seen that when his mother comes he seems hardly to know her and no longer cries when she leaves – on the face of it a peaceful situation but in fact a cause for concern that a child so young should have lost his attachment to his mother.

Finally, if his stay is still longer, and if the nursing system gives the usual kind of fragmented care, he will in time seem not only not to need his mother but not to need any mothering at all – a peculiar state which, if it were seen in a child in the family, would rightly cause considerable concern. Yet it could be seen in many long-stay children's wards where it drew little or no comment.

During the three years from 1948 in which I made my observations I took every opportunity to talk with paediatricians and nurses on the wards about the problem as I saw it. But the myth of the Happy Children's Ward that had sustained the hospital professions for several decades was very resistant to what I had to say. I came to recognize that I was up against more than familiarity with distress, that even more profoundly there were unconscious defences which were largely inaccessible to my written and spoken descriptions of distress and deterioration.

The young medical or nursing student beginning training was as hurt as I by the distress, but had no options other than to repress disturbing awareness in order to get on with the work or to leave the training. The defences against personal upset became stronger and stronger with the passage of time, reinforced as they were by the inadequacies of training and the hospital culture of avoiding emotional involvement. Ultimately, feeling became repressed and the views of the outsider could be smilingly dismissed, as they had been in my case, as those of a sentimental psychologist. I came to the realization that even the most senior paediatricians and nurses had gone through these stages before reaching the apparent serenity of status and authority.

I was up against a blank wall.

TACKLING RESISTANCES

The problem was how to pierce the enormous resistances against acknowledging distress and the danger of emotional damage to young patients. In several of the hospitals to which I had entry, some senior people were interested in the research aspects although not knowledge-able about the psychological development of young children. One of these was Dr Alan Moncrieff, Professor of Child Health at the Hospital for Sick Children in Great Ormond Street, London, who obtained an invitation for me to present some of my findings to the twenty-first anniversary annual weekend conference of the British Paediatric Asso-ciation to be held at Windermere in the Lake District in early 1951.

Somewhat daunted by my inexperience, and by the prospect of being the only lay person amongst this gathering of urbane medical specialists, in fact the first non-medical person to have spoken to the conference, I nevertheless gladly accepted. I was somewhat reassured by knowing that amongst those present would be Sir James Spence, distinguished Pro-fessor of Child Health at the University of Newcastle; for thirty years he had had as part of his department at the Royal Victoria Infirmary the well-known Babies' Hospital where mothers stayed with their infants and very young children. I was puzzled that his example, which to me was the height of humane paediatrics, had not been emulated or much influenced British paediatrics. But I confidently expected his support for my fifteen-minute talk.

I briefly outlined my observations of Protest, Despair and Detachment and gave some case examples. To my extreme dismay, Spence stood up in the large gathering and sweepingly attacked me in a fluent and biting vein of irony. This tall distinguished-looking man, whom I respected, referred dismissively to what I had said about 'emotional upset' in young patients in hospitals. 'What is wrong with emotional upset? This year we are celebrating the centenary of the birth of Wordsworth, the great Lakeland Poet. He suffered from emotional upset, yet look at the poems he produced.'

Dr Leonard Parsons, Professor of Child Health at Birmingham University, came to my rescue, saying nothing about my material but defending my right to express my views. Over drinks afterwards several paediatricians were considerate of me, but no one appeared lit up about my concerns. As someone only a step away from the tenements, inexper-ienced and without status as yet in this realm, I felt much diminished by the unexpected attitude of Professor Spence whom I had expected to be an ally.

Having gone on to visit my family in Scotland, and finding that I was still hurt and puzzled, I got off the train at Newcastle on the way back to London and bearded the great man in his room at the Royal Victoria

Infirmary. My call was unexpected, but Spence was friendly and made time for me – he was quite unperturbed by my hardly controlled disappointment and irritation. It became clear that I had been a whipping-boy for his antipathy towards psychiatrists. He spoke scathingly about psychiatry, which in his view fragmented people's individuality so that the essential person was lost sight of. He talked about his belief that every paediatrician should not only have a concern for the entire family but should express this by doing home visits and carrying the responsibility unaided. Spence would not employ a psychiatrist or social worker; his paediatric registrars were taught to be respectful and courteous to child patients and their parents and to hold family units together.

I was much impressed by his kindly and gracious manner and by the example of courtesy and consideration that he set his registrars, and I said so; but I did not understand how paediatric registrars could acquire the skills of psychiatry and social work under this regime, let alone find the time to do home visiting. It seemed to me that James Spence had an almost mystical view of paediatrics as an all-embracing vocation, none of which could be delegated.

As we talked, he unbent towards me. He thought me sincere in my concern for young children in hospital, but misguided in being associated with a psychiatric clinic. He took me on a visit to his small Babies' Hospital and my heart warmed to the gentle and courteous way in which he spoke to the mothers about their babies and their families. He was deeply committed to the mother being together with her sick baby; but this was a small unit, and I asked how he dealt with the children of mothers he could not accommodate or who could not come into hospital. He took me across the corridor to a typical children's ward of the times, where visiting was only twice a week. I immediately detected there the phenomena of Protest and Despair that I had seen elsewhere.

When I asked how he could reconcile the fact that in one part of his domain mothers and children were kept together, while in the open ward visiting was restricted to two hours a week, he patted my knee as if to comfort me in my unnecessary concern and said, 'Robertson, I know how much these children need. Twice a week is enough.' The kindly Professor Spence seemed to me to be as defended as the average paediatrician. It struck me forcibly that kindliness, however genuine, was no substitute for understanding the emotional needs of infants and young children.

Spence put a high value on the mother's sensitivity towards her sick baby. He believed that she could detect a change in the baby's breathing long before a nurse or doctor would be aware of it. Therefore she had an important part in the care of her sick baby. But it appeared to me that Spence's motivation to have mothers and babies together stemmed primarily from a concern to sustain the mother, rather than from understanding the emotional needs of the baby. His chivalrous attitude put the mother on a pedestal, where she got all his empathetic attention, and the babies got a spin-off. He felt the mother's need to be with her baby but did not have a comparable sense of the baby's need to be with the mother. In the open ward mothers could visit twice a week as in other hospitals; in his view, that was enough for the unaccompanied baby or young child.

I thought I understood then why the good things about the Babies' Hospital had not been emulated. It seemed to me that they were not based upon general principles that could be taught but upon the idiosyncrasies of one man, his particular fusion of empathy and blindness. I was to discover that this could also be true of other leading paediatricians.

These encounters with Professor Spence and other paediatricians led me to a view about how defences worked throughout the hospital professions in Britain, a view confirmed when I later travelled around the world – how paediatricians could have kind intentions towards children, and from these kind intentions have developed areas of considerate practice; yet also have areas of harmful practice to which they were blind because they were not trained in psychological development and because anxieties about distress in children became repressed in order to sustain a peaceful status quo.

As I investigated further in British hospitals it became even clearer, in my view, that there was an enormous meshing of defences against acknowledging the distress and psychological deterioration in young patients. I saw defences so powerful that the kindest of staff could be wholly unaware of the emotional abuse they were practising and colluding in. My talking had little effect upon the massive defences against the anxieties roused by working with sick and distressed young children. A paradox was that some of the paediatricians I got to know were themselves fathers, tender and protective towards their own (healthy) children, yet unable to extend that empathy to young patients.

In the wards the emotional states of young patients were not seen in continuum. A child was 'content' or 'cheerful' or 'friendly' or 'unfriendly' or 'tearful' or whatever; but although physical changes were noted with care day by day, progressions of behaviour were not. When I managed to get a paediatrician to look at a young patient who concerned me, the attention was brief and only the behaviour of the moment would be remarked upon. It was not related to behaviour of the previous day or the day before that.

With colleagues at the Tavistock Clinic to whom I reported on my work I had a sense of the inadequacy of words to convey what I saw and how I understood it. By professional aptitude they were ready to accept what I said; but for me the problem was one of description and evaluation. How was I to find the correct words with which to describe objectively the shifts of behaviour in a young patient in distress on the first day, the third day? How to choose adjectives that would convey the subtleties without distortion?

Although I believed I was objective, despite the intensity of my concerns, I knew that no matter how well I chose the words each listening colleague could construe them differently and have differing impressions of the child. It seemed well nigh impossible to convey satisfactorily my images of the child's behaviour: to paediatricians because they were too defended, in my view, to empathize with the subject, and even to well-oriented colleagues because of the limitations of words.

The answer came by chance. I read somewhere that visual communication pierces defences as the spoken word cannot do. It allows what is shown to be examined and re-examined. That was the answer. I decided to attempt a film record of a young child throughout a short stay in hospital, with two main uses in mind. One was that in reporting to Tavistock colleagues, with their clinical and scientific interest in behaviour, misunderstandings of verbal descriptions would be avoided; everyone in a group would see the same scenes, while sequences could be viewed and reviewed in order to heighten perception and understanding by repetition. The second was that paediatricians could be shown the visual record over and over again, until the gaps in understanding between us had been narrowed. The child would be seen longitudinally, day after day, following the changes of state and behaviour usually not noted amid the preoccupations of ward work. Both groups would thus see for themselves the behaviour of one child over a number of days without the intermediacy of the spoken word and make their own judgements.

In 1951 Dr Tom Main of the Cassel Hospital, Richmond, loaned £150 from a fund, which together with Tavistock money bought a Bell and Howell spring-wound 16 mm cine-camera with three lenses and a hand-held light meter, plus eighty minutes of black and white film stock at 100 f.p.s., the fastest film then available. The camera did not have through-the-lens viewing, nor a tripod. It would be hand held, and I would have to depend on light from the ward windows. These, fortunately, stretched from floor to ceiling and in the approaching month of August would be a reasonable source of daylight.

Even more hazardous, however, was the fact that I had never before handled a cine-camera. I studied a handbook over a weekend, then exposed one of the precious rolls of film on the family. With that amount of practice I had to begin the single-handed project, to load and unload the camera without assistance and to keep the ward accepting of what I was doing.

The consultant paediatrician in charge of the medical/surgical ward of our parent hospital, the Central Middlesex, selected the child for my project by sticking a pin in the four-page list of those waiting for minor elective surgery. A surgical patient was necessary so that I could have advance notice of admission and could observe the child's behaviour and relationships with the parents at home before being separated from them.

Although the ward staff appeared to have no insight into my views, and therefore did not feel threatened by the project, there was some suspicion that I would film the child only when she cried – that I would not film her 'when she is happy'. I for my part knew that a child of two put into hospital and separated from her parents could not be happy. But, to anticipate later charges that I had selected shots with bias, I had the consultant's agreement that I would film time samples of behaviour during two forty-minute periods at the same times each day. These would be filmed to the dictates of the sweep hand of a large clock next to the child's cot in order to establish that no other consideration determined the daily sequences and to obtain material that could be compared day by day in order to observe changes in behaviour; secondly, there would be *ciné vérité* filming of main events such as medical examinations, premedication, relations with staff and visits by parents.

It should be borne in mind that the 1951 ward was typical of the times. The nurses were hard-working, busy keeping order, giving medication, making beds, feeding and cleaning the children. They were cheerful and friendly, with ready smiles for the younger patients as they went about

24

their work. But they were not allowed to stop and play with them or to give comfort. They interacted freely with the older children but went to the younger ones only when there was a physical need to be dealt with.

It was believed that for a nurse to stop with a young patient was to waste time and that to try to be friendly or to offer comfort made the child unhappy, as was shown by his beginning to cry having previously been quiet and 'settled'.

There was no bedside play and there were no play ladies. Patients were kept in their cots for twenty-three hours of each day. Those fit to walk were allowed late in the afternoon to go for an hour into a playroom containing a rocking horse and other large toys.

There was a premium on quietness and tidiness. Cots were tidied frequently and the nurse who went too close to a young patient and so 'made him cry' was rebuked. Visits by parents were allowed grudgingly, because these were thought to make young patients unhappy and to disturb the calm of the ward.

Visiting by parents was restricted to once a week for two hours on Sunday afternoon. (But, because of my interest in how the research child's attitude to the parents might change during eight days in hospital, they were allowed to visit every second day.)

There was no deliberate unkindness. Sister and nurses were friendly people whose inadequacy, in my view, derived from their conditioning to a traditional concept of nursing which concentrated on physical care and did not recognize the emotional needs of young patients. They shared with nurses in general the misconception that quiet young patients were contented and that their contentment should not be disturbed by friendly contact, however well intentioned.

2

Film:

A Two-year-old Goes to Hospital

IN THIS CHAPTER I give a very full account of Laura in order to convey to the reader the complexity of her experience and to try to capture something of the film's attention to detail. This account refers to plates 1–10. The reader should bear in mind that the film, made in 1952, was silent, with spoken commentary. A record of everything said was made, however, and some of this is reproduced here.

Laura was two years and five months old, awaiting surgery for an umbilical hernia, when in 1951 the prick of a pin in the ward waiting list brought her into my research. She was the only child of devoted working-class parents, a pretty and characterful little girl. Mother was pregnant with a second child. My heart sank, however, when I met Laura in her home. For several years I had been talking about the acute distress reactions of young patients, but I saw that in Laura I had found a child in a hundred who was not going to react openly. Her parents applied pressure for good behaviour; she was a 'little madam' who talked well, was very well behaved and had unusual control over the expression of feeling; a child discouraged from crying or making a fuss.

I was tempted to return to the hospital and ask the consultant to make a second choice, to find a more typical two-year-old. But that would have cast doubts on my objectivity, so I persisted with the project although dismayed that Laura's behaviour was not going to illustrate the overwhelming unhappiness that I had been describing.

Both parents expressed anxiety about the distress Laura would feel, yet reassured themselves by adding that perhaps she would be so interested in her new surroundings that she would not miss them too much. Mother had talked to the child about going to hospital, about doctors and nurses, and had got her to help pack the few things she would need there. But Laura had never been out of her mother's care, except for an occasional afternoon with a familiar person. To me it was doubtful how far a child so young could anticipate being alone in hospital in the care of strangers.

First Day in Hospital

Laura was smartly dressed as if for a summer outing and talked cheerfully with her mother as they approached the hospital. She walked briskly through the hospital corridors, confident and self-possessed, and even in the ante-room to the surgical ward she was bright and friendly to the nurse who took her admission details. She sat on a chair beside her mother with her teddy-bear tucked comfortably under one arm. Despite her mother's attempt to prepare her, Laura had not understood that she was to be left there.

When the nurse invited her to 'come and see the rocking-horse', Laura said, 'You come too, Mummy.' But when her mother did not move she went off with her hand placed trustingly in that of the nurse. They paused in the playroom and Laura touched the rocking-horse. But when she was then led further into the ward she began to resist slightly, trying to release her hand from the firm grip of the nurse. When they reached the bathroom she was suddenly afraid, refused to enter and cried loudly, 'I want my mummy.' The nurse pressed her inside and began to remove her pretty frock and the ribbon from her hair. Laura struggled, crying bitterly for her mummy, and when freed for a moment she ran naked to the door in an attempt to escape.

Ten minutes later, after an unnecessary but routine bath, her unusual control over the expression of feeling had asserted itself. But the animation had gone from her face and she talked quietly to the nurse about her teddy. She was taken into the open ward and the continuing strangeness of the new experience seemed to confuse her further. She pointed and asked, 'What's that girl in bed for? Why's that boy in bed?' Then she found that she, too, was in bed, being tucked under the covers. When the nurse tried to take her temperature under an arm, Laura burst into uncontrolled sobbing for her mother. But as soon as the temperature had been taken her composure returned.

Mother was then allowed in from the waiting-room to say goodbye. Laura began to cry, but as her mother talked she quietened and showed interest in what she was being told. Her mother pointed to the road

27

below where the buses ran, and said she would come on the bus to see her next day. This reassurance, coupled with her mother's insistent 'Don't cry', kept Laura quiet; and although her mouth drooped as her mother prepared to go she recovered herself and returned her mother's parting wave. This was exactly an hour after Laura had entered the hospital, sprightly and bright-faced. Now her expression was dull and was to remain so for most of the eight days to come. This two-year-old was now alone and unsupported to face the fears, frights and hurts of a hospital ward.

At the moment of parting, her mother had given Laura an old piece of blanket she had had since infancy and which she called her 'baby'. During the days in hospital the blanket 'baby' and the teddy-bear were a great source of comfort to her when she was sad or frightened.

After her mother had gone, Laura stood in her cot looking out at the twenty other children whose cots ranged both sides of the ward, some of whom had broken legs suspended from pulleys, and at the busy nurses and orderlies who were doing the morning's work. She talked with five-year-old Victor in the next cot, flicked over the pages of a comic and put the hem of her blanket 'baby' into her mouth. She appeared solemn and bewildered but not manifestly unhappy. When another new patient cried, she watched him with quiet interest.

Gradually she emerged from her preoccupation with the crying child and put down her blanket 'baby'. She brushed a crumb from her cot and sang to herself, apparently quite relaxed. But when a nurse came at 11.15 a.m. to begin the morning play period, which I had arranged in order to discover how Laura would react when brought close to someone, she looked at the nurse with a tense expression and said, very quietly, 'Where's my mummy?' The nurse ignored the question and Laura did not repeat it – typical of her behaviour on many subsequent occasions when she would ask quietly and without insistence for her mother. She joined in the nurse's play with her teddy and talked as if untroubled.

A few minutes after the nurse had gone, Laura stood up and called out, 'Mummy, Mummy, Mummy. Come here.' She sounded quite cheerful, as if free of anxiety. But when the ward sister came to do something for her a few minutes later, Laura said in a plaintive voice, 'I want my mummy.' The sister said, 'Mummy's gone to make Daddy's dinner. She'll come on the bus tomorrow.' Laura grumbled, 'But I want her now.'

She refused to let the sister put on her bib and pushed her away in determined fashion. Nor would she allow the nurse to do so who came to give her lunch. She ate well but said repeatedly, though quietly, that she wanted her mummy.

At rest time she settled herself down with blanket 'baby' in one arm and her teddy in the other, and with her flannel basket tucked under the covers. There she lay, with those familiar things tucked in around her. As the day went on she became more and more subdued, with none of the bright interludes that leavened the morning. She had begun picking her nose during rest time and continued to do so throughout the afternoon. Her thumb frequently brushed her mouth without ever going in. But when sister gave her a stick of candy rock, she sucked it with noisy relish.

Several times during the afternoon a baby in a cot across the ward cried, and each time Laura asked me, 'Why is that baby crying?' On the first occasion I returned the question, 'Well, Laura, why is that baby crying?' – and got no reply. Another time, she called out, 'I not crying, see!' Nor did she cry during that day, though it appeared that to achieve this all her ability to control the expression of feeling had to be brought to bear. She sucked, picked her nose and did not demand attention. But each time the nurse came to do something for her, in a quiet little voice and without insistence she asked, 'Where is my mummy?'

The children were allowed out of their cots for an hour each afternoon, and at about 3.30 p.m. Laura went with them into the playroom. In those days, as I have indicated, there were no play ladies, but she played purposefully and with concentration. She took little notice of the other children, except to assert herself when they intruded on her play.

In that hour, there was a first indication of positive feeling both for the nurse who had been her attendant all day and for me. When the nurse left the playroom, Laura seemed undecided whether to follow; but when I answered to her unease by calling to her from the corner where I sat with a book, she responded immediately, talked to me and remained in the playroom. She played most of the time near me, including me in her activity with the occasional flicker of a smile. On later days, it was increasingly evident that she found some security in my presence – probably both because I made a link with home and because I was a constant figure, being near her during most of her waking day.

For most of the time I sat with a magazine in an easy chair a few yards from her cot, occasionally using my hand-held cine-camera. I never initiated anything between us, but always responded to her. When she called, 'Come and do up my dolly's dress,' I did so, and smiled in response when she made some comment through the bars of her cot.

When she was put back into her cot after her visit to the playroom, she whimpered for a few minutes then lay quietly with her teddy and blanket 'baby' by her side. The surgeon came to make her acquaintance. He was gentle and unhurried in his approach, but Laura was apprehensive. She turned away, clutching her 'baby' and teddy. She resisted having her nightdress lifted so that he could see the hernia and thrust his hands away, exclaiming repeatedly but without crying, 'I don't like it – it's better now.' Afterwards she insisted that the surgeon should examine her teddy with his stethoscope and this he did.

At 7 p.m. a nurse came to prepare Laura for bed. As her hair was brushed she asked, 'Where is my mummy?' The nurse did not reply and Laura did not repeat the question. Suddenly she began to co-operate in the preparations for the night. She reached out and touched the drop side of her cot and said, 'Put it up.' But she was restless; she sat up, looked around, lay down, cuddled and kissed her teddy and 'baby'. At 10 p.m. she was given a sedative which settled her for the night.

Second Day: Day of Operation

When I entered the ward at 6 a.m. there was a chorus of 'Daddy' from the older children. But when I neared Laura's cot she looked at me intently and said 'Where is my mummy?' several times over. Then she seemed to thrust the mood aside and became conversational with the nurses. She did not resist their washing her and brushing her hair.

Two hours later breakfast was served and cleared away in the general activity of night-shift nurses handing over to day shift. The nurses were good-humoured and kindly, but because of the 'job assignment' organization of duties Laura did not have the sustained attention of any one of them. Five nurses shared in serving and clearing her breakfast within fifteen minutes and Laura could not have differentiated between them in their white uniforms. She took their ministrations quietly, even submissively.

Twenty minutes later she attracted my attention and, when I went to her, insisted, 'I want to see my mummy. I want to see her now. I want to go on the bus.' She was flushed and looked miserable as she spoke, but almost immediately her feelings came under control once more and she appeared calm. Her expression was more tense than yesterday, her eyes smaller and slightly sunken. During the next hour or two, she alternated between gazing along the ward with a solemn expression and cuddling her 'baby'. Once she lay for ten minutes with her face pressed into the pillow. From her irregular breathing it seemed that she might be crying, but when she sat up her eyes were dry. There were no doubt that she was under considerable stress, but, although her expression and bearing reflected the struggle going on inside, the tears did not come.

When the nurse came for the play period, Laura was not interested in the toys. Her face was strained and she announced vehemently, 'I want to see my mummy. I want to see my mummy now.' There were no tears, but when the baby across the way began to cry Laura was disturbed. She asked, 'What's he crying for?' then turned away and looked out of the window on to the road below with its stream of lorries and buses.

At 12 noon lunches were being served and Laura had said she was hungry. But she could not be given food or drink because it was time for pre-medication. The operation was due in about thirty minutes. A screen was put around her cot and a rectal anaesthetic was administered with tact by the sister and a nurse. After a few seconds of frightened crying as the slender tubing was inserted, Laura grew quiet. Ten minutes later her unconscious body was dressed in operation cap, gown and long socks that she had earlier refused to have put on. Her teddy and 'baby' were tucked in beside her and she lay in a deep sleep awaiting the theatre trolley.

Shortly afterwards it was learned that the operation list had been rearranged and that Laura would not be dealt with until late in the afternoon. The sister was deeply angered; first, because of the hardship this meant for Laura who had been unnecessarily anaesthetized and would go hungry for some hours more, and secondly (as I inferred) because it had exposed a defect in the ward procedures to me and my camera. She tried hard to have Laura's time reinstated but failed, and said bitterly that this was a not uncommon happening because there was insufficient co-operation between surgeons and nursing staff.

Laura roused from the anaesthetic two and a half hours later at 2.30 p.m. and began to cry miserably. Her distress mounted; for ten minutes she cried bitterly for her mummy and chewed at her blanket 'baby'. She was hungry and several times during the next few hours she asked plaintively for food, which could not be given to her because of the impending operation. These hours were very trying for her. The screen that had hidden her from the ward during the pre-medication had been removed, and at tea-time she could see the other children being fed while her plaintive requests for something to eat were ignored by the hurrying nurses. When she saw the baby being fed, she called out, 'He's had enough.' She grizzled, rolled around in her cot as if frustrated beyond endurance and lay with an arm across her eyes crying for her mummy.

Just before 5 p.m. the theatre trolley came to fetch Laura for the operation. The sister's discretion had prevented her from giving the child further pre-medication, so Laura was fully conscious and sitting upright on the trolley when wheeled off to the theatre. Her face puckered unhappily, but there were no tears and she did not resist. At 5.30 p.m. she was returned to her cot, the operation over, and ten minutes later she began to stir. The nurse rubbed her face briskly with a wet flannel, and at 6 p.m. Laura murmured that she had a sore tummy and asked the nurse to rub it. This the nurse did intermittently for twenty minutes and it seemed to soothe the pain.

At 6.30 p.m. Laura was drowsy and listless, lying back on the pillow. When her parents appeared in the doorway, she immediately burst into tears. As they leaned over the cot she turned away from them with an arm over her eyes, desolate in her crying – as if overcome by anger and despair. After about a minute, during which they talked soothingly to her, she turned towards them, sat up and tried hard to get to her mother. However, saying this was dangerous for the stitches, the nurse gently but firmly restrained Laura who in a short time gave up trying.

But she wept heart-brokenly, crying repeatedly, 'I want to go home. I want to get up.' This was the first really loud and uncontrolled crying that had been heard since her admission. The nurse put an arm across to prevent the parents from trying to pick Laura up. They were helpless, unable to comfort their child. When they began to say goodbye, Laura quietened but caught hold of her father's tie and exclaimed pathetically, 'Don't go, Daddy.'

Her father and mother were upset by Laura's distress but could not leave the ward without somehow getting reassurance from her. They both leaned over the cot rail, trying to elicit a smile or a parting gesture. Suddenly she responded to their wish by lifting her hand and waving feebly – a gesture pathetically inconsistent with her misery and need of them. Thus reassured by the child they had been unable to comfort, the parents left. Laura lay silent, with a puckered brow and a thumb that brushed her mouth but did not get inside.

That night she had a sedative and slept, her teddy and blanket 'baby' tucked in beside her.

THIRD DAY

Laura awoke about 6 a.m. and was quietly miserable until breakfast at 8 a.m. Occasionally she brightened to chat with nurses, and twice she cried bitterly for Mummy and Daddy. She ate a large breakfast, evidently very hungry after a day without food. When the twelve-month-old baby in the next cot cried, Laura watched him quietly for several minutes before asserting, 'I not crying. I not crying, see!' Then she sat quietly, fingering her face and lips and picking her nose – her teddy in one arm and 'baby' in the other. She did not cry and she did not demand attention.

When the nurse came for the play period Laura was quiet and controlled, but when the nurse touched her 'baby' she snatched it away and burst into violent and uncontrolled crying for her mummy. Contact with the friendly nurse had cracked the façade and allowed the pent-up longing to break through – an effect that was noticed on other occasions. Nurse was embarrassed by Laura's distress, in part probably because she thought a film shot of a crying child would be to the discredit of the ward, and offered, 'You mustn't cry – look at that little boy. He isn't crying', and similar inducements to stifle the tears. But Laura's tears were in full flood and she continued with shaking sobs, 'I want to see my mummy now. Go and find my mummy.'

When the nurse left, Laura's control gradually returned and she quietened. Twenty minutes later she was sitting quite still, with only the twitch of her mouth and the occasional flutter of her hands across her eyes to hint at the precarious control over the turmoil within. Just then two doctors came to look at the plaster that covered the wound. They were friendly and gentle, but she hid her face in her hands and was as motionless as an animal gone into hiding.

I had realized that an error in focusing had possibly spoiled the film record of the six-minute play period, and the nurse willingly returned to repeat it thirty-six minutes later. She was glad to have a second opportunity to cheer Laura up and set about it determinedly with toys and jolly words. But for several minutes Laura's face was averted and stony. Then the baby cried out. Laura looked at the nurse, her mouth trembled and she asked, 'What's that baby crying for?' and immediately burst into tears. The baby's distress was her own. For the second time Laura had greeted her nurse in the same impassive and unresponsive way and had then broken down.

After crying loudly, while trying to curb her tears with poignantly adult manipulation of a handkerchief, Laura quietened. But she ignored the

33

nurse's attempts to interest her in play. After a while the nurse gave up trying to amuse and responded directly to the child's need. She put down the toy and talked about Laura's mother. She pointed out of the window and said her mummy would come on the bus 'out there', the first time the cause of Laura's distress had been acknowledged. Laura immediately came to life. She stood up and looked down into the busy road. A bus appeared and she tensed with interest.

Two hours later, during the afternoon, Laura was awake but lying down and muttering to herself as if disgruntled. Her mother appeared in the doorway and Laura greeted her with a loud, protesting 'Mummy', but made no attempt to sit up, although she had been sitting up all morning. Mother was patient with Laura but also reluctant to have her cry. Probably for that reason, and because she was uncertain what was permitted, she did not caress or attempt to pick Laura up. Ten minutes later a nurse came and lifted the still unresponsive child into a sitting position. Gradually Laura's face cleared, but it was fifteen minutes before she came to life in course of a hand-clapping game initiated by her mother. Then her face lit up with a radiant smile, the first in three days, her eyes opened wide and she looked with affection on her mother – her confusion and resentment for the moment forgotten.

Several times, quietly, she asked to be taken home. When her mother said she could come home when her tummy was better, Laura seemed to understand and repeated, 'When my tummy better.' After several warnings that Laura seemed to ignore, her mother announced, 'I'm going home now.' Laura's expression was instantly tense and unhappy. Her mother said, 'Don't cry', pointing an admonitory finger, and Laura nodded uncertainly. As her mother left, and before she was out of sight, Laura turned away with an expression of the deepest misery.

The relief of tears which would have come to most children of that age in that situation was not readily available to Laura. As she tried to keep her feelings in check, she idly turned the pages of a book, fingered her hair and both hands fluttered impotently before her face as if she had been momentarily disoriented. Then, although it was still early afternoon, she asked to be tucked down and ensured that her teddy, 'baby' and flannel basket were with her under the covers. The nurse said, 'You cannot be tired.'

An hour later another nurse removed the chair on which her mother had sat, which provoked Laura to exclaim sharply, 'Don't take away my mummy's chair.' The nurse returned the chair to the cot side and Laura lay looking at it.

For the remainder of the afternoon her behaviour was subdued, with occasional spells of quiet crying. Various nurses tended her in brisk fashion without eliciting any response. But when a nurse sat down to give her supper she cried loudly; again, sustained contact with a nurse had evoked expression of her feelings. (The sister had tried to keep the same nurse for Laura, but after the third day the job assignment system could not bear this special attention and Laura was thereafter tended by changing nurses.)

That evening, after being tucked down for the night, Laura sat up repeatedly and appeared withdrawn. But when I went to her she looked up and said, 'My tummy's better. I'm going home in a minute.' She remembered her mother's promise and was apparently resisting sleep in the hope that something would happen. An hour later, at 7 p.m., she was again sitting up. I asked, 'Aren't you going to sleep?' and she replied, 'No. It's not night-time yet.' It was 9.20 p.m. before she finally submitted.

FOURTH DAY

In the morning Laura continued to be plaintive and quietly tearful. The ward was busy, and had I not been present it is likely that her subdued behaviour would have been deemed that of a 'settled' child. However, there was an illuminating incident later in the morning. A steam-roller appeared in the road below the ward, and Laura and several other children whose cots were near the windows looked down with interest as it puffed to and fro to complete a minor road repair. After a few minutes the steam-roller moved on and out of sight and the children's attention turned away from the road. Laura sat quietly gazing into the ward with an expressionless face, the only movement the twitching of her fingers. Then she began to cry, quietly at first as if trying to stem the flood, then bitterly. 'I want to see the steam-roller. I want to see the steam-roller. I want to see my mummy. I want to see the steam-roller.' The intensity with which she cried for the departed steam-roller was explained by the slip of the tongue. It was her mother she was crying for, but she had tried to conceal her wish as she had done at other times as part of her unusual control; as when she said, 'I not crying, see! Fetch that boy's mummy.' Laura was expected not to make a fuss.

During the day she wanted someone always to be near her cot. In various ways she tried to detain the nurses who did things for her and to induce me to bring my chair closer. As bedtime approached, Laura's play became noisy and defiant. When allowed into the playroom she banged a door after being told not to and cried and protested when put to bed. She became quiet and ate a pensive meal. Two hours later, when the ward was quiet and most other children asleep, she was still sitting up in her cot – eyes drooping, but stubbornly pushing off sleep.

Mother did not visit.

FIFTH DAY

This morning Laura was solemn and refused part of her breakfast. Several times she cried loudly but briefly for her mummy. A nurse threatened impatiently that her mother would not come if she cried, and this sobered Laura momentarily. She had made a precarious adaptation to the ward; however, she did not feel safe. There were frights and fears. As a nurse passed with a thermometer for another child, Laura whimpered, 'I don't want some of that'; and when, shortly afterwards, a trolley was wheeled along the ward she began anxiously, 'I don't want . . .' The complaint petered out as the trolley rolled past her bed.

When I held my exposure meter near her face preparatory to filming the morning-time sample of behaviour, she brightened a little and exhibited the self-conscious and beatific smile she reserved for this daily event. She asked for the flower in my buttonhole, which I gave her. She began to sing. I was a familiar and safe person who made a link with home.

When her mother came in the afternoon, Laura was still asleep. She roused slowly when her name was called, was confused and querulous and for a time averted her face. She seemed resentful, her face rigid and unsmiling, and she wiped away her mother's kiss. Then when her mother, still uncertain what the hospital allowed, said she could not take Laura on to her lap, Laura began to cry for her father. 'I want my daddy. Get my daddy.' Nor did she quite recover the good humour of the visit two days previously. She seemed not to hear her mother's several warnings that she would soon be leaving. When her mother announced, 'I'm going home now', Laura's lip trembled. Her hand touched her mother's cheek in a futile gesture and she turned away with the struggle for mastery distorting her features.

Laura's eyes followed her mother to the ward door; but again, as on the previous visit, she turned away before her mother had quite disappeared. Her mother's final hand-wave was to the back of Laura's head.

She was solemn, bit her lip, then stood up and quietly looked down on the road where the lorries and buses streamed past.

Sixth Day

The morning was long and tedious for Laura as the ward went about its business. This was to be a day without a visit. As the surgical trolley came along the ward Laura exclaimed with some anxiety, 'I don't want to go on that trolley. Put that boy on the trolley', pointing to a three-year-old across the way. The sister explained that no one went on this trolley, that it was for dressing bad legs and so on. Laura was anxious to convince the sister that she did not have a bad leg.

A few minutes later, when a nurse momentarily rested a tray of surgical instruments on a table near by, Laura began to cry and protested, 'I don't want to have one.' The nurse moved on and Laura became active. She took a many-petalled flower, shredded it over the side of the cot and gazed down on the litter with an expression of quiet satisfaction unexpected in a child so afraid of mess.

During tea-time a porter carried a newly admitted child through the ward and placed him in a distant side room. The boy was eleven months older than Laura. A more typical new admission, he cried loudly for his mother in a heart-broken way that Laura rarely permitted herself and she was visibly affected. She ate slowly, head turned in the direction of the noise, her expression tense. Several times she inquired of the ward in general, 'What's that boy crying for?' but made no reply when I put the question back to her. When I continued, 'Shall I go and say something to the boy?' she retorted, as if my remark had been quite stupid, 'Don't "say" to him. Go fetch his mummy. Go on. Go on. Go fetch my mummy', her voice shrill with her own unhappiness. She loitered anxiously over her tea, all her attention on the wailing boy. When allowed up a short time later she went first to say a gentle word to the boy, nearly a year older than she.

Mother did not visit.

Seventh Day

In the morning, while two nurses tidied her cot Laura was quiet and subdued. As her hair was brushed she asked with a choking voice, 'Where is my mummy? Is my mummy coming today? I want to see my mummy now.' The nurses made no reply and Laura began to sing to her teddy.

Just before lunch-time the surgical trolley began its morning journey through the ward, and this time the anxiety with which she watched its progress was justified. The sister and a nurse had come to take out her stitches. She began to grizzle and her hands fluttered uncertainly as she complained, 'What are you going to do to me now?' The sister explained simply and with tact; the removal of the plaster and the snipping of the stitches was a brief and apparently painless procedure which Laura watched with alternating tears and moments of quiet interest. As soon as it was over, the sister lifted her from the cot and comforted her. Laura said, uncertainly, 'I want to go home now my tummy's better.' She had remembered her mother's assurances.

Although Laura knew her parents were coming, the imminence of the visit brought no sign of excitement. Her mother arrived first. Laura was sitting on a chair playing with a doll when her mother entered the ward and called her name. She looked up with bright interest, succeeded immediately by a blank expression. Her mother's kiss she took impassively, and when her mother joined in a game with the doll Laura's expression remained subdued. The occasional trace of a smile at her mother's play with a balloon did nothing to relieve the tension. She did not touch her mother, nor try to get close to her. With each visit the initial phase of frozen behaviour towards her mother had intensified, and today it was more marked than before. There was neither welcome nor manifest resentment, just a muted response.

When ten minutes later her father arrived from work, he got a much warmer welcome. She squealed, 'Daddy', and for a moment appeared delighted; but by the time he reached her the exuberance had subsided and she was merely friendly but undemonstrative. At his request, she gave him a kiss. Then she directed him to a chair and thenceforward gave the impression of controlling the family party. She showed no more emotion than if she had never been parted from them. Most of the play was with her father who took her on to his knee to look at books; but while she was there, and as if to make certain mother did not go away, she ensured that her mother, too, had a book to look at. Later, when she and her mother played with dolls, she thrust a book into her father's hands as if to anchor him, too.

Although earlier in the day Laura had shown that she expected to go home now that her stitches were out, she put no pressure on her parents. Just once, as her father prepared to leave to return to work, she said quietly, 'I come with you.' In indirect ways she tried to delay her father's going. She said to her mother, 'You go home and make Daddy's tea. Daddy stay here.' After her father left, with a kiss and a parting wave, Laura was quiet. The balloon Mother had brought burst with a loud pop and Laura broke into tears which were quickly brought under control.

Ten minutes later her mother left. The sister had drawn discreetly near in case there was a scene, but Laura made no protest, although there had been no mention of her going home and the disappointment must have been intense. For a moment, she looked up at her mother with a pained expression and the back of her hand passed across her eyes as if to deter a tear. Then she lowered her head and gazed at a little bag which turned slowly at the end of a string in her hand. She seemed completely to ignore her mother's parting words and gestures. At the doorway, her mother turned with a smile to give a final wave, but Laura still stood with head bent.

A few minutes later, however, she slipped out of the ward and hurried along the long corridor. She caught up with her mother, who had stopped to talk to a nurse. She said in a quiet voice, 'I go with you.' Her mother said she could not do so just yet. Laura said nothing more and waved an obedient goodbye from the top of the stairs. Then she returned to the ward and sat on the window sill looking down on the traffic. 'I'se looking for Mummy and Daddy on the bus,' she explained to me. But when I tried to talk more about it, she turned away in a defensive gesture and busied herself with her doll.

The three-year-old boy was still crying in his cot in the side room. Laura went to him and said in a comforting and very grown-up manner, 'You want your mummy. Never mind. You get her in a minute.' The boy had refused to leave his cot for the playroom; Laura was very anxious that he should do so and looked everywhere for his slippers.

Late that afternoon I was aware that Laura's attitude to me had changed. She was treating me with the caution and withdrawn behaviour that she had shown her mother. When I said goodbye as I left that evening she continued with her play and did not look up. Some days later I learned from her mother that just before leaving she had whispered to Laura that she would be going home next day. Laura's hopes had been raised, but were so checked by doubt that she could not confide in me.

EIGHTH DAY: DAY OF DISCHARGE FROM HOSPITAL

I arrived in the ward about 8 a.m. and saw that Laura was talking brightly to the three nurses who were making her bed, but when I spoke to her I got only a meagre response. I asked, 'Do you want me to go away?' and Laura answered, 'Yes.' 'Don't you like me any more?' 'No, don't like you.' She then urged me to go and talk to other children, not to her; and all the time she did not look up. Anxiety about whether or not she was going home must have been great.

During the next hour she was restless and unhappy, crying off and on for her mother in a way not seen hitherto. She shook with heavy sobs, tears streaming down her cheeks, as if the control of the past seven days had at last given way. Although she had been told she was going home today she had not mentioned it to anyone and, not knowing she knew, I could not account for her changed behaviour. Hitherto, when I held the exposure meter near her face she had affected an amusingly sublime expression, but this morning she had no patience with it and turned her face to the pillow.

After about an hour of this behaviour, she became quiet and stood up in her cot to look out of the window. Her face was still, but suddenly it lit up with a brilliant smile. She turned to me and exclaimed eagerly, 'I'm going swimming tomorrow.' Puzzled, I asked, 'Are you? But who with?' Her face clouded over, and when she spoke again it was with a stammer as if to cover up an indiscretion. She answered, 'With Sister, and that little boy', and pointed across the ward to where a three-year-old lay with a fractured femur strung up on a pulley. I knew she went swimming with her father. She was saying obliquely that her mother was taking her home, an expression of trust that she had immediately to cover up in a feat of mental acrobatics remarkable for one so young. Just then she wet her bed.

At 10.15 a.m. Laura sat shaking with sobs when her mother arrived and came towards her smiling and saying, 'Are you coming home, Laura?' Laura did not respond immediately. She sat watching with a cautious expression as her mother came round the cot, then suddenly exclaimed, 'Oh yes! Yes!' and began to come out from under the covers. After a moment, she sat back in a corner of the cot as if still uncertain about her mother's intentions. But when her mother produced her outdoor shoes, Laura's face lit up with delight. She scrambled to her feet and threw her arms round her mother's neck in the first embrace of the eight days. Even at that point, however, uncertainty remained and her elation subsided. As her mother dressed her she sought assurance in quaint, negative statements, delivered quietly and with a flat expression. 'I'm not going home,' she said. Her mother assured her that she was going home, but Laura's face remained still. Then, 'I'm not going on the bus', and contradicting herself, 'Can we go upstairs on the bus?'

Elation returned and, as her dress was pulled over her head, she called to me, 'I'm going home – with my mummy', in a tone of confidence and great joy. She quickly gathered up her personal possessions – her teddy, blanket 'baby' and flannel basket – into a bundle she could hardly embrace. Mother tried to persuade her to leave a tattered book behind for the other children, but Laura insisted that everything belonging to her should be taken home. Nothing of her should remain in the ward.

Henceforward it was Laura who set the pace of departure. Within a few minutes her feelings were so reorganized that no one mattered except her mother and herself. I was ignored, and when I tentatively lifted my exposure meter she pushed my arm aside and snapped, 'Don't, I'm going home.' On the way out the tattered book slipped from the bundle in her arms and staff nurse picked it up. Laura snatched it back, screaming with temper, the fiercest display of feeling during her whole stay.

At her mother's request Laura said a polite 'thank you' to the nurse. Then she led the way from the ward. On the stairs she was two steps ahead of her mother, and in the long corridor she gradually increased her lead to perhaps fifteen yards, hurrying towards the outer door with all her belongings held about her. In the courtyard she stepped out smartly, refusing to take her mother's hand.

ON RETURNING HOME

I called on the family forty-eight hours after Laura returned home and was struck by the change in her expression. I noted at the time, 'It was as though a lamp had lit up inside her.' The blanched look of the days in hospital had gone, but from her parents' observations a more complete picture emerged.

Like most young children who return home after a stay alone in hospital, Laura went through a period of marked anxiety and irritability. She had temper tantrums, wetted and soiled herself and became very upset if her mother went momentarily out of sight – as if fearing she might be abandoned once more. She slept badly and for the first few nights her mother had to sleep beside her. However, although Laura clung to her mother there was also aggression against her. Laura would seek embraces, then suddenly punch and scratch. Towards her father she was still consistently friendly, as she is seen to be in the film when he visits her in hospital. Her mother, who had been closest to her and who had protected and cared for her in everyday life while her father was at work, was therefore the one who got the brunt of disappointment and anger over having been left in the hospital.

Laura did not talk about hospital and turned a deaf ear to anyone who mentioned it. But she reacted with anxiety to seeing shop assistants and others wearing white overalls, the colour of nurses' uniforms, which presumably reminded her of the unhappy hospital experience. The disturbed behaviour gradually lessened; but six months after return home she accidentally saw a few scenes from the end of the film record when I was showing it to her parents. She burst into violent tears and said angrily to her mother, 'Where was you all that time?' Then she turned away and cried on her father's shoulder. Her mother said with dismay, 'Laura seems to blame me for something.'

After that unplanned cathartic happening, Laura talked about hospital and seemed less anxious. But three months later the family went to an Ideal Home Exhibition which had a crèche where young children could be left while parents toured the exhibits. Laura did not seem to mind being left there among the toys, even though the assistants were in white. But as the parents left the building they heard Laura scream. They hurried back and found her 'hysterical' and it was an hour before she was calm. When they investigated what had happened, they were told that an official photographer had pointed his camera at her whereupon she had become 'hysterical'. Whereas in the hospital my camera and I had made a positive link with home and security, the camera in the crèche had made a reverse link back to the hospital with its distressing associations.

Fourteen years later I took the film to the home to show to a family gathering. Laura, now a big girl of sixteen years and dressed in school uniform, seated herself in a far corner of the room. After the film the relatives were quiet as they recovered from the sadness of the child. Laura stood up and said firmly, 'That meant nothing to me', but she could not maintain the cover-up and reached out and took hold of her father's tie. The relatives were much amused. I was told that when Laura was unhappy she had a habit of clutching her father's tie. Now they understood that this went back to the scene in the hospital where in her unhappiness she seeks to detain her father by holding his tie and saying, 'Don't go, Daddy.'

3

Reception of
A Two-year-old
Goes to Hospital

M Y ANTICIPATION that Laura would understate the problem, by not showing the florid distress I had been describing, proved correct. But to many viewers of the film, the struggle of a child aged two-and-a-half to control her feelings proved very painful, possibly even more than a film about a continuously crying child would have been. Understated or not, and over time, the film was to make a big impact upon the hospital professions.

In 1952, when the film was first shown, *Nursing Times*, journal of the Royal College of Nursing, published the results of its inquiry into the practices of eight well-known hospitals in relation to the visiting of children (1952b).

Senior nursing and medical staff had collaborated in preparing the detailed statements submitted. These show a remarkable uniformity of attitudes, in which there is no reference to the emotional needs of young children.

It can be reasonably inferred that what the staffs had in common was defensiveness against recognizing the plight of young patients, which allowed them to share the view that all was well in their establishments. The descriptions of visiting arrangements, commonly once or twice a week for thirty minutes, sometimes once or twice a month, imply that, whatever problems the administrations were aware of, these had not to do with the emotional well-being of young patients. Visits were rigidly controlled as to frequency and duration.

At the première screening in November 1952, before a large audience of doctors and nurses at the Royal Society of Medicine, the film encountered much resistance (*Lancet*, 1952). Some accepted its truths, but the majority reacted negatively. Various speakers said hotly that I had filmed an atypical child of atypical parents in an atypical ward; that young patients in their wards were happy; that they had never heard parents complain; that I had slandered paediatrics; and the film should be withdrawn.

This had to be understood, in my view, as a desperate attempt to maintain the myth that had sustained the hospital professions for generations – the myth that children's wards were happy places, that young patients 'settled' and became content in the absence of their parents – and to do so by attacking the man whose film brought paediatric beliefs and practices into question. For the visual rendering had succeeded in doing what the spoken and written word had failed to do. It had pierced the defences and compelled attention to the problem; but in order to do so it had touched on anxieties that had been repressed. The strength of the attempts to rebut what I was showing indicated the force of the reawakened anxiety. Mere disagreement would not have justified the furore.

After that meeting a number of younger paediatricians made known their agreement that there was a problem – but what to do about it? Although that had to be taken up, my immediate preoccupation was in dealing with the resistances. Some of the wards to which I had had free and friendly access became closed to me. A professor of child health wrote to the chairman of the Tavistock Clinic complaining of my lack of objectivity. He gave as example that in the film I had 'unfairly' panned down from Laura's impassive face to her twitching fingers. That shot had upset the professor of child health. Like most of his contemporaries he had been accustomed to the quiet faces of 'settled' young patients and drawn comfort from them. As I saw it, instead of realizing that the shot of twitching fingers had touched on his repressed anxiety, he now sought to blame me for unfairly 'causing' the upset he felt.

The matron of the hospital in which I filmed Laura convened a meeting of nurses there and angrily chaired my showing of the film. The meeting ran at an abusive level, with charges that I had prevented the nurses getting to Laura, that I had put screens around her so that she was isolated (in fact the one scene with a screen showed usual ward practice of putting a screen round any child sitting on a chamber-pot), and the children in the paediatric wards were 'happy'. The operation of such fierce unconscious defensiveness, as I formulated it, was remarkable to experience; the senior nurses believed what they said, blind to the reality of the everyday situation in their paediatric wards.

Then the medical superintendent learned of the project and heard of it in terms of the fierce criticisms by senior nursing staff. He requested a viewing of the film. His reaction was: 'Well, I am sorry it is my hospital. But I accept that it is an objective record which should be shown widely.'

EARLY SHOWINGS IN BRITAIN

The reception given to the film at its première at the Royal Society of Medicine alerted me to the resistances it would meet from the hospital professions throughout the country. It was decided the subject was so explosive that the film would be withheld from general release until the professions had had time to come to terms with it, lest the premature mobilizing of public discontent with the treatment of young patients should provoke attacks on hospitals and cause hardening of resistances.

The professional reviews of *A Two-year-old Goes to Hospital*, written by people who were not involved in anxiety-making ward situations, were uniformly positive. 'This is an objective and important film which must be taken seriously. It explodes the belief that a "good" child is well adjusted' was the tenor in medical and nursing journals (James Robertson, 1953b). And I was aware of more and more paediatricians and nurses who came some way along my thinking.

Thus fortified, and with good expectations, I returned to Newcastle and a large staff meeting presided over by Professor Spence. I thought that since my film was an objective and non-critical record the professor would give it his blessing. But my wishful expectations of appreciative acceptance were dashed. After the showing he was as caustically negative as before and his lieutenants followed his lead. Why?

One possibility was that, having made a good relationship on my previous visit to Newcastle, on my second visit Professor Spence had not expected to be confronted by a presentation that would offend him as my talk at the Windermere Conference had done.

When a few months later we flew together to a seminar in Paris, he told me he preferred the simple if misguided honesty of my orientation to the 'more dangerous attitudes' of Dr Bowlby. And it seemed that despite the apparent invulnerability of his rejection of my views there was a touch of conscience. He wrote an obituary of Sir Leonard Parsons, the Birmingham professor of paediatrics, in which he recalled how that distinguished man had come to the defence of a younger man who had been attacked at the Windermere Conference a year or two earlier. Even so, Spence omitted to acknowledge that it was he who had been the attacker.

45

Attempts to discredit my work continued and took forms which showed the depth of anxiety that had been aroused in paediatricians of status. A main charge was that I must have been very selective in editing the film since the child was never shown when 'happy'. A consultant paediatrician in a London teaching hospital insisted that the young patients in his ward were happy and that I should make a film there. I said I would be glad to do so on condition that he stayed with me and shared the observation. This he declined to do, so no film was made. I was also frequently accused of having invented the poignant remarks attributed to the child. To cope with this the Tavistock Clinic engaged the headmaster of a school for the deaf to lip-read the film; he confirmed that there were no discrepancies between the lip movements of the child and the words attributed to her.

Wherever I went in Britain the resistances and accusations were predictable. Usually led by senior medicals, they were often stated with such emphasis and sometimes with such hostility to me that whatever acceptance there might have been among junior staff in the meetings was stifled. Sometimes juniors approached me afterwards to say how much they agreed, and to talk about the changes they would make if they had sanction.

I flew to Belfast for a meeting of the Ulster Paediatric Association; news of the film had gone ahead and the amphitheatre at the university was packed. The criticisms were fierce and familiar and the chairman, another professor of child health, failed in his task of mediation by joining in.

When the assembly dispersed I was left alone in the hall. Only the fact that I had overheard the name of my hotel got me into a bed. Such was the emotional confusion created by the film in usually civilized men that they had abandoned normal courtesies.

At the Royal Hospital for Sick Children, Yorkhill, Glasgow, within a short distance of where I had been reared, the experience in Belfast was repeated. The chairman, again a professor of child health, did not give protection from the abuse that was directed at me but instead joined the critics. As I walked away from the hospital that evening with the film can under my arm, I heard the patter of running feet behind me. It was the matron. Catching up, she said breathlessly, 'Yon may be true of a wee English lassie, but it's not true of a Scottish bairn!'

At the same time, positive influence of the film was spreading, although through quieter events. Nursing journals reported many study days and conferences at which much agreement had been reached about the truth of the film and the implications for care.

In addition, the World Health Organization bought twelve copies for use in its projects in various parts of Africa and India, and this provided capital needed to make prints for sale and rental.

IN THE UNITED STATES

In 1953 I was appointed a short-term mental health consultant to the World Health organization and sent with the film to the United States on a six-week tour of universities, hospitals and learned societies. Having heard that mental health concepts had permeated further in American hospitals than in Europe, I was eager to discover how well paediatric care could be provided. I therefore asked that on this visit I should see only the hospitals regarded as progressive.

Nevertheless, having had such a bruising time in Britain from paediatricians of status, I anticipated similar aggressive resistances. But my first two presentations in Washington, to a gathering of academics and to the staff at the distinguished Children's Hospital, gave me a quite different experience from that which I anticipated. There was warm appreciation of *A Two-year-old Goes to Hospital* and general acceptance of its truth – for Britain! I was told that, however true the film might be of Britain, it was not true of the United States. American children, I was told, did not behave like Laura; American children were less cosseted than British, were accustomed to being out of the home and were therefore not upset by being in hospital. Even so, it did not take long to detect that the problem of young children in hospital was as acute in the United States as in Britain, although masked by social and cultural differences.

In Britain we had already moved into the Welfare State; already there was an awareness in the community that our hospitals belonged to the people, were paid for by taxes, that everyone had a right to free medical care at the point of need and the right to comment. But the United States was not a caring society in that sense: there was no provision of hospital services to which everyone was entitled as of right and which were used by people of all social classes. Hospital care was a commodity, available in differing qualities according to capacity to pay.

This was clearly shown in Washington Children's Hospital. There I discovered three levels of care.

Private patients were on the top floor. Each mother and child couple shared a room with cot and bed, and the mother was there round the

47

clock. Those mothers I spoke to knew the benefit to their children and themselves, but the costs were so high that some whose children had chronic conditions needing lengthy periods in hospital were in grave financial difficulties. But no mother expressed a wish for government assistance. In the great American dream everyone stood on his own two feet. As in a shopping centre, there was choice and one got what one could afford to pay for.

There was also tension between nursing staff and mothers. The facility for mothers to stay was on a purely commercial basis, not one of what was best for the child. Nurses felt that resident mothers treated them as waitresses and interfered with their work. In mute hostility senior nurses tended to frustrate mothers trying to help in the care of their children.

The Semi-privates were on a lower floor, at a lesser charge. Each room was shared by two mothers and two children, and mothers could stay for twelve hours each day but not overnight. Otherwise the situation was as in the Private ward, including the tensions between nurses and mothers.

The Indigents were in two wards on the ground floor, one for black children and one for white. Indigents were parents who did not have the means with which to meet hospital charges and whose minimum costs were met by a municipal charity called the Community Chest. I judged the Indigents to be ordinary working class, and poorer.

Visiting was twice a week for two hours. The younger patients showed signs of distress that were familiar to me, but although some of the black parents to whom I spoke were concerned about this none complained of the restrictions. I guessed that, although poor, they identified with the American ideology of the time; they accepted the lower level of facility as appropriate to their status as recipients of charity.

In discussion with a senior administrator I pointed to the three different levels of involvement of mothers in the care of child patients – twenty-four hours a day for the Privates, twelve hours a day for the Semi-privates, and twice weekly visiting for Indigents in the 'Straight' wards. He said that the provision in each section was adequate and he did not seem to have criteria of emotional well-being which would have detected the inconsistencies.

I had gone to America with a conviction that young patients need care by the mother as a priority, or in her absence by a substitute mother to provide continuity of mothering-type care. I used this as a measure by which to test the compatibility between intellectual attitudes and ward practice. I found that although there was much acceptance of the principle that the main factor in Laura's distress was absence of the mother, and although it was often agreed that similar behaviour could be seen in their wards, there was generally little motivation to solve the problem by including mothers in the care of their children in hospital. There was a tacit assumption that if staff could become skilled enough all problems of care could be solved by staff activity – including separation distress.

Mental health and child development were much discussed, but practical implications avoided. There was a not untypical instance of an intern taking a crying child firmly from the admission room towards the ward and showing the limits of his mental health training by saying, 'I know why you are crying. It's because you want your mother', instead of considering how to prevent the distress of separation. In my view, this form of facile mental health understanding was a kind of group *folie* which, together with the universal perception of the child as 'settled', defended staff from anxiety.

Some hospitals believed they provided continuity of substitute mothering care when in fact they did not. In one university hospital much credited in the literature with each nurse having a family group, I discovered from talking to the nurses that they were 'affiliates' (students in general training at other hospitals) on ten-week placements during which they moved from department to department before reaching the paediatric ward for their final two weeks. Each was then given a 'family group' of three or four children; but because they spent only two weeks in the paediatric ward the composition of each family group was changed each day in order to give the student nurses experience of different ages and different ailments. The notion that they gave continuous substitute mothering was a myth.

CONTINUING MY CAMPAIGN

Much travelling in the United States and Europe had confirmed that the attitudes of hospital staffs towards very young patients, in particular the resistances to recognizing their plight, were determined by ignorance of emotional development and repressed anxiety about distress in children. In those days of restrictions on parental access, one could see that the behaviour of young children in hospital was similar everywhere in the Western world, regardless of national and ideological boundaries. The resistances proved to be strongest at the most senior levels of paediatrics and nursing, stances that reflected the defensive myths of the time.

Returning to Britain I continued my campaign within the professions. Thirty years later my film *A Two-year-old Goes to Hospital* is accepted as an understated illustration of the problem, but in the early 1950s it continued to bring shock and hurt to the hospital professions, and I think it is difficult for the present generation to realize the climate of the times and the deep emotions that were aroused. Lecturing up and down the country I continued to meet opposition, accusations that I had 'rigged' the situations shown in the film and denial that the behaviour shown had any importance. On the other hand, the number of professionals who shared my concerns and wished to use the film in their regions was growing. I continued with tutoring events in the Tavistock and else-where. But the film was still withheld from general release.

Despite this high level of ambivalence towards me, improvements began to appear unevenly in hospital wards in and out of London: one hour a day visiting, two hours a day, three hours a day and even four hours. But institutional inertia was so great that each increment of improvement was achieved with difficulty and tended to be regarded as sufficient, as if nothing more was needed. There was anxiety that if mothers had more access to their children they would behave hysteri-cally, would give them sweets, would make 'settled' children cry and would bring chaos into the wards.

In my view, however, visits by parents did not *make* their children unhappy, but merely revealed the distress that lay behind the 'settled' mask. Doctors and nurses tended to misperceive mothers, whom they saw mainly in crowded out-patient departments where long waits and the restlessness of anxious children could make mothers agitated. When parents were restricted to once a week visiting they would sometimes give sweets and cakes, even if asked not to; they had only an hour or two in which to try to comfort their sick and unhappy children and some sought with sweet things to make up for their feelings of inadequacy. I suggested that mothers would not behave in this way if brought more fully into the care of their sick children.

I have to admit that throughout the campaigning of the early 1950s for more visiting my own cards were close to my chest. I had an objective which could not be pressed for prematurely: that mothers of under-fives should be admitted to hospital with them to help in their care and prevent the dangerous stresses of separation. On the few occasions when

I ventured to suggest this during film presentations it was dismissed as fanciful and wholly impractical.

But in my reserved view, increase of visiting periods to four or more hours a day, which was becoming common, did not meet the need. It could be an improvement for older children, who because of their greater maturity might be more able to understand and to cope better with periods between visits; but for the younger ones, the under-fives, even four hours a day visiting still left many hours without the mother – long hours during which the young patient was exposed without support to the frights and hurts of the hospital ward. I was confident the only satisfactory solution was that when a young child was admitted to hospital the mother should be encouraged to stay with him, to continue with the comforting and bodily care to which the child was accustomed at home and through which he knew her love and protection.

4

Second Film:
Going to Hospital with Mother

IN 1954, fate intervened to give us first-hand experience of mother and child in hospital. Jean, our four-year-old daughter, had a series of ear infections that could not be treated medically because she was allergic to antibiotics; a tonsillectomy was recommended. Dr Ronald MacKeith, consultant paediatrician at Guy's Hospital and fully supportive of my campaigning for increased visiting, agreed to go a step further by having Jean and her mother together in his ward. In the event he had to overcome a few anxieties in himself when Joyce made clear the amount of involvement she sought in addition to being resident with Jean.

Dr MacKeith did not think it would be useful for Joyce to be with Jean in the recovery room, being genuinely concerned that Joyce was unfamiliar with the sight of a post-operative child and would be upset by the pallor, restlessness and bloodiness; he said that Jean would still be under the effects of the anaesthetic and unaware of her surroundings. But he deferred to Joyce's wish and also supported her request to be with Jean in the induction room. The surgeon and anaesthetist reluctantly agreed; but, impatient of the whole idea of the mother's involvement, the surgeon sarcastically invited Joyce to be present at the operation. Joyce naturally declined, but was with our daughter during induction and throughout the post-operative period.

In the recovery room Jean seemed unaware of anything in her restless and disoriented state, but next day she showed clearly that she had been aware of her mother's presence: 'Mummy, you kept telling me to keep my head on the pillow.' And, said with emphasis, 'You told me my throat would be sore, Mummy, and it is.' Having been told the truth about the pain, she retained trust in her mother.

Jean returned home in good spirits and had no problems arising from her stay in hospital. She started nursery school two weeks later in a confident mood. But a playmate of her own age had been at the same time as Jean in a tonsils ward that did not allow visiting. After several days, the parents were sent for because of severe bleeding, but were not allowed to stay after the bleeding stopped. While Jean was going cheerfully to nursery this child was at home, pale and unsettled by her tonsillectomy without mother.

Joyce kept a daily diary of what Jean did and said before, during and after her hospitalization. That detailed account of the subtleties of a young child's anticipation of an anxiety-making experience, and the working through afterwards, are incorporated in Joyce's article 'A Mother's Observations on the Tonsillectomy of her Four-year-old Daughter: With Comments by Anna Freud', which, headed by an excellent editorial 'The Mind of a Young Child', was published in *Nursing Times* (Joyce Robertson, 1956). The journal's support was a significant step and the article produced a lengthy and controversial correspondence. It ranged from those who fully supported what they had read to others who were angered by the 'rubbish' of the mother's account, scolded the editor for publishing the article and threatened to cancel their subscriptions to the journal. A professor of child health criticized us as parents who had transferred our anxieties to the child; he was admirably answered by Dr MacKeith. The correspondence reflects the differing professional attitudes of the times (*Nursing Times*, 1957–8).

Moving into Europe, I made presentations of *A Two-year-old Goes to Hospital* during 1953–4 to professional audiences in Denmark, France, Germany, Holland, Norway and Yugoslavia. I found the familiar mix of kind intentions limited in effectiveness by lack of knowledge and defensive blindness, particularly at the higher levels of paediatrics. As in Britain, at presentations it was the more senior who were most resistive, the more junior being more open. Continental reviewers were uniformly accepting of the film.

MAKING THE FILM

In 1953 I met Dr Dermod MacCarthy, consultant paediatrician at Amersham General Hospital. At the première of *A Two-year-old Goes to Hospital* at the Royal Society of Medicine in November 1952 he had been one of the many who were angered by the film, a humane paediatrician who felt that he and his profession were slandered. Driving back to

Amersham with his ward sister, Ivy Morris, he spoke crossly about 'Robertson', who had said such untrue things about children in hospital. Sister Morris pulled him up with the words, 'But what Mr Robertson says is true.'

Next day Dr MacCarthy found, as he himself admitted, that he could no longer walk down his children's ward with his former complacency. He was suddenly aware of Lauras among the younger patients. He wrote, 'I was angry, but after the film I really heard children crying for the first time.' Unlike some of his fellow paediatricians who remained angry and unchanged after the film presentation, Dr MacCarthy put his roused anxiety to good use. He had long been easy about visiting and occasionally had mothers stay; but now he recognized the full implications of the young child's need of the mother. He quickly opened the ward to unrestricted visiting and encouraged all mothers of under-fives to stay. He did not pick and choose between them on grounds that some were more suitable than others; family doctors in the community could tell the mother of any young child they were sending to hospital that she could stay with him. In the opinion of Dr MacCarthy and his like-minded colleagues, Sister Ivy Morris and Registrar Dr Mary Lindsay, the young patient needed his mother; no matter what the staff's view of her might be, their task was to get on with healing the illness and to keep mother and child together.

Dr MacCarthy's relaxed ward was heart-warming to see. When brought fully into their children's care, most mothers were as competent and sensible in the ward as they were at home. The occasional one who was feckless or fearful got more nursing support; there was no question of excluding her. The anxiety about mothers who fed sweets and cakes to their children had been dispelled; mothers whose affection and concern were not obstructed by restrictions had less need to bring sweet things. There was no increase in infection. Student nurses were a greater source of infection than were mothers to their own children.

Although our teaching was about the special needs of the under-fives, accommodation was not restricted to that age-group. The mother who felt an older child needed her to stay could do so; sometimes there was special need because the child was fearful after having been alone in hospital when younger. And as the presence of mother (or father) was not an amenity but essential for the contentment of their children, there was no charge for accommodation or meals. Parents became valued members of the care-giving team.

That was the model I needed to make a second film, *Going to Hospital with Mother*. Again I had to have a child undergoing an elective operation, so that I could begin filming in the home. Perhaps because my first film had incidentally drawn attention to the undesirability of performing non-urgent operations on very young children, there were only three children on the waiting-list. Two of them were circumcisions to be done at the request of general practitioners under pressure from mothers. These Dr MacCarthy did not wish to have filmed, he personally being against the operation; now that the matter had been raised he doubted if the surgeons would do them.

The remaining child was Sally, aged twenty-one months, younger child in the kind of working-class family that I knew well and whose qualities gladdened me. Her mother was not at work, but stayed home to care for her children – able to housekeep, cook and care for them with quiet competence. Sally had an umbilical hernia of a kind that did not recover spontaneously.

So I was able to make a film that demonstrated that having mother and child together in hospital is eminently practicable and protects the young child from excess of anxiety; the film was released to professional use in 1958 (James Robertson, 1958a).

THE STORY OF THE FILM

The following is a scene-by-scene account of the film and accompanies plates 11–16.

We see Sally as a twenty-month-old child, the second child in a working-class family. She is lively and impatient of interference, never far from her mother's skirts. When her face is washed she resists and cries loudly, but the tears are dry in a moment. Her mother, busy about her domestic jobs, has the ordinary mother's competence to do many things while meeting her children's needs.

When Sally and her mother go to hospital they leave her four-year-old sister Angela at her grandmother's house where she will stay in the daytime, going home each evening with her father on his return from work. At the hospital they are met by the ward sister who shows mother the amenities, including the kitchen where she can make a cup of tea. Then the sister leaves them in their cubicle containing a locker, cot for Sally, bed for her mother and a wash-basin. Through the glass walls mother can see other mothers with their children.

When the surgical registrar calls to make a preliminary examination, Sally protests loudly at the interference. She does not like the examination any more than having her face washed; but with her mother there to hold her the protest is brief and of little consequence. As she is tucked down for the night, talking up to her mother and full of fun, it is clear that it is the presence or absence of a mother that matters to a child of this age and not whether her cot is at home or in hospital.

Next morning, Sally is prepared for the operation – skin cleansed and pre-medication given by mouth and injection. She is held throughout by her mother, whose lips press tightly together as she shares the reaction of Sally to the needle. Sally resists and cries, then is quickly consoled by cuddling down into her mother's arms. As the trolley wheels her away, she stirs and comes to her knees, but her mother is there with a gentle hand and a quiet word to soothe her. In a moment she is tucked down again and on her way to the theatre. While the operation proceeds it is good for her mother's morale that she can sit chatting to another mother.

Within a few minutes after her return to the cubicle, Sally has an injection to put her to sleep. Mother takes over from the sister and sits quietly beside the sleeping child. As Sally recovers, her mother intuitively meets her need for comfort – wiping her brow, smoothing her hair, sitting quietly by. Being unaccustomed to the aftermath of an operation, the mother has moments of anxiety. The sister and registrar quietly reassure her. The atmosphere is so permissive and supporting that when the consultant surgeon calls to make a check, the mother talks freely about her anxieties. At intervals, the six resident mothers also meet in the ward kitchen to make tea, wash up and chat about their children. They are of different social groups, but it is clear that in their common experience they are mutually supportive.

At no time does Sally show any of the fretfulness or withdrawal commonly seen in unaccompanied young patients. On the fifth day, when she is fully recovered from the operation and about to be discharged, she is as bright and mischievous as before admission, in a state of good-humoured well-being never seen in unaccompanied young patients of this age on the fifth day. On return home there were no temper tantrums or regressions such as are usually shown by young children who have been in hospital by themselves. Sally resumed family life as if she had never been away. In a sense she had not been away; she had always been in her mother's loving care.

It took a week to shoot the film, and about a year to complete. Before filming I had offered the hospital right of veto, knowing that afterwards there would be staff anxieties to be worked through. The consultant surgeon asked for the scene of Sally struggling while her stomach is cleansed to be deleted, since in the future such cleansing was going to be done while the child was unconscious; but he agreed that, although the sequence would no longer represent practice in the departments in his charge, it should remain as a caution to surgeons elsewhere. The surgical registrar asked that a 'friendly' poke of his finger in Sally's stomach be removed, but he eventually agreed it should remain as a teaching point about the anxiety that could be caused to a young child by a gesture kindly intended. The matron was upset that a nurse's uniform was untidy and that bandages were to be seen drying on hot water pipes, fearing she would be criticized by the Royal College of Nursing. But these, too, were allowed to remain.

In an appendix to the film guide, Dr MacCarthy made clear that his approach was not based on mental health considerations but was that of the humane paediatrician: 'Our primary concern is to prevent the unhappiness that is caused to young patients by separation from the mother. The possibility of after-effects or lasting harm has always been a secondary consideration. To prove it is difficult' (MacCarthy, 1958).

By 1956 the practice of Dr MacCarthy had gone further than any other British paediatrician by kindliness in the tradition of Spence and other humanizing paediatricians, remedying every visible risk of detriment to his child patients. But for lack of a theory of psychological development there were gaps in his understanding and practice. For instance, because infants of under six months do not show classical separation distress, and after brief restlessness may smile at anyone, he held for some time to the then common paediatric belief that there was less need for the mother to be there than with a toddler. My psychoanalytic views on the critical stages of psychological development before six months did not prevail against the 'happy' behaviour of these infants.

Going to Hospital with Mother was well received as a contrast to *Two-year-old*. It showed that staff attitudes were more important than physical structures, that ordinary mothers were indeed sensible and competent and that a young child supported by mother and empathetic staff during a hospital stay and a minor operation could come through without special upset and have no emotional disturbances after returning home.

5

Years of Change

A LTHOUGH there was lingering denigration from some top medicals, reviewers around the world acknowledged the importance of my films and there was evidence of growing support in the medical and nursing professions. By 1957, professional and public concern had become sufficient to cause the Minister of Health to appoint a Committee on the Welfare of Children in Hospital (the Platt Committee), which invited professional and lay organizations to submit evidence.

I wrote a lengthy memorandum on 'Young Children in Hospital' which was submitted on behalf of the Tavistock Institute of Human Relations, under my own name. When invited to show my two films, *A Two-year-old Goes to Hospital* and *Going to Hospital with Mother* to the committee, I asked Dr MacCarthy to accompany me so that he could expand on his approach to mothers and children as shown in my second film. We appeared together before the committee.

Knowing that the report of the committee would be published in 1959, I gained the co-operation of a BBC producer to make a programme around excerpts from the two films. Preparations were quite advanced when in 1958 I was asked to meet the Director of Television, Mr Kenneth Adam. Expecting a commendation for preparing a unique programme in readiness for the publication of the report, I was astounded to be told he had decided not to allow the project to go further. Having 'consulted medical opinion', he said, he did not wish the BBC to cause anxiety to ordinary families by showing hospital care that was not generally available. Evidently resistance in high places still operated. I was left angry and wondering which of the professors of child health had intervened.

On the recommendation of Sir Harry Platt, Bt, chairman of the committee, I quickly shaped my memorandum into a book *Young Children in Hospital*, which was published in 1958 (James Robertson, 1958b) in anticipation of the Ministry of Health report on *The Welfare of Children in Hospital* (the Platt Report, DHSS, 1959). The Platt Report adopted virtually all the recommendations in my memorandum and the book drew much attention in the professional and lay press in Britain and throughout the world. It went quickly into eight European languages and into Japanese. Reviews were consistently positive.

The Minister of Health accepted the Platt Report and declared its recommendations to be Ministry policy, but said that since these touched on matters of clinical judgement they could not be made compulsory. He encouraged the hospital professions to implement the recommendations at their own pace, even though the Platt Report had stressed that 'as a matter of urgency' the training of medical and nursing students should be improved to give greater understanding of the psychological development of children.

There was now a task of professional and public education. In January 1961 I contributed a series of three articles to the *Observer* newspaper, and some weeks later an article in the *Guardian*, on the care of young children in hospitals (James Robertson, 1961).* In a one-hour BBC television programme two months later (the BBC having softened its attitude in light of the Minister's acceptance of the Platt Report), I presented sequences from *A Two-year-old Goes to Hospital* and *Going to Hospital with Mother* in discussion with Joyce Robertson and Dr Ronald MacKeith, and with Dr Dermod MacCarthy and Sister Ivy Morris whose liberal ward practices at Amersham had anticipated the recommendations of the Platt Report.

In those days there was no video recording; television was live. Taking advantage of this, and ignoring direction from the producer, in the last two minutes I spoke directly to camera and invited parents to tell me about good and bad experience of paediatric wards. The first response was a telephone call that awaited my return from the BBC. A man with a working-class accent said he and his wife had seen the programme just after leaving their young child in hospital that afternoon, shocked to

---

* The *Observer*'s obituary of James Robertson, on 22 January 1989, acknowledged its pride in having played a part in disseminating his views; the *Guardian*'s obituary on 13 January also recalled 'the significant correspondence from doctors and parents' in Mary Stott's Mainly for Women page. – *Eds*

learn that visiting was not allowed. They had peeped into the ward and seen their little girl lying on a bed in a state of distress. A neighbour had now told them of a nearby hospital which did allow visiting. They were very upset. What could they do?

I asked what he and his wife would like to do, to which he said they would like to move their child to the other hospital, but of course that would not be possible. I told him to remember that the child was theirs, not the hospital's, and that he could ask for the transfer to be made. His reply, 'Well, we'll get on the motor bike and see what we can do', was music to me.

That evening he phoned from a call box in a state of elation. He and his wife had gone back to the hospital, and after some argument at lower levels had seen the medical superintendent. He had told them they were being foolish – that the child would 'settle down'. Having just seen our programme they had the answer for that and had the satisfaction of following on the motor cycle the ambulance taking their child to the other hospital. First they had had to sign that the transfer was made against the first hospital's advice!

From the television programme and the *Observer* articles came more than four hundred letters. Joyce and I sorted them on the sitting-room floor under headings taken from the Platt Report, showing how the recommendations had or had not been implemented and what this had meant for the recent experience of young patients and their parents. The outcome was a book of letters from parents, *Hospitals and Children: A Parent's-eye View* (James Robertson, 1962), with a foreword by Sir Harry Platt, Bt, chairman of the Ministry of Health Committee on the Welfare of Children in Hospital, in which he said:

> Mr James Robertson's pioneer studies on the psychological trauma inflicted on young children during periods of stay in hospital have brought this important aspect of child welfare vividly before the notice of a wide public. Much has been done to mitigate the consequences of the hospitalization of the young child since the publication of the author's first book on the subject (1958) and the production of the documentary film *Going to Hospital with Mother* (1958). Both these works had a strong influence on the Central Health Services Report, *The Welfare of Children in Hospital* (DHSS, 1959). In the last few years the admission of mother with child, and the encouragement of unrestricted visiting, have been increasingly welcomed by children's hospitals. But tradition and the difficulty of adapting existing hospital

structures have curbed the pace of reform. It is therefore of great importance that Mr Robertson should continue to remind us that all is not yet well.

In this new book he returns to the attack armed with the powerful evidence of those who, best of all, can speak for the inarticulate child – the parents.

The letters from parents are arranged in themes linked to recommendations of the Platt Report. Apart from topping and tailing, they are given as written. In their simplicity and directness the letters make moving and convincing reading.

They cover a wide range of hospital practices and attitudes. They show, on the one hand, how adequately a children's ward can meet the emotional needs of families when it is organized to do so; and, on the other hand, how the persistence of out-of-date restrictions can cause the kindest of doctors and nurses to affront family feeling and endanger the mental health of young patients. Here are some examples.

Letter 7:

When my young son was just over two years old it was discovered that he would need to undergo a serious operation.

Remembering childhood experiences of my own when left to my fate in hospital, I asked whether it would be possible for me to stay in hospital with him. The surgeon attending his case made the necessary arrangements and I remained in the hospital for over four weeks during my son's first stay there and for a further two weeks when he was admitted for a final operation.

He never for a moment experienced the feeling of insecurity and bewilderment which even now I can remember from my own early experiences, and except for the seven or eight days when he was recovering from the operation, actually enjoyed his stay in hospital and the company of the other children who were allowed almost complete freedom of movement in the ward if they could take advantage of it. He was sorry to leave the friends he had made, and had no objection to going back when it became necessary – which I regarded as the final proof of the success of the experiment.

I had half expected that the nurses and sisters would not take kindly to the presence of an outsider in the ward who might be in the way at odd times. On the contrary, I found that they did everything possible to make things easier for me. Everyone in the hospital, from consultants down, was as helpful as possible.

I shall be eternally grateful to the doctors and nurses of
Pendlebury who brought my son through a difficult operation
successfully, and sent him home without the memories of a bitter
experience which can be so shattering to a young child. If he had to
go into hospital tomorrow he would be quite ready to do so –
whereas, even now, the smells and sounds of a hospital still bring
back to me an echo of the wretchedness I felt so long ago as a child.

The state of my son's mind, as much as the healthy condition of
his body, is a fine proof of the humanity and kindness of the modern
approach to these problems, and to the medical and nursing staff
who make it possible.

Pendlebury Hospital, Manchester

*Letter 58 (girl two years nine months; suspected appendicitis; six days in
hospital; half-hour daily visits):*
Two strange men, kindly but nevertheless strange, came in, wrapped
her in a blanket and carried her into this weird motor car. She was
very frightened, but with the infinite trust of a little child she could
be brave as long as I was with her. On arriving at the hospital she
was submitted to the usual proddings and testings that are necessary
with a new admission, and just endured this by tightly clutching my
hand. She would not let go, but as long as she had my hand the
doctors were able to go ahead with their examinations. It was found
that she did not have appendicitis, but they were not satisfied and
said that they would have to keep her in hospital in order to make
various tests.

I was left with her for quite some time during which I tried to
explain that she would not be coming home with Daddy and me, but
must stay for a little while till they had made her better. Have you
ever tried telling a two-year-old that? Suddenly without warning a
male nurse came along and without a word picked my little girl up
from the examination couch and set off at a spanking pace for some
unknown destination. Ann (my little girl) screamed in terror. I ran
after them and was told that I could go up to the ward – following at
almost a sprint, and trying to reassure her over the nurse's shoulder
was no mean task.

On reaching the ward, and still travelling at this high speed, the
nurse took her to a cubicle about half-way down the ward, but I was
stopped by the staff nurse until, as I thought, they had put her into
bed. I could hear her asking this male nurse, 'Where is my mummy

gone?' And just as I was about to at least kiss her goodbye I was told that I could not see her then, but could come back the next evening.

From then on her case was almost identical with the film *A Two-year-old Goes to Hospital* which was shown in your programme. I was never allowed to see her except at the authorized visiting time 6.30 to 7 p.m. each evening, and during her stay, which lasted for six days, she just lay taking no interest in anything. She ate nothing at all during the whole of this time, which including the day at home when she first had her pain was seven days. She just lay consumed in her own misery all this time.

I might add that Christmas Day came and went without any relaxation of visiting times. At the end of this period I was told that she would be better at home as she was fretting so much and therefore not making the hoped-for progress. I was given instruction for carrying out the treatment myself, and once home she got well rapidly.

Of course I had the usual remarks passed by the sister-in-charge that Ann was spoiled because she fretted so, but my great fear is that should she ever again need hospital treatment she will have this experience in her mind, and I feel it has done untold damage. She is now quite recovered from it, apart from her terror of doctors and nurses. Even our own doctor she fears in case he will send her into hospital again.

Warwickshire

The letters impress with their reasonableness, with their warmth when describing good experience and with their lack of rancour even when recounting harsh experience. The devotion and kind intentions of hospital staffs are constantly acknowledged and the problem of making children's ward practice compatible with good intentions emerges clearly.

An outstanding impression is that parents who were brought fully into the care of their sick children found staff attitudes supportive and understanding, so that no matter how dangerous or distressing their child's illness they found the strength to cope. In contrast, the greatest stress for parents and child patients occurred when parents were frustrated in their wish to help their sick child; this caused intense distress to the child while in hospital and disturbances of behaviour on return home.

The contrast in outcome for parents is vividly seen around the death of a child. Several mothers wrote about being in hospital throughout a child's illness and death and how, although grief-stricken by the berea-vement, they were comforted by the fact that they had been there to do everything they could for their child and by having seen the devoted attention of doctors and nurses who had tended their child day and night. Below are some examples.

Letter 12:
I feel the need to write and tell of the most horrible experience of my life, as parent of a two-year-old child. She was an intelligent little girl and we had a happy relationship. On learning that she had to go into hospital, my first overwhelming feeling of frustration was that of being powerless to make her understand why we would have to part. I gave her two of her favourite cuddly toys to take with her and she clung to these all the three months she was in hospital as if her life depended on them, and indeed I believe it did.

Her reaction to my first visit was a shock to me. She didn't cry until I made to go, then she flew into a most terrible rage – even standing on her head. After two more visits her attitude to me changed; she became quiet and solemn, appearing on the surface to be indifferent. She watched eagerly for me coming in the door, but then soon as I reached her she turned her head away from me and ignored me for the rest of the visit. It was plain that she was terribly hurt and distressed. Her condition was such that her food was most valuable to her, but she ate hardly anything. After about a month her mental and physical state had become so deteriorated that I felt I had to plead with the doctor to let me stay with her, although I knew this was frowned upon in this hospital. The strict visiting time is one hour each day. However, after hearing my plea the doctor allowed me to stay. My child's first reaction to this was good, in fact she objected strongly to anyone else doing anything for her. She would say with what seemed to be a note of fear in her voice, 'Mummy do it', and when I left the ward for a short time she would shout, 'Mummy, come back'; and from time to time she would show her anger and resentment to me as she did at first – just as if she could never really forget my cruel treatment of her. Thank goodness the doctor let me bring her home to die. She was with her dad and I for just two weeks during which time I was free to lavish upon her all the love and attention which a mother longs to give her sick child, and I nursed her till death. If I was ever fortunate enough to have another child I feel I could never let it go away from me unless

I was allowed to go also. I would rather risk nursing the child myself than condemn it to such brutal unhappiness at two years old. I fail to see how a child as young as this who is very ill can recover when in a distressed state of mind. The hardest thing for me to bear now is not the loss of my dear child, but that she had to go through such a thing before her death; and I know that in this same hospital and others children are going through the same terrible experience.

Yorkshire

Letter 11:

A year ago my daughter died in hospital at the age of twenty months. I was one of those mothers who was fortunate my baby did not go into hospital alone.

You probably know all about this hospital, but I will describe it from the mother's point of view. Small, wildly inconvenient for the nurses. Mothers and children in pleasant bed-sitters, unaccompanied children either in cubicles or a smallish nursery. Meals for mothers – a cooked midday and evening meal, the makings of breakfast and tea – a mothers' kitchen for cups of tea, etc., and (a great boon) a telephone which could be used at all times without troubling the staff. I shall never forget the kindness of staff. I was filled with admiration for them all. Dr —— who came in at 10 p.m. that first night to see how Mary had settled; sister-in-charge, who was so kind but who could inspire awkward mums with great respect, who could allow informality and dignity.

It was through no fault of the hospital that things took the course they did. She thrived in the summer, and in the autumn had a cough. The doctor sent us again to the Babies' Hospital for tests which confirmed his suspicion of fibrocystic disease. The next stay for a fortnight was much more harrowing and worrying. We came home to carry out the treatment. A fortnight later her chest became worse. She went back to the hospital into an oxygen tent and died three days later – her heart gave out.

To have sent her into a ward alone might not have mattered much at two-and-a-half months; it would have been cruel at nineteen months. She had been ill for three months and had had my undivided attention all the time. To have been catapulted from that to loneliness would have been dreadful. As it was, although she fought the treatment every time, and got frightened, I was with her and she had many happy hours right up to the last week.

65

Apart from the child, who is the prime consideration, the mother, too, is better for being with the child. You know what is going on and how things are. When things go badly mothers help each other. Without any conscious arrangement the mothers of dangerously ill and doomed children gravitate together, and we did get help from one another in different ways according to our natures.

We saw the work, tireless and unceasing, which went on to help our children. I have seen doctors and nurses who were tired out after a heavy day turn to deal with some problem. So I knew that if human endeavour could have saved my child, she would be living.

Because we knew the doctors so well, and saw them so often, we could feel like a family. When Mary died, Dr —— was able to say things which were a real help and consolation. He couldn't have done so if we hadn't 'lived together'.

There were all kinds of mothers. What struck me was that the child wanted his mother, even if by my standards she was ghastly. One in particular was dreadful by any standard, but was there because her child had pined for her when there alone. He would rather have the mother who knocked him about than the kind conscientious and often dedicated nurses. There were things that were not perfect. I won't bother to enumerate them, but I mention the fact in case you think that over enthusiasm has destroyed my power of judgement. But I would do anything to help popularize the idea of the Babies' Hospital.

Newcastle Babies' Hospital

However, several mothers wrote about restrictions imposed on their involvement and the terrible shock of learning that their child had died during their absence. Some imagined that if only they had been there to give comfort the child might not have died, and felt they would be haunted for ever by a sense of failure.

One mother wrote objectively about an instance where the parents' intuition about their child had been more reliable than medical opinion. Their young son aged two years five months had been in hospital because of an acute asthma attack. They were not allowed to visit him but could peep through a curtain as he lay alone in a cubicle. They became alarmed to see him struggle with asthma and separation distress. They felt that the sudden separation and the rigorous exclusion of the mother might well prejudice his chances of recovery, so after forty-eight hours they took him home against the medical director's advice and after signing a statement that they took responsibility for their action.

On the way home by car the child came to life, sat up and began to chatter and exclaim about familiar scenes. The parents had some anxiety lest their action endangered the child's life and had taken the precaution of arranging that the family doctor would be in their home when they arrived. The child, now very lively, ran up the garden path and quickly joined his siblings in play. The family doctor pronounced him fit and well. His deteriorating condition in hospital had been caused by separation and unsuitable care (James Robertson, 1962, p. 149).

In that book all the hospitals referred to, satisfactory and unsatisfactory, are named. It was reviewed in positive terms around the world.

Around this time I gave a talk on BBC radio about young children in hospital. When discussing what parents could do if they wanted more visiting than was allowed, I went through the usual sequence – talk to the sister and, if she refuses, talk to the paediatrician; if he refuses, talk to the hospital secretary. Soon I came up against the question: what to advise if all approaches fail? I could not lamely say that parents should give up. I wrote into the script that if parents decided to stay quietly by the cot of their sick child they could not be evicted. The BBC producer was taken aback at my apparent incitement to unlawful behaviour and the legal department were consulted. They confirmed that parents staying peacefully could not be evicted, so I gave my talk as written. Several parents then wrote to say they had taken the advice and sat on chairs by their child's cot through the night against regulations, and that after being ignored they had in some instances been given cups of tea. Quiet assertion had discovered kindliness and helped to modify attitudes by showing that parents were reasonable people.

The response to the broadcasts, the newspaper articles, the book and the films, which were now on general release, brought heavy mail and a telephone which rang throughout the day with requests for advice and help from parents and professionals from all over Britain. The burden of work was very heavy and would have been difficult to sustain without the efficiency and commitment of Pat Willard, my full-time secretary and assistant from 1953 to 1973.

6

Involving the
Community

LATTERLY I HAD WORKED for the emergence of a parents' movement which would take over the burden, and this development was now due.

As I have said in my book *Hospitals and Children: A Parent's-eye View*, in a three-part series of articles for the *Observer* and in an article on 'The Plight of Small Children in Hospitals' (Robertson, 1962, 1961, 1960), I urged parents to organize themselves in order to work for implementation of the Platt Report. A group of young mothers from Battersea in London came to the Tavistock Clinic to seek my help. They were delighted that the views of someone with specialized knowledge of child development should support their wish to combat hospital restrictions. Mother Care for Children in Hospital, later called the National Association for the Welfare of Children in Hospital (NAWCH), came into being in 1961.

During the next few years I conducted public meetings throughout Britain to encourage support for the new movement; twenty-five years later it is difficult to convey the atmosphere of these early meetings. The films were timely. They mobilized community experience of children's wards. People wept with Laura and rejoiced over the security and contentment of Sally and her mother in the care of Dr MacCarthy and his colleagues at Amersham. Feelings that had not previously had public expression came freely in animated discussions full of anecdotes about good and bad experiences of children's wards.

Sympathetic doctors and nurses throughout the country joined NAWCH groups in spreading understanding of the problems of young patients and their families. In the 1970s NAWCH members were co-opted on to hospital management committees and helped in many ways as volunteers, providing play and other services. The films were brought into training in some schools of nursing. NAWCH, in good standing with the Department of Health and Social Security, campaigned ceaselessly through national and regional conferences and the activities of its local groups, sustaining pressure for adequate involvement of parents in the care of sick children in hospitals.

In 1983, NAWCH reported that about 50 per cent of children's wards offered accommodation for parents and about 50 per cent had unrestricted visiting (Thornes, 1983). There have been no national surveys since then. NAWCH says that exact figures are hard to come by but believes that there is steady, though patchy, improvement. At the time of writing – 1988 – there are also wide variations in the quality of the provisions throughout the country. In some wards there are too few beds for parents, so that not all who wish to stay with their children can do so. In others there are beds, but the ambivalent attitudes of staff do not encourage their use. Sometimes parents, not realizing the benefits of accompanying their children, do not ask to stay.

Some hospitals offer beds, but at a distance from the children's ward, thereby negating the whole idea which is to prevent separation of mother and child – especially at night. It would seem that some wards have not fully understood the purpose of the arrangement. In some hospitals, medical wards are satisfactory but surgical wards are restrictive. In the many wards where mothers-in and unrestricted visiting have been fully implemented, the benefits for children, parents and staff have been great. A visit to such wards is gladdening to the heart, as the following quotes from nursing officers received by NAWCH in 1985 show (Thornes, 1988): 'In the last six months only one toddler has stayed unaccompanied' (Ingham Infirmary); 'Almost without exception, the children are accompanied by a parent, and it is the usual practice for the parents to be accommodated overnight' (Westmorland County Hospital); 'For the under-fives, 85–90 per cent of parents have been resident for the duration of their stay' (Mount Vernon Hospital, Northwood, Middlesex).

THE CONTINUING NEED FOR NAWCH

Many doctors and nurses became committed to having parents in their wards as members of the caring team, but these new attitudes were not a consequence of improved training of medical and nursing students in the psychological development of children as urgently recommended by the Platt Report. Little improvement in training had occurred (James Robertson, 1971).

There had, however, been a great advance in public sentiment. Positive images of mother and sick child together in hospital were reflected on television and in the press. Doctors and nurses, being themselves members of the community, shared in the public sentiment. Furthermore, the reduction of distress in accompanied child patients, the easing of relations between parents and staff working together for the children, and the reduction of previously unacknowledged anxiety in doctors and nurses about distress in young patients, freed them to be more relaxed in their care. It was this wave of public sentiment, encouraged by the campaigning of NAWCH and the general release of my films, which were the main determinants of change.

Nurses and paediatricians will continue to vary in their understanding and commitment until their training is extended. So the need remains for an active and vigilant NAWCH composed of parents, doctors and nurses who will work together to educate each new generation of parents on the need to accompany their young children in hospital; to inform parents of the facilities that are available, and of their rights; to sustain pressure for the maintenance of facilities, and for improvement in the education of medical and nursing students in the basics of child development and parent–child relationships; to bear in mind that the stresses which caused generations of doctors and nurses to become blind and deaf to the plight of young patients, and to impose extreme restrictions on parents, are still present – the stresses of seeing young patients who are fretting for a mother who is not there, who are ill and in pain, who may die; the human tendency to become defended against the unbearable, could again affect doctors and nurses and lead to blind spots.

There is further to go.

The efforts of the past thirty-five years have been directed towards keeping mothers and their young children together in hospital. But this has been narrowly focused on children who have mothers ready and able to stay with them. Little attention has so far been given to the great number of infants and young children who for whatever reason are alone in hospitals and who for their good emotional development also need 'mothering' – that is, to be in a stable and continuous relationship with a mothering person who is always available to give comfort, care and protection; someone who will understand the child's needs and respond to them as the 'ordinary, devoted' mother would. Some of these children are in short-stay wards; others in long-stay wards far from home, where they may remain for months or longer, sinking through the damaging stages of Protest and Despair into the misleading phase of Detachment.

In a short-stay ward a nurse specially assigned and willing to work long hours might be able to give a particular child continuous mothering-type care; but nurses working on conventional shift systems could not do so because of times off duty and the relatively short working week. Experiment has shown that even with best effort the number of nurses attending a child could not be reduced below six in a twenty-four hour working day (Jolly, 1974). In long-stay wards expedients cannot approach a solution.

There is something to learn from the experience of local authority social service departments which deal with healthy young children in need of care. These have recognized that institutions with their inevitable fragmentation of care are harmful to good psychological development. Social service departments therefore no longer use residential nurseries for the under-fives. In an attempt to provide family life and continuous mothering-type care, these healthy young children are placed with foster-mothers.

But hospitals continue to give fragmented care which, no matter how kindly the nurses may be in their individual attentions, frustrates the children's need of stable relationships. Even in wards which welcome mothers to stay, one can still find unaccompanied young patients who are no better off than is Laura in A *Two-year-old Goes to Hospital* (Jolly, 1974; Robertson and Robertson, 1973b; *Nursing Times*, 1957), where the stress of separation from the mother is aggravated by fragmented care and lack of protection from the fears and frights of the hospital ward. Moreover, since nurses cannot provide this quality of continuous mothering care it may be that hospitals could follow the example of social service departments and provide a foster-mother for each unaccompanied child. This may seem an extreme and impracticable proposal. But thirty years ago it seemed equally extreme to consider having mothers resident in hospital.

Whatever the solution may be, the plight of unaccompanied young patients is now a challenge for the future of hospital paediatrics. But because early psychological development is so subtle and complex, damage and deterioration in infants and very young children can be less obvious than in older children and therefore go undetected and unattended to. The level of knowledge and experience required to provide for the emotional needs of the under-threes is, I think, greater than

71

could be incorporated in the trainings of paediatricians and paediatric nurses. I believe they will need the support and guidance on the ward and in seminars of qualified child psychotherapists.

POSTSCRIPT, 1988

Twenty-seven years after its founding as a pressure group, NAWCH is aware that although there have been many improvements in the provisions for young patients and their parents there is a need for new initiatives. NAWCH, in association with the British Paediatric Association, National Association of Health Authorities and the Royal College of Nursing, set up a steering group to investigate current attitudes to unrestricted access and the provision of overnight accommodation for parents, with a view to obtaining overnight accommodation for 100 per cent of the parents of under-fives, and scaled-down accommodation for parents of older age-groups. This return of NAWCH to first principles is to be welcomed; indeed it is essential if what has been achieved is to be held and built upon.

PART 2

Young Children in Brief Separation: A Fresh Look

James and Joyce Robertson

Introduction

FIFTEEN YEARS of strenuous research and campaigning on the care of young children in hospital came to a climax in the early 1960s with the Minister of Health's acceptance of the Platt Report on the Welfare of Children in Hospital, the acknowledgement by Sir Harry Platt that my work had had a substantial influence on its findings, and the founding of Mother Care for Children in Hospital (now NAWCH). This ginger group of parents took over the burdens I had carried alone for so long. Now, although I was much preoccupied with the world-wide responses to my books and films, and with a certain amount of supportive work for NAWCH, I was free to take up another project which Joyce and I decided to do together.

In 1956, when our two children were established at school, Joyce had returned to work for Anna Freud in the Well Baby Clinic of the Hampstead Child Therapy Clinic, there to pursue her interest in infant development and mother–infant relationships. She had already published on these themes (Joyce Robertson, 1956, 1962, 1965).

We had discussed my hospital research and, as her work progressed in the Well Baby Clinic, I was familiar with the developmental studies that she was doing. We were well prepared for the next stage in our lives, that of research colleagues.

7

Background to the
Separation Project

DURING THE PREVIOUS QUARTER of a century, much had been published about the general effects of separation from the mother in early childhood, mostly in the form of retrospective or follow-up studies. The few direct observational studies had been done exclusively in hospitals and other residential institutions (Burlingham and Freud, 1942, 1944; Freud, 1974; Heinicke and Westheimer, 1965; Micic, 1962; Prugh *et al.*, 1953; James Robertson, 1953, 1953a; Schaffer and Callender, 1959; Spitz, 1945; Spitz and Wolff, 1946). Institution-based studies had the limitation that the data they provided did not permit responses to separation from the mother to be reliably differentiated from the influence of associated adverse factors such as illness, pain, cot confinement, multiple caretakers and the confusion which follows transfer from home into a strange environment. Some writers cautioned the influence of associated factors, but without being able to indicate their relative importance. For lack of means of differentiating, the literature on early separation therefore remained substantially a literature on an assortment of factors of unknown weight among which loss of the mother was only one.

This was the point at which we and John Bowlby began to see things differently. Bowlby (1960), theorizing principally on the hospital data collected by James Robertson, made what we saw as a sweeping generalization:

> that acute distress is the usual response of young children (between about six months and three to four years of age) to separation from the

76

mother, regardless of circumstances and quality of substitute care; and, by implication, that there is no distinction between the responses of these infants at different levels of development.

Anna Freud (1960), criticizing Bowlby's generalizations, involved herself in the discussion, conducted within the *Psychoanalytic Study of the Child*:

> Neither the Hampstead Nurseries nor hospitals and other residential homes have offered ideal conditions for the study of separation *per se*. We, as well as Dr Bowlby, used data collected under circumstances where the children had to adapt not only to the loss of the mother but also to the change from family to group life, a transition very difficult to achieve for any young child. Whereas the mother herself had been the undisputed possession of the child, the nurse as substitute mother had to be shared inevitably with a number of contemporaries. Also, inevitably, it is never one single nurse who substitutes for the all day and all night care of the mother. Anna Freud stresses the lack of relevant data without which it is not possible to make statements about separation *per se*: 'we need to supplement our observations, excluding group or ward conditions'.

The paediatrician and psychologist Yarrow (1961), in a definitive review of research in this area, showed that 'maternal separation has never been studied under pure conditions'; that is, other, complicating factors were always present. Bowlby's colleagues Heinicke and Westheimer (1965), discussing their observations on young children in a residential nursery, acknowledged that their data could not determine the influence of institutional factors, including that of multiple caretakers. They speculate that 'if it were possible to contrast a minimal care situation with one involving highly individualized care, then one might get quite different results'.

But in Bowlby's book *Attachment and Loss* (1969, Ch. 2), although there is a passing reference to the complexities of the institutional situation, there was a disappointing emphasis on the assertion that regardless of age and conditions of care the young child's response to separation is usually the mourning sequence initiated by acute distress:

> The subjects of various studies differ in many respects. For example, they differ in age, in the type of home from which they come, in the type of institution to which they go and the care they receive there, and in the length of time they are away. They differ, too, in whether they are healthy or sick. In spite of all these variations, however, and

despite the different backgrounds and expectations of the observers, there is a remarkable uniformity in the findings. Once a child is over the age of six months he tends to respond to the event of separation from mother in certain typical ways.

Without citing the evidence regarding the influence of each class of variable, Bowlby asserts that 'by far the most important variable' is absence of the mother, and dismisses other variables as relatively unimportant. He deals thus with strange environment, previous mother–child relationship and the state of the mother as in pregnancy; and he omits to consider other variables such as quality of substitute care, multiple caretakers, age and level of maturity of the child at separation.

Moving on from our previous work, Joyce and I decided to try to clarify the subject by looking more closely at the influence of variables on the behaviour of healthy young children during a ten-day separation from the mother. In order to achieve maximum coverage we would become foster-parents to a series of young children, giving care for twenty-four hours a day and making written and filmed observations while doing so.

We made a proposal to Dr Bowlby, then director of the Tavistock Child Development Research Unit, for a project to refine the earlier studies by getting closer to separation *per se*. Unfortunately he was not as responsive as we would have liked.

But ultimately £1,000 of unit funds were earmarked for our use. Joyce left the Hampstead Well Baby Clinic where she had worked for the previous ten years and joined me at the Tavistock Clinic.

In a pilot study we took into our foster care Kate, aged two years five months, referred by a social worker in the maternity hospital where the mother awaited the birth of a second child. Our research experience hitherto had been of young children who had reacted with acute distress to admission to hospitals and other institutions. We were therefore apprehensive that Kate would do something similar right in our home. But she did not. For the first three or four days of the separation she was cheerful and controlled, only gradually showing signs of anxiety. There were subtleties of behaviour that were observable only because of the intimacy of her care by Joyce and never previously described in the literature.

During the month's separation she formed a strong attachment to her substitute mother, and it was clear that in this instance the acute distress asserted by Dr Bowlby to be inevitable did not occur. We judged that this had been prevented by the quality of care during the separation. (See full case report on p. 100). We were excited by our findings, and eager to continue with the project; but unfortunately, as so often happens in research departments, other projects were considered more important and the balance of the £1,000 that had been allocated to the project was now put to other purposes. The balance having been withdrawn, we were left without funds. That was an unexpected blow which threatened to put an end to the project. It was serious, bearing in mind the difficulty of finding subjects; a second child, Jane, was already lined up for our foster care in two months' time.

We were angered and bewildered that our project which promised to throw new light on separation behaviour was to be jettisoned, but so sure in our own minds of its value that we set about finding our own funds. Time was short. We decided to approach the Grant Foundation in New York. Adèle Morrison, the general secretary, had a very positive attitude to us, partly through my work on children in hospital but more importantly because of her appreciation of the reports on the Hampstead Well Baby Clinic that Joyce had written over some years.

It happened that we were to be in the United States to lecture at Yale and Harvard, so we arranged to go first to New York for a preliminary discussion. Adèle Morrison listened with keen interest to our ideas, said she would consult some colleagues and, a few days later, telephoned across the United States to say the Grant Foundation would give an advance to enable us to proceed with Jane on our return to London. In New York a few days later we picked up a cheque for £1,000 in advance and had assurance that funding for three years awaited formal application. Our satisfaction that our previous work should have merited such a positive response from the Grant Foundation, and relief that the study of Jane could go ahead, knew no bounds.

This made us independent, free of the danger of obstruction of our research. (The Grant Foundation financed this project for the next eleven years, supplementing the salary of James Robertson as a psychiatric social worker in the National Health Service. Adèle Morrison, the most knowledgeable and considerate general secretary, not only read our running accounts of observations but visited us frequently to discuss them in insightful detail – visits usually scheduled for a morning but always lasting all day. This was the most rewarding relationship with a foundation that any researchers could wish for – funding and deep interest.)

During these years we studied and filmed four young children taken into our foster care and one child filmed in a residential nursery generously funded by a personal award from Kodak. This became the series *Young Children in Brief Separation: A Fresh Look*. Plates 17–58 show selected stills from the films.

8

Film:

John, Aged Seventeen Months, for Nine Days in a Residential Nursery

Pᴀʀᴛ ᴏғ ᴏᴜʀ ᴏʙsᴇʀᴠᴀᴛɪᴏɴs on young children in the 1950s had been done in residential nurseries, and each of us had written about the unsatisfactory care of children in such institutions. We had seen young children taken into residential nurseries because of family breakdown or because the courts had deemed the parents unsatisfactory, and that in residential nurseries they got another form of unsatisfactory care. New-born infants awaiting adoption often lay month after month in impoverishing conditions, not getting the experiences of stable relationships that infants need for normal emotional development. Under-threes placed there for safety suffered fragmented care and passed through the stages of Protest, Despair and Detachment without raising concern in staff or visiting social workers.

Staff, administrators and social workers seemed to be as defended against distress and deterioration in the young children in their care as I had described of paediatricians and nurses in hospitals. Social workers had trainings which included the writings of Dr Bowlby on maternal deprivation, but the implications were lost in the stressful actuality of field situations.

Having made a dramatic impact on the hospital professions with *A Two-year-old Goes to Hospital*, Joyce and I wished to make a film on the reactions of a young, healthy child to life in a residential nursery, in order to draw attention to the dangers of institutional care. In the search for a well-parented child going into a residential nursery, we toured social services departments in the London area, asking them to refer any child

81

about to be admitted who met our criteria. There was some interest, no apparent anxiety about institutional care and no apprehension that we might discover something that would embarrass. It became clear that the majority of young children dealt with by social services departments came from disadvantaged families and had had previous adverse experiences. The social service departments were genuinely unable to find a young child who met our criteria of previous good experience, including that they had not previously been separated.

Ultimately a suitable child was found, John aged seventeen months, about to be admitted to a typical residential nursery where care was fragmented between changing nurses, and where food and routines took no account of children's previous experience and individual needs.

The nursery and training college was a handsome building in a leafy suburb, which as a non-profit making trust operated with a vestige of the philanthropic intention to give care to disadvantaged children, which had been its purpose when founded in 1910. There were about fifty children under five years of age. Most were placed there by social services departments; the remainder were privately placed children. There was a two-year training course for nursery nurses.

The management committee consisted largely of the wives of prosperous business men. The setting, together with the pretty picture of young nurses walking well-dressed children in the nearby park, gave to the establishment a deceptive aura of charm. It was only if one got inside with knowledge of emotional development that it became obvious that this was no place for the care of infants and very young children. The staff were mainly young students, who moved between departments in the course of training and gave no continuity of care. Training had priority over the needs of the children – sometimes quite consciously. (When we mentioned our misgivings about combining care and training to a committee member, she said, 'That cannot be helped. If you run a motoring school you must accept that some cars will be damaged.')

Management by a committee who had good intentions but little knowledge of young children, and who were diverted by their antics instead of understanding the negative signs, created a climate of management self-satisfaction which was inaccessible to discussion. Senior staff and visiting social workers from the departments were as blinkered as had been the hospital staffs of twenty years earlier. The conditions of care were typical of residential nurseries of the time. The matron, who had moved there after thirty years in hospitals, had a motherly attitude to the children; but there were long-established defences she would retain until she retired.

We visited the home and talked with the parents about the distressing experience this would be for the child. John and his mother had a quiet and harmonious relationship. He was a sturdy, good-looking boy who ate and slept well and said a few words. His parents knew that John would be upset in the nursery and were uneasy about it, but felt there was no better arrangement they could make. It was not possible for his father to be at home to care for John and, as newcomers to London they had no friends or kin to look after him. Also, John's mother did not wish him to be looked after by a foster-mother. She feared he might get too attached to the foster-mother; furthermore, she said, no one could know what might happen to a child once he was left inside a foster home. What went on in the nursery was open to view. There were trained staff, and she assumed that the social workers and Home Office inspectors who visited regularly approved the care that was given. The nursery had also been recommended by the family doctor.

So we observed the commonplace happening of a seventeen-month-old non-verbal toddler spending nine days in a residential nursery while his mother was in hospital having her second child.

John accompanied his parents when they visited the nursery, but at seventeen months he did not understand the purpose of the visit. The parents were reassured by the liveliness of the group of four under-two-year-olds that John was to join and by the friendliness of the young nurses. The mother's labour began in the night and John was left in the nursery as she was *en route* to the maternity hospital. He cried for a short time then fell asleep.

As before, the following is a scene-by-scene account of the film. The accompanying stills appear on plates 17–24.

When John awoke he found himself in a strange setting, in a room with four other children of his own age all clamouring to be dressed. He watched as they were attended to, and when an eighteen-year-old nurse, Mary, approached him with a smile he responded in a friendly way.

At breakfast it was another young nurse, Christine, who fed him and to her he was also friendly, as he was to two others who gave part of his care during that first day. Any one of them could have become a substitute mother, but this the system did not allow. The young nurses were not assigned to individual children but turned to whatever tasks came to hand. Although the nurses were friendly, the contacts were fleeting and unsatisfactory to John. He tried hard, but failed to find one who would stay by him.

Three of the other children had been in the institution from birth and were noisy, aggressive, self-assertive and demanding; they had never known stable relationships and in many ways fended for themselves in a violent little community. They knew from experience that they could not expect their needs to be anticipated and met. They were not attached to individual nurses, had no pleasure in relationships, were not upset when nurses left the room, did not greet returning nurses with smiles. They laughed gleefully when they snatched from each other. The exception was Martin, aged twelve months. For the first eleven months of his life he had been with a foster-mother and, after a month in the nursery, he still struggled to be in a relationship with a nurse – any nurse. His tearful insistence frequently defeated John's quieter attempts to find a nurse to care for him.

John was bewildered by the noise, occasionally putting his hands to his ears. A cared-for family child, he was taller and physically better developed than the institution children; but he was no match for their aggression. He stood in quiet surprise when he was pinched and smacked. When his father visited that afternoon John looked blankly at him before widening into a smile of recognition. He made no objection when his father left. It was Mary, the nurse who had dressed him in the morning, who put him to bed that evening. He was again ready to make a relationship. But Mary had to move on to other duties and John gave a shout of protest and disappointment as she walked away.

On the second day John still coped quite well. While the institutional children rushed about, snatching and fighting, he played constructively with little cars as he had done at home – in a corner away from the commotion. Occasionally he still sought to get close to a nurse. But usually his tentative approaches were overlooked as the nurses responded to the more clamorous children; or, if he got a nurse's attention, he was either displaced by a more assertive child or the nurse dropped him to do other tasks. The young nurses were not concerned about John; he ate well, was quiet and undemanding and cried only when put into his cot.

When his father made to leave after visiting, John's quiet uncomplaining manner changed to crying and struggling to go home with him. Nurse Mary comforted John, and he soon emerged into a smiling exchange and expectation of play. But again the young nurse could not linger and John shouted in tearful complaint as she walked away from his cot.

From the third day John began to show distress. His overtures to the nurses did not bring the care and affection he was used to. His needs were overlooked and he was assailed by the noisy clamour and attacks of the other children. He still cried little, but either stood forlornly at the end of the room or played quietly in a corner with his back to the group. When his father visited, John smacked him crossly and pulled at his glasses.

On the fourth day there was marked deterioration. There were lengthy spells of sad crying which merged with the din of the other children and went unnoticed by the nurses. His play was listless; he sucked more, and his fingers often strayed over his face and eyes. He ate and drank hardly at all and walked with a slow, shambling gait. After lunch the children were put down to rest. But John was restless and only ten minutes before the end of the rest period did he drop off to sleep. Then it was time for a walk in the park for which he was too tired.

He still tried, though with less effort, to get close to one or another of the nurses. But in this he was generally unsuccessful and several times crawled under a table to cry alone.

On the fifth day his misery attracted some attention from the nurses. But they could not comfort John or interest him in toys and he ate nothing all day. And as no nurse had direct responsibility for him their concern was dispersed and ineffectual. His face was drawn and his eyes swollen. He cried in quiet despair, sometimes rolling about on the floor and wringing his hands. Occasionally he shouted angrily at no one in particular and in a brief contact smacked Mary's face.

John now made fewer direct approaches to the nurses; and, as if defeated in his attempts to get comfort from them, he turned to a teddy-bear larger than himself. While the other children were rushing about or clambering over the young nurses, John would be sitting somewhere burrowed into the teddy-bear. Sometimes he stood looking around at the adults as though searching for one who would cuddle him. Nurse Mary made herself more available than did the other nurses, but she came and went according to the duty rota and not according to John's need of her. So she was not much help to him.

John's father was unable to visit on the fourth and fifth days.

On the sixth day John was miserable and inactive. When Mary came on duty, her face registered concern for him, but the system of group care frustrated them both and her concern was lost in the babel of the other toddlers. John's mouth trembled with tears held in check. In contrast to the beginning of his stay, when he stood out as the brightest and bonniest of the children, he was now unhappy and forlorn. Nurses picked him up briefly and put him down when other children claimed their attention. He cried a great deal. He manipulated the big teddy-bear, twisting it this way and that in desperate attempts to find comfort from its short arms.

When his father came, John pinched and smacked him. Then his face lightened and hopefully he went to the door to show mutely his wish to go home. He fetched his outdoor shoes and, as his father sought to humour him by putting them on, the child's face broke into a little smile as if this presaged going home. But when his father made no move to take him, John's face became overcast.

He left his father and went to Mary, looking back at his father with an anguished expression. Then he turned away from Mary, too, and sat apart from them both clutching his cuddly blanket.

On the seventh day John did not play, did not eat, did not make demands, did not respond for more than a few seconds to the fleeting attempts of the young nurses to cheer him. He stumbled as he walked, unhappy and whimpering. His expression was dull and blank, not like that of the lively, good-looking boy who had been admitted a week earlier.

John got some comfort from being held, it did not matter by whom. But always he was put down within a short time. Towards the end of the day he would walk towards a nurse, then turn away to cry in a corner. On one occasion he stopped short and fell on his face on the floor in a gesture of despair, his brow pressed to the ground. He huddled up against the large teddy-bear.

His father came late and John was asleep.

On the eighth day he was even more miserable. There was an angry note to his cries when another child sought to oust him from a nurse's knee. But there was no respite to his unhappiness. For a long time he lay in apathetic silence on the floor, his head on the large teddy-bear, and was impassive when other children came to him.

He still ate little. When his father came at tea-time and tried to help, John was so distressed that he could neither eat nor drink. He cried compulsively over his cup. At the end of the visit John was abandoned to despair and no one could comfort him, not even his favourite nurse, Mary. When she tried to take him on to her knee, he squirmed down on to the floor and crawled into a corner beside the teddy-bear. There he lay completely unresponsive to the troubled young nurse.

On the ninth day, the day of reunion, John cried from the moment he awoke, hanging over the side of his cot. All but one of the nurses were new to him. He was slumped motionless on her lap when his mother came to take him home. At the sight of his mother John threw himself about, crying loudly, and after stealing a glance at his mother looked away. Several times he looked back at her, then turned away over the nurse's shoulder, crying with a distraught expression.

After a few minutes his mother took John on to her knee, but he continued to struggle and cry, arching his back away from his mother, and eventually got down and ran crying to Joyce. She calmed him, gave him a drink and passed him back to his mother. He lay snuggled into her, clutching his cuddly blanket and not looking at her.

A few minutes later his father entered the room and John struggled away from his mother into his father's arms. His crying stopped, and for the first time he looked directly at his mother. It was a long hard look. His mother said, 'He has never looked at me like that before.' She wiped a tear from her eyes and a few minutes later wrapped John in his coat and hurried from the nursery.

In discussion afterwards, the young nurses agreed among themselves that 'we have had many children like John'.

In the first week after returning home John had many temper tantrums. He rejected his parents at all levels – would not accept affection or comforting, would not play with them and removed himself physically by shutting himself in his room. He cried a great deal and could not cope with the slightest delay in having his wishes met. He was aggressive and destructive in his play. Instead of carefully manipulating his toys, he now scattered them angrily.

During the second week the tantrums stopped and he was undemanding. For much of the time he played quietly alone in his room. But in the third week there was a dramatic change. His behaviour became more extreme than in the first week. The tantrums returned; he refused food so resolutely that he lost some pounds in weight; he slept badly at night and did not rest during the day; and he became clinging. The parents were shocked by this deterioration, particularly by the gulf that had appeared between them and their son. They reorganized family life around the task of supporting John and giving him maximum attention in an attempt to help him regain whatever had been lost.

A month after returning home the relationship to his mother had much improved. But his 'good' state was precariously held and a visit by Joyce which he seemed to enjoy threw him back into the original state in which he refused food and all attentions from his parents. He recovered after a few days, but three weeks later (seven weeks after returning home) another visit by Joyce again elicited extreme disturbance which this time lasted for five days and included a new feature of aggression against his mother. Presumably, seeing Joyce reactivated anxieties and fears related to the separation experience.

Three years after his stay in the residential nursery, when John was four and a half years old, he was a handsome, lively boy who gave much pleasure to his parents. But there were two marked features which troubled them. He was fearful of losing his mother and got upset if she was not where he thought she would be. And every few months he had bouts of provocative aggression against her which came out of the blue and lasted for several days. These features seemed to be legacies of the traumatic experience of being for nine days in a residential nursery which did not meet his emotional needs.

John's story is in the well-established pattern of institutional separations. 'The infant is at the mercy of the compliance of its environment, and of the ability of the institution to provide an adequate substitute mother' (Spitz, 1945).

9
Reception of *John*

JOHN is a simple story of a type found in journals, short case notes which make little impact before the page is turned over. But, as with *A Two-year-old Goes to Hospital* twenty-five years earlier, when told by the visual medium the story was powerful; it pierced defences and caused much disturbance in viewers. The reactions of a few colleagues convinced us we had a bomb on our hands.

In Britain

With the status resulting from the success of the hospital campaign, we had no hesitation in confronting the principals at the Children's Department of the Home Office which was responsible for staff training and the inspection of residential nurseries throughout the country. Those dealing with training welcomed the film as something they needed; but the inspectors with responsibilities in the field were intensely angered. They had never seen a place like that, said one, quite unaware that she was the inspector for the nursery in which we had filmed and occupationally blind to the state of the young children. We did not expose her, realizing that others shared her defensive blindness.

The Inspectorate continued in irritated rejection of *John*, much as many paediatricians had done when confronted with *A Two-year-old Goes to Hospital* many years before. They said the nursery was not typical, that there were many better in the London area to which they could have directed us. We said we would be glad to make a film in a residential

89

nursery of their choice where the emotional needs of young children were adequately provided for. A month later we had a telephone call to say that on investigation none of the London nurseries were better. Would we be willing to go out of London?

A senior inspector took us to a small, well-recommended nursery in the countryside forty miles away, where we found that two of the nurses had gone shopping in the village, another had the day off and of the few remaining one was alone in the garden with ten young children. While we stood there, a four-year-old had a fall from a climbing frame, unseen by the nurse who was looking elsewhere. The child did not cry out but, as is common with institutional children who do not expect to be comforted, clutched his back with a grimace until the pain had eased. In a walk around the house the senior inspector saw through our eyes that this was a typical situation of fragmented care which could not meet the emotional needs of the children; she shrugged her shoulders in dismay that the nursery had not come up to the Department's image. Another day she took us to a large mansion house in the other direction out of London. The day was fine and the children made a pleasant sight as they played on the lawns. But the matron had been forewarned about our visit and, as we approached, she said, 'It's no use. We cannot do it.'

That was the end of opposition at the Home Office. In July 1969 a special edition of the *Bulletin* of the Home Office Inspectorate devoted all of its thirteen pages to *John*, accepting its message and considering the implications for policy (Home Office Children's Department Inspectorate, 1969). This marked a turning-point in the provisions for young healthy children in care in Britain. Moreover, the great number of reviews in professional journals in Britain and around the world were without exception keenly appreciative. A leading medical journal predicted, 'This film is a landmark. What *A Two-year-old Goes to Hospital* did for paediatrics *John* will probably do for residential care' (*Lancet*, 1970).

Below is a selection of quotes from the great number of reviews:

A horrifying film which forces us to look at what despair is for a young child . . . What is so frightening is that the behaviour of the young nurses is kindly, but the system results in total failure to meet John's need of a stable substitute mother (*British Journal of Psychiatric Social Work*).

Should be compulsory viewing for everyone engaged in child care. It forces the observer to identify with the plight of this little boy, and through him with that of all young children in care (*British Journal of Medical Psychology*).

No words could convey John's stress reactions as powerfully as the camera does. The impact of John's hour by hour increasing misery and deterioration becomes almost unbearable (*Journal of Child Psychotherapy*).

Superb photography, a disquieting film which upsets our complacency (*Nursery Journal*).

John is an individual who is defeated by a system which fails to recognize or meet his needs. The nursery can be seen as a microcosm of many other caring institutions, and perhaps of society itself and the many thousands who are damaged (*Child Care*).

Shows with disturbing clarity that institutional care is not geared to meet the emotional needs of small children. The camera does not allow us to ward off John's mounting misery or to disregard his desperate need for comfort. It becomes quite harrowing to watch (*Mental Health*).

Again, as with the first hospital film, it was when *John* reached the rank and file that the impact brought varying reactions. Two principals of a national children's charity, whose name was tainted in the community because of its large-scale use of institutional care, reacted positively and invited us to conduct a weekend seminar for staff who would be brought in from the regions. But the plan was aborted by a prominent psychologist who acted as consultant to the charity; he advised strongly against the film and the seminar was abandoned.

The dangers of early separation had long been known intellectually. Every social worker and child-care officer had answered examination questions about separation. But it had not been known with appropriate affect. A story that could be told in twenty lines of textbook without causing comment, in its visual form struck deep and provoked emotional turmoil in most viewers. Although we had many grateful communications we also had others which verged on the abusive. Some said the film was 'obscene'. Some reacted as bereaved persons can do, searching in their pain for someone to blame – the parents, the nurses, the authorities, the Robertsons. We were accused many times of having sacrificed John to research, of having sat by without doing anything about his plight, about being heartless; some thought the nurses could have played more with John and were critical of the parents for having left him in a nursery, etc. All this was avoiding the essential communication about the vulnerability of the very young. The film touched upon childhood fears of loss and, in some, reactivated forgotten memories of events that had scarred their lives. The hostile reactions were classic examples of 'shooting the messenger'.

A university tutor wrote that she would not use the film again for teaching, because it had been too upsetting for her social work students; I replied that if she could not help her students to learn from this piece of reality in the classroom, how would they fare when they entered the field and were exposed to situations which could set up defences? A committee which recommended films for use with church groups blacklisted *John* as 'unethical' – as if we had caused John's distress, instead of merely showing it.

Those who could use the experience of seeing *John* were helped by it, but some others seemed to lock into their irrational responses. These ignored the fact that the four minutes shown of John's behaviour each day were focused on the stages of John's deterioration under fragmented care and gave no basis for making judgements on what, for instance, the Robertsons did or did not do. For some people reality was more than they could bear, whether for John or for forgotten parts of themselves. Even some consultants in psychiatry and psychoanalysis could not see through their defensive antipathy. 'I could kill you,' said a distinguished psychoanalyst.

But to return to the positive. In addition to the abuse there were the rewards of widespread plaudits and the knowledge that, as *A Two-year-old* had given a fillip to major improvements in the hospital care of young children, *John* had given a great push towards the closure of residential nurseries, especially training establishments. Social services departments throughout Britain rented *John* for in-service training and, although the initial response of some was explosive denial reminiscent of my experience with paediatricians, this phase was of short duration. Fostering became the officially approved form of care. After the initial shock reactions, the truth of *John* was generally accepted and influenced policies.

John gained a Silver Medal at the 1969 Venice Film Festival; a Silver Medal from the British Medical Association; and in 1972 the Occasional Award for a Film of Outstanding Merit from the British Life Assurance Trust, Britain's top award for medical and health educational films. The Trust Awards were to be presented at an event which did not include showings of excerpts of films, but as Sir Keith Joseph, who was then

Minister of Health, was to make the presentations I thought the opportunity should not be missed. By sheer muscle power I got a projector
erected in the auditorium and showed ten minutes of excerpts from *John*
which much affected the minister.

Shortly afterwards the minister invited us to make a presentation of
John at the Department of Health and Social Security. We showed the
full-length version to him and a large gathering of staff. Afterwards,
visibly moved, he asked, 'Is this true?' The head of the department said
after a moment that it was true, whereupon Sir Keith asked for statistics
about the numbers of young children in care, etc. When the Heath
government fell, a promising opening disappeared with the minister. But
the permanent training staff continued to collaborate with us. In the mid-
1970s ministers of the succeeding Labour government came for their
own showing at the Tavistock Clinic, including Shirley Williams and
Lady Serota. Dr David Owen, Minister of Health, came privately and
said that as a medical student he had been reared on *A Two-year-old Goes
to Hospital*, so was ready for *John*.

Abroad: 'It Doesn't Happen Here'

Prints of *John* were sold to universities, colleges, schools of nursing,
psychoanalytic societies and the like in most countries of the world
except in Eastern Europe and the Soviet Union.

Invitations to present our material to universities, learned societies and
congresses took us to many places in Europe and further afield. On one
visit to the United States, our sponsors, the Grant Foundation, assem-
bled a distinguished gathering at their headquarters in New York where
we showed *John* and *Lucy* to their great satisfaction at the outcome of
their investment in us. Then on a six weeks' tour we travelled the East
Coast including Harvard, Yale, Washington, Cleveland, and the
universities and psychoanalytical societies of Los Angeles and San Francisco in the West. Everywhere we were well received because of the
unique records of very young children, the impact of *John* and the
novelty of a couple with a shared concern and enthusiasm. It was an
experience to see that even distinguished psychoanalysts, for instance,
who were accustomed to hearing without upset much emotional material
from the couch could be brought to tears by *John*.

Inevitably, we met defences of the kind we had become accustomed to
in Britain. Being a mental health oriented country, at least on paper,
there was legislation forbidding institutional care for the under-sixes. We

applauded the intention, but felt sure that in the populous centres there must be provision for placement in group care when emergency made it impossible to place directly with foster-parents. But everywhere we went this was denied: after each presentation we asked about group care and were told sincerely that there was none for very young children. That assurance followed us down the East Coast, across to Washington and Cleveland, to Los Angeles and to our final stop in California. My insistence that 'there must be' institutional provision brought no concession until our last few days in San Francisco.

There we showed *John* and *Jane* to large professional audiences at the University of California at Berkeley on two consecutive evenings under the chairmanship of the professor of social work. During discussion he confidently told the audience that he had assured us there was no group care for young children in California, that foster placement met all emergencies. To his surprise, a woman stood up and contradicted him. If we joined her next day she would take us to visit a state shelter containing 130 young children. We went with her and found a residential nursery much more arid than that in which John had been placed, with a minimum of furnishing and no toys, children dressed uniformly and without personal possessions, staffed by black women who gave physical attention without sign of tenderness or playfulness. The place was custodial and not at all caring. The often criticized nurses who looked after John were paragons by comparison.

The male superintendent was a pleasant administrator without child-care qualifications. He told us what we had known must be true, that every state had its shelter; that although in theory his was a short-stay place from which the children would be transferred to foster care very quickly, in fact they commonly lingered there for years. It seemed to us that American social workers, having decided that institutions were damaging to mental health, sheltered under the illusion that these had been successfully abolished. As a result state shelters, being out of sight and out of mind, did not get the social work attention they needed.

The wider relevance of our films became increasingly obvious. Several times in the United States psychiatrists said with strong feeling that they must now look at their admission wards; it could be, as with *John*, that environmental stresses in the admission ward aggravated the condition of patients newly admitted and made accurate assessment impossible. Another psychiatrist intended to look at his schizophrenics; he must give more attention to the need for supportive relationships, so vividly shown in *John*. Interestingly, at a conference in Chicago for business men, *John* was found to relate to the feelings of disorientation they often had as they moved between airports and hotels around the world.

We could see that *John* spoke to a universal problem and its foreign-language versions brought the familiar mix of applause and irrational rejection. One lesson we did learn was to anticipate a defensive 'It doesn't happen now', or 'It may happen in Britain, but it doesn't happen here.' For instance, on a visit to Holland to present *John* at the University of Leiden, we took the precaution of arriving a day early and asking to see two residential nurseries. One we had learned about on the plane going over, having found in the literature package an illustrated folder advertising in collaboration with KLM a residential nursery by the sea. Couples attending conferences or doing business in Amsterdam were invited to leave young children there, and without hindrance have a pleasant break. Their children would 'enjoy the company of an international group of children'. On visiting that nursery we found not one John but several, all very young children deposited for some days by professional parents who accepted the assurances given. The other nursery was run by a religious order for short and long stays, peaceful but as lacking in meeting emotional needs as any we had seen. At the university next day, true to expectation, the first person to stand up after *John* had been shown said, 'That may happen in England, but it doesn't happen in Holland.' Prepared, we said we could take him to two nurseries we had just seen where the situation was no better – as it could not be better, because fragmented care was inevitable in institutions.

Or again, although put in a different form of words, at a conference of the International Scientific Film Association held in Leipzig, East Germany, the Communist adjudicators decided, contrary to sustained applause from the international audience, that *John* was 'technically good but not true to socialist reality'. This ideologically determined judgement recalled the attitude of the Russian delegation in Berlin twenty years earlier to *A Two-year-old Goes to Hospital* and we realized that at that time we could make no further progress.

10

Four Children in
Foster Care

IN ORDER TO get closer to separation *per se*, we sought to create a separation situation from which many of the stresses that complicate institutional studies were eliminated; and in which the emotional needs of the children would be met as well as possible by a fully available substitute mother. This would also give us an opportunity to observe the influence of variables including level of ego maturity and object constancy, previous parent–child relationships, quality of substitute care and length of separation.

We took a series of four children into our foster care, one at a time. All were between one year five months and two years five months of age. None of them had been previously separated from the mother.

The children were

Kate, aged two years five months, who stayed for twenty-seven days;
Thomas, aged two years four months, who stayed for ten days;
Lucy, aged twenty-one months, who stayed for nineteen days; and
Jane, aged seventeen months, who stayed for ten days.

The children had in common that their mothers were going to hospital to have a second baby, that as was usual at that time the maternity units did not allow children to visit, that their fathers were unable to stay home to look after them and that they had neither kin nor friends to take over their care.

During each separation Joyce made written observations on the child's behaviour and I did economical cine-recording with a simple hand-held camera. In the month before the separation each child visited the foster family several times with his parents, so that at separation the child came into the care of someone he knew and into a setting with which he was familiar. Joyce learned from the mother about his routines, comfort habits and the food he liked. The child brought with him his own bed and blankets, toys and cuddlies. Fathers visited as much as they wished and could stay for meals, put their child to bed and so on.

Our observations on the fostered children showed that when the stress factors which complicate institutional studies had been eliminated, and adequate substitute mothering provided, four young children separated from the mother for ten to twenty-seven days were often anxious and sometimes angry or upset, but none reacted with the acute distress and despair that had been described as usual in young children alone in hospital.

In varying degree, reflecting their differing levels of object constancy and ego maturity, all made a relationship to the substitute mother. Because they were not overwhelmed, as young children admitted to institutions commonly are, their inner resources were available to cope with loss of the mother. Individual differences in response, which are obscured by the severity of institutional separations, became apparent.

During the first few days all four showed an increase in laughter and activity, which were understood as defensive against anxiety. The crying that occurred was mainly when the father left after visits and lasted no more than one or two minutes. By the time the children might have been expected to show despair (according to institutional studies), that is, on the second, third or fourth day, there was some sadness, a lowered frustration tolerance and some aggression. But this did not have the quality of despair. By that point each child had developed a relationship to the foster-mother sufficient to sustain him and had begun to cling to her. The relationship to the foster-mother held these children in a state of what we called 'manageable anxiety'. They used her increasingly and with growing intimacy.

The differences between the children aged one and a half (Jane and Lucy) and those aged two and a half (Kate and Thomas) in terms of level of development were most vividly seen in their relationships to the foster-mother and the absent mother. The children aged one and a half could not carry a clear memory of the absent mother; quickly, and without sign of conflict, they became warmly attached to the foster-mother.

97

The children aged two and a half, in their greater maturity, did carry clear memory of the absent mother and could talk about her; photographs helped in the recall. Kate remembered her mother's expectation of good behaviour, and in the foster home she tried to be the good girl her mother wanted her to be. Thomas remembered his mother clearly and talked about their life together. He needed and sought attention from the foster-mother, but when that was given he often reacted with 'Don't do that to me. My mummy does it', as if feeling that to accept mothering from another was being disloyal to his mother.

At reunion, the two older children had no hesitation in returning to the mother. The foster-mother had served her purpose and could be given up without difficulty. But the younger children's memories of the mother had dimmed. They had become attached to the foster-mother and had difficulty in giving her up.

Lucy, aged twenty-one months, whose separation had extended to nineteen days, had special difficulty after reunion. Her behaviour showed that she wanted to be with her mother, but that she was in conflict over her strong attachment to the foster-mother. This had to be dealt with by her mother and foster-mother over several weeks in order to wean Lucy from the foster-mother; the pain of conflict for the child was considerable.

There were indications that had the separations of the older pair become longer their attachment, too, would have shifted away from the mother to the foster-mother.

Although under considerable strain, all four fostered children functioned and related well, learned new skills and new words and at reunion greeted their mothers warmly after initial shyness. The separations had not been traumatic. The children had not been overwhelmed.

This was in contrast to John, the seventeen-month-old child observed in a residential nursery. He had been denied responsive substitute mothering and exposed to the multiple stresses of the institutional environment. These stress factors, additional to loss of the mother, converted separation anxiety into trauma. At the beginning of the separation John tried without success to find a nurse to mother him. He protested and despaired, deteriorated in all areas, and at reunion rejected his mother with struggles and desperate crying.

In our view, the difference between the responses of the fostered children and those of John was qualitative, not merely of degree. But the fact that the fostered children came through so well does not mean that the hazards attached to early separation can be eliminated entirely. At that early and vulnerable phase of development, even the best of substitute care is not a certain prescription for neutralizing the risks. After return home there was in all four fostered children an increase of hostility against the mother which, although infinitely less than with John, carried some potential for disharmony in the mother–child relationship.

THE FILM SERIES

Joyce had made detailed notes on each child's behaviour. These were written up every evening and at the end of each child's separation the data on him were integrated into a narrative. Out of the narrative record Joyce created a summary account of our understanding of the child's experience and behaviour. We made a rough cut of each film. The editor had no latitude to cut for emphasis or drama and was scrupulous in respecting our scripts.

A film was made of each child (John, Jane, Lucy, Thomas, Kate). These were published between 1967 and 1973 under the series title 'Young Children in Brief Separation' (Robertson and Robertson, 1969, 1967, 1971, 1973a, 1968).

11
Film:
Kate, Aged Two Years Five Months, in Foster Care for Twenty-seven Days

Kate was the first and much loved child of an immigrant Irish
Catholic family. She had lived quietly with her parents in a small flat
on the fifth floor of a working-class tenement and was unused to
spending time away from her mother.

We first met Kate in her own home. She was a bright, attractive child
who, after a few minutes' initial shyness, made contact easily and talked
well. During subsequent visits to our home Kate was increasingly
relaxed and friendly. There was sometimes an over-excitedness in her
manner, which perhaps denoted awareness of the part Joyce Robertson
was to play.

Kate's upbringing had been on the rigid side. Her father employed
smacks, but relied as much on prohibitions couched in quiet but firm
tones. Although her mother was softer, and Kate had more latitude with
her, mother's demands were high.

Kate was more self-controlled than is usual for a child of her age, yet
she was lively and spontaneous. The bond between mother and child was
close and had intensified because of their isolation together in the top-
floor flat. There was little body contact between them; their close
relationship was maintained by looking and talking.

The parents had explained to Kate why she was going to stay with the
Robertsons, and she was included in their discussions of arrangements;
but it is unlikely she could have anticipated what being away from her
parents and home would be like. (Moreover, no one then knew that,

because of complications in the birth, her mother would be detained in hospital beyond the expected ten days.)

First Week

Day of Separation

The moment of separation came more suddenly and earlier than any of us expected. The mother's blood pressure had not responded adequately to home bed rest and the doctor ordered admission to hospital. My afternoon visit to the home that day was prolonged into the early evening, during which time final preparations for the separation were made by the parents, helped by Kate and me.

As we packed her case Kate made no comments other than practical ones. She came willingly, leaving her mother in bed and her father at home, too, to go to 'Jean's house'. At father's request she kissed her mother goodbye, adding of her own accord, 'Kate come back soon.'

In the taxi she chatted about the buses and the lights. Once she slipped in, 'Where's my daddy?' and went on chatting cheerfully about something else. She also said, 'Kate see the lights going home.' I assumed she was really asking to be told that she was going on an ordinary short visit but suspicious that this one might be different.

That evening she behaved as though contented and happy to be with the Robertsons. She ate a good supper, coped with her own toileting, went to bed with a beaming and untroubled face and slept immediately. She did not stir until 8.30 the following morning.

During the second and third days Kate was cheerful and good-humoured, but although friendly was reserved and did not allow body contact. The strain she was under showed mainly in activity and excitement, alternating with quieter moods when she referred in one way or another to her parents and home. She occasionally spoke directly – 'Where is Mummy gone?' 'Mummy wasn't there in the night' – and she asked to have her shoes on so that 'Kate go home.' She repeated to herself what her parents had said to her: 'Don't worry, Kate. Won't be long.'

She played out home situations. For instance, she pretended that the rent man knocked at the door; she found a window-ledge like the one next to her parents' bed and arranged small toys on it; she got a bowl of water and industriously 'washed' our windows. Her play was punctuated by comments such as 'Be careful, Kate; silly Kate; saucy Kate'; as though she was supplying both her own and her mother's part in the play.

Kate searched our house with her eyes, sometimes silently, sometimes commenting on the differences between the Robertson home and her own. These references to or memories of home were usually followed by stillness or quietness, a twisting of her fingers and rubbing of her face or eyes. Sometimes she became awkward and negative, but these episodes were short-lived; they were over within seconds and over-active gaiety took their place.

Kate behaved according to the standards set by her parents, and reminded herself, 'Mustn't talk with my mouth full', 'Must eat my potatoes first', 'Must keep it tidy', etc. She found a magazine and showed it to me. 'Kate mustn't touch it', she warned, and even when I gave permission for her to look at it she still acted on her own instructions. She put the magazine back carefully, saying, 'No, Kate mustn't touch it.'

Kate also reprimanded herself for trivial misdemeanours. After a mild caution that she should not unwind a roll of cotton wool, she said, 'Kate mustn't do it. Kate mustn't touch it. Kate get smacked bottom. Kate won't do it.' She told me of naughty boys and girls and the dire consequences that would befall them.

If one of the Robertsons initiated talk of her parents (as distinct from responding when she mentioned them), Kate behaved as though deaf.

During these first three days she ate well, slept well, did not have a wet bed or wet pants and did not cry. The Robertsons respected her reserve and her wish to manage by herself, but were responsive and ready to invest their fostering roles with more warmth and support as soon as she wanted it or could accept it.

Several Tavistock colleagues saw us in a coffee house with Kate. They had anticipated that she would be in a state of Protest or Despair and were very surprised to see us with a composed and cheerful little girl.

By the fourth day Kate showed in various ways, but most clearly in her relationship to me, that she was less able to cope with this new and strange situation. The ability to control her feelings was diminishing.

What began as a watching of my movements now became a real clinging. She followed me from room to room, calling, 'Where are you?' This gradually became abbreviated to 'You' and for a while 'You' became her name for me. If I moved out of sight she asked where I was. She voiced the fear that we would lose each other and became unable to play at hide-and-seek. She terminated the game with some anxiety: 'Kate is not all gone; Kate is not lost; Kate is under the table; Kate not lost you.'

She began to control me aggressively. 'Sit there. Lie down. Go to sleep. Don't knit', and became cross when I did not comply. Occasionally she was directly aggressive. She came in from playing on the balcony and without warning smacked my hand, then hit me with a book. She pointed a finger at me, looked cross, stamped her foot and smacked me again. I asked, 'Am I naughty? Are you angry with me?' Her answer gave nothing away. 'No, you not naughty,' she said; but her negative feelings continued to find expression. Then, after a series of negative responses, she would make conciliatory offers: 'Kate will shut the door. Kate will do it for you', as if she could not risk being out of tune for more than a few minutes.

Kate's father visited daily during the first week. On the sixth day he volunteered that Kate seemed as cheerful and active as she was at home. Watching her during his visit, and comparing her behaviour then with what we saw at other times, we became aware of some differences. With her father she giggled and laughed heartily, but on the rare occasions when she laughed with the Robertsons it was forced. She would say, 'Kate is laughing. Ha ha ha.' Kate smiled a lot with us, but it seemed this was less friendly than to ensure a benign environment.

After brief time-lags of reserve, Kate enjoyed her father's visits. They had fun together, playing well-loved games from home. She was affectionate, climbed on to his knee, kissed him when asked to, patted him gently when he coughed, allowed him to leave her without complaint at the end of each visit. But after an enjoyable visit on the sixth day Kate implored, 'Daddy, stay with Kate. Take Kate, too. I want you, Daddy. Kate will cry.' Father responded calmly to her pleading and showed no hurry to escape her obvious distress. He asked her, 'Why will you cry?' and when she repeated her plea he said, 'No, you won't cry. Babies cry.'

Although she looked tearful, her lips trembling and her breathing uneven, Kate held back the tears and obeyed her father's request to give him a kiss and one for Mummy. She waved to him from the window, and stayed there until his car was out of sight.

In other ways Kate betrayed how hard she was trying to be the big and good girl that her parents wanted her to be. Of her own accord she constantly tidied up, put things away, wiped up spills – real and imaginary. When I asked her to put away the building bricks that were scattered over the floor she tried to put them symmetrically in their box as a much older child would have done. Some of the behaviour had an obsessional tinge, but I was more inclined to see it as being 'good' in her parents' terms.

During these first six days Kate had managed to hold herself together, to behave according to her parents' expectations almost as though she could hear their approval and reprimands ringing in her ears. She was a 'good girl' who didn't cry. She quickly controlled the slight outbreaks of negative, aggressive or regressive behaviour and her efforts were reinforced by father's daily visits.

But the uneasy equilibrium maintained in the security of the foster home was shaken when she found herself in a strange setting. On the afternoon of the sixth day her foster-father and I took her to spend an hour in my toddler play group with three mothers and three two-year-olds. Kate stayed very close to me, her inactivity and drawn face showing the tension she was under. When I moved a few yards across to the other side of the room, Kate burst into tears – the first tears of the separation.

It was there, in the unfamiliar surroundings, that Kate reached out for the first time to her foster-father – recognizing him as familiar and safe. Prior to this she had regarded him with reserve and caution.

The first tears on the sixth day were followed by others during the next week, usually brief episodes connected with feared separation from me. In the early days, anxiety had shown by nonsense talk, hilarious laughter, exaggerated body movement, and part-playful, part-aggressive kicking and smacking. But by the end of the first week she often looked pensive and drawn, her eyes dark as though she needed sleep, and she cried more easily.

When her mother was mentioned she became pseudo-deaf or she pointed to me and said, 'That is my mummy.' She now cried if separated from me for even a minute and her fear of being lost increased. She said, 'Kate not get lost, Kate stay with you'; and on the street she manoeuvred to get and stay as close to me as possible. When she got in front and could not see me she said accusingly, 'You lost Kate.'

She developed a sensory alertness, and sometimes looked like a little hunted animal. Every sound had to be explained and investigated. She searched the room with her eyes, commenting on what she saw: what was like or unlike her own home; what had changed since the previous day, even to the detail of flowers that had been rearranged.

There was less aggression and less hilarity. She did not smile as much, but instead laughed extravagantly and without humour. She was quieter and sadder, as though some of the spirit had gone out of her. She wanted the comfort of extra bottles during the day as well as at sleeping times and she welcomed body contact.

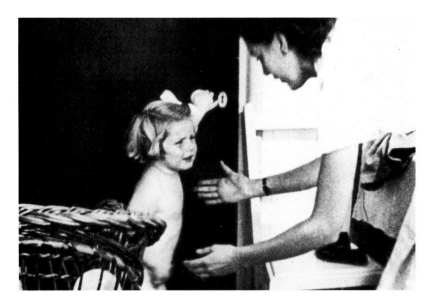

1 Laura tries to escape back to her mother

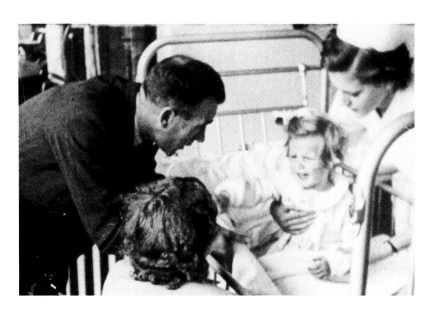

2 The nurse's arm keeps Laura from her parents

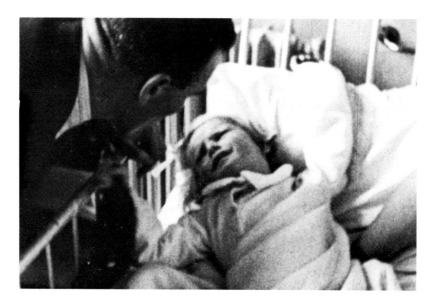

3   'Don't go, Daddy!'

4   The 'settled child': she does not cry or call for attention

5   'Where is my mummy?'

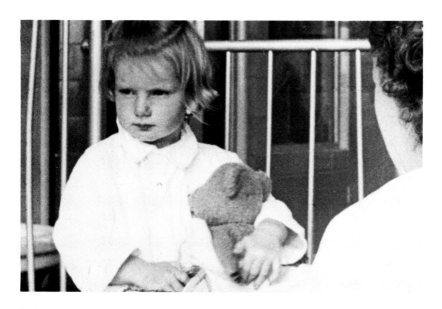

6   Laura is unresponsive when the nurse offers play

7　Laura is happy during her mother's visit

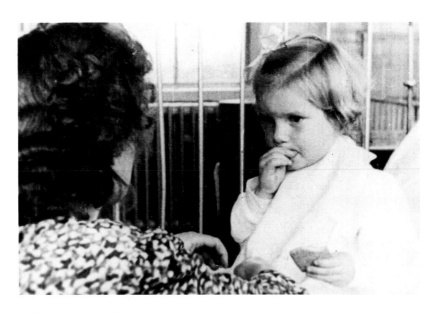

8　Her mother says, 'I have to go home now.'

9 'I want my mummy.'

9a Looking for mummy's bus.

10   Laura steps out, refusing to hold her mother's hand.

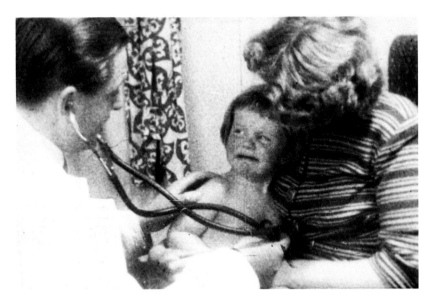

11 Sally is able to express her objection to the examination

12 Sally is secure because her mother is there

13 The mothers support each other

14 Mother is there to comfort as she does at home

15 Sally and her mother share an unhappy moment

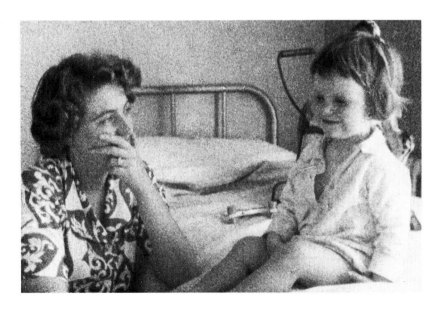

16 Sally in good spirits rarely seen in a young child alone in hospital

17   At first John watches the other children with interest

18   John turns his back to the group and plays with his little car

19 The nurse is unaware that John needs her attention

20 Nurse Pat tries unsuccessfully to comfort two unhappy children

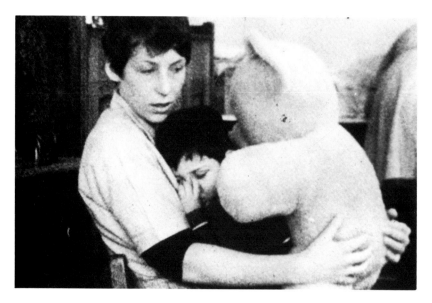

21　John finds some peace with Nurse Mary

22　John forlornly turns to the inanimate teddy-bear for comfort

23 On his last morning John cries continuously

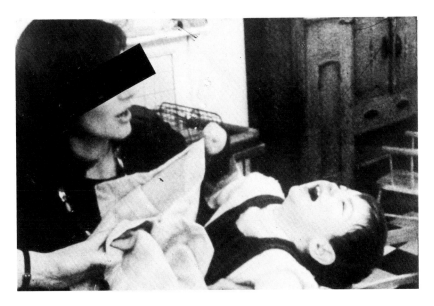

24 John struggles away from his mother. He cannot accept her

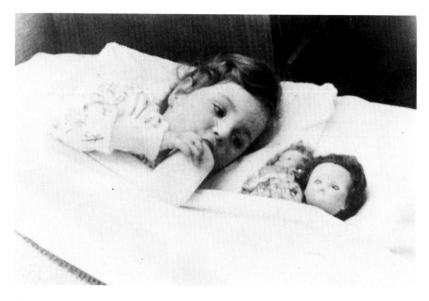

25 Kate has her own bottle and cuddly toys

26 She surprised us with her lively good humour

27   Kate avoids looking at her mother in hospital

28   After the visit she is confused and tearful

29 Doll play helps Kate understand the separation

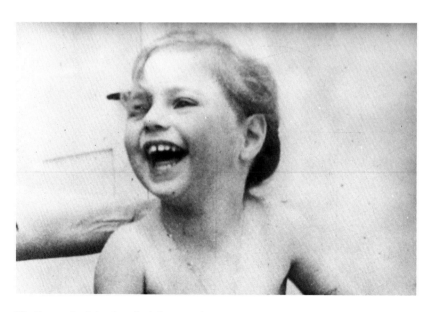

30 For much of the time she is happy and secure

31 Kate enjoys her father's visit

32 Kate objects to leaving the hospital

33   On the last day she needs much comforting

34 Father promises to come back tomorrow

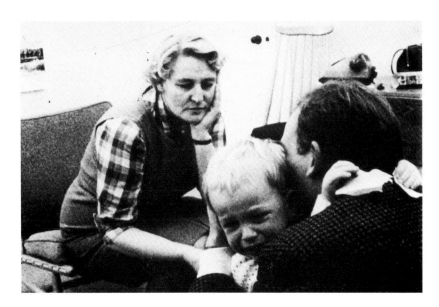

35 Thomas enjoys the visit but hates the goodbyes

36   The foster-mother is ready to comfort him

37   Thomas has his familiar table and chair from home

38 He resists going to bed

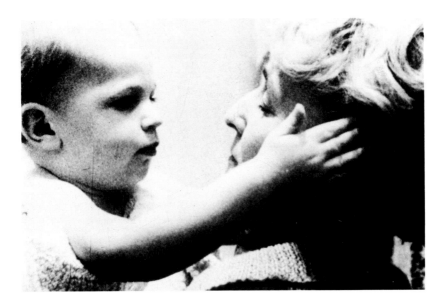

39 Thomas needs to give and take affection

40 Sudden anger: 'Don't cuddle me, my mummy cuddles me.'

41 He gently caresses his mother on reunion

42 Thomas tells his father, 'My mummy came back.'

43　Lucy cautiously gets to know the foster-mother

44　A comforting cuddle after Father's visit

45 An old and familiar book from home

46 As she grew in confidence, Lucy became cheekily playful

47 Her play became constructive and concentrated

48 On reunion Lucy indicated, 'This is where we all belong.'

49 Lucy had difficulty reconciling two mother figures

50 Jane and her mother before the separation

51 Initially Jane laughed a lot in a tense, artificial way

52 The artificial grin alternated with a puzzled, anxious expression

53 Jane eats independently and with pleasure

54 She turns to the foster-mother at moments of anxiety

55 Jane investigates and becomes familiar with her foster-mother's face

56 Jane and her foster-mother share an unhappy moment

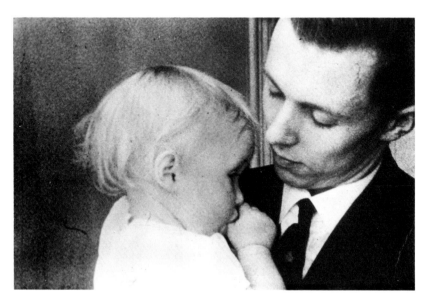

57 She is sad as Father says goodbye

58   At reunion Jane is delighted to see her mother

Her relationships showed new features. In the latter part of the first week the spontaneous recollections of her mother were punitive ones. For example, she recalled with feeling how when she talked in church her mummy smacked her bottom. This she told me several times in various forms.

On her father's visit on the eighth day she pointed a finger at him accusingly. 'You smacked Kate's bottom.' Kate then for the first time directed aggression towards her father, but his response aborted its expression. While building she held up a brick menacingly and said to him, 'Kate will smack your face with it.' Her father answered quietly and without taking his eyes off her, 'Kate won't.' Kate immediately echoed his words. 'Kate won't.'

A few seconds later she tried again. 'Kate will get very cross with you.' Her father answered again, quietly but with clear meaning, 'Daddy will get cross, too.' Kate reverted to her usual good-humoured sweetness.

To her foster-father Kate became increasingly warm and friendly, asking for his attentions and initiating rough-and-tumble games. She called him 'Daddy', watched his movements and asked for him when he was out of the house. Some of her happiest times were spent with Jean, her thirteen-year-old foster-sister. This relationship developed from both sides into a warm, spontaneous and uncomplicated one. Whatever had gone before, Kate's mood lightened when Jean appeared and played with her.

Something more dramatic was happening in Kate's relationship to me. As the memory of her mother became less clear she sometimes seemed unable to remember that she existed. Although sometimes Kate said to me, 'You are not Kate's mummy, you are Jean's mummy', there were times when only one mummy existed and that was me. When shown photos of her mother she fluctuated between uneasy flickering recognition and absolute denial that it was her mother. When asked where Kate's mummy was, she increasingly answered, 'You are my mummy', or 'My mummy is over there', pointing to me.

This had begun on the sixth day, when Kate called me 'Mummy' forty times in two minutes – as though unable to stop saying the word 'Mummy' and attaching it to me. She was now more clinging and controlling, more dependent and more affectionate.

SECOND WEEK

When Kate first came to us we were impressed by her competence in all areas. She managed her toileting; she climbed, walked and ran with free, co-ordinated movements; she was fearless but careful; she played constructively and with concentration; she was alert and in contact with her caretakers.

By the end of the first week this had changed and Kate seemed aware of her diminished competence. She may have feared a breakdown of her newly acquired toilet training when she told me and herself for seven minutes, non-stop, 'Boopy is nasty – mustn't eat it – nasty in mouth.'

Likewise she warned herself on the stairs, 'Kate won't fall, Kate will hold on tight'; but Kate did tumble, and generally did not manage herself as well as previously. Although our extra vigilance avoided serious hurt for her, she continued to have minor accidents and she feared to have more. 'Pins hurt you very much'; even the elastic bands with which she had played happily all the week now became dangerous. 'Hurt you, hurt you,' she said.

Often she did not comprehend what was said to her and answered vaguely, 'Uh-uh', as if preoccupied. She quietly manipulated small objects as though these kept her hands busy and allowed her thoughts to be elsewhere. Or she walked about dreamily, and on one occasion called to me to rescue her from her fog: 'What is Kate looking for?'

Her play, too, changed. She did not concentrate; she was not really involved. The building bricks which had previously given her such delight were now tipped out and scattered, then forgotten. Her doll and its pram were left standing in the corner untouched.

Soon after she got up on the ninth day, Kate demanded, 'I want to see my mummy. Take me to see Mummy. Put my coat on.' I explained why she could not go to her mummy, but this only served to displace the wish to see her mummy on to other people and things. 'I want to see Daddy. I want to see Jean's daddy.' When told that Jean's daddy had gone to work, she answered, 'I want to see Jean's daddy gone.'

The day was coloured by 'I want to see . . .', and we made trip after trip around the house to 'see' things in answer to her urgent 'Show me, show me'.

This intense need to see whatever came to her mind continued unabated for several days, even after Kate had actually seen her mother in the hospital on the tenth day. A new theme then added itself: 'Mummy wasn't there, was gone, then I found her.'

First Visit to Mother in Hospital

Like many others in Britain at that time, this maternity unit did not allow visiting by children. But when by the tenth day the baby had not been born and we realized that the separation was going to be extended, the foster-father put pressure on the unit to allow Kate to visit her mother by identifying himself as the maker of *A Two-year-old Goes to Hospital.*

Kate was at first shy with her mother, then gradually warmed up. But she was limp as a rag doll, allowing herself to be cuddled and talked to while withholding any vital affect. When the half-hour visit was over, Kate left her mother with the same bland, smiling acquiescence. Not until we were home again did some real feeling emerge: 'Take me to see my mummy. Kate get into Mummy's bed.' A tantrum followed soon afterwards.

This visit to the mother was important to Kate. She now knew where her mother was and could agree when I said, 'Mummy is in hospital', whereas previously she would usually say, 'No, Mummy is in bed at home', which was where Kate had last seen her. She now said, 'I found my mummy.'

Doll Play

When Kate came to us we gave her a family of small dolls – a mummy, a daddy, a little girl and a baby doll; the baby was 'just' a baby – neither girl nor boy – to represent the baby-to-come. We hoped that through her play with dolls we might understand more of her feelings than she could put into words, but initially this did not happen. For the first ten days she re-created situations from home. A baby was not part of the life she knew, so she put the baby doll aside. One day the three dolls were sat together on the edge of a stool so that they could go for a ride in Daddy's car, and with an eager pointing finger she identified them as Mummy, Daddy and Kate. My helping hand was pushed away. I was not of the family.

I used the dolls to explain that she would be going to visit her mother in hospital, but not to stay; with a child so young it was uncertain that words alone could convey this important difference. After the first hospital visit I again used the dolls to go over with her what had happened at the hospital – the mother's pleasure at seeing Kate, her demonstrations of affection, yet the inevitable parting. Kate joined in with enthusiasm. She inserted an imaginary stool for the girl doll to stand on by the mother doll's bedside, a true recall of her experience on the visit. She also remembered that her mother had patted her bottom, a warm memory that could not have been expected from the cool way in which Kate had behaved during the visit.

It was after this that Kate began to use the dolls in a lively and telling way. Again and again she demonstrated her wish to be reunited with her parents. Sometimes she tucked them all into the same bed or put them into a 'flat' she had constructed from bricks. Sometimes she arranged them in her 'car' and drove them home; later, when she was feeling less hopeful, she took them all on an interminable train journey which never arrived anywhere.

After the visit to her mother on the tenth day, several changes occurred in Kate's demeanour. On arriving home there was a first temper tantrum and it preceded a period of more overtly aggressive and negative behaviour. In the main these outbursts were fairly quickly controlled by Kate herself, or converted swiftly into a safer and permitted activity. An angry plucking at my clothing became 'I am washing your jumper, making it nice and clean'; but the occasional bite was accompanied by a scowl and no conversion.

There was more variety in her affective expression and more spontaneity. We heard laughter which had some real amusement in it and some crossness which did not become aborted but was carried through to its end. She was more affectionate, too. When I kissed her good-night on the thirteenth night, she commented, 'You kissed Kate', then put up her arm and wound it round my neck affectionately. Her moods were more varied – less compliant, more defiant, more crying, more warmth. She was still, however, one of the most mature and controlled two-year-olds that I had ever dealt with.

Her good verbal communication made clear that she still carried within her the wishes and warnings of her parents and memories of their punishments. She was trying to behave according to their standards.

Although her parents were rather demanding they were also loving, consistent and truthful. What was happening to Kate, and their expectations of good behaviour, had been explained to her; during his daily visits to the foster home her father reinforced this reality.

The latter half of the second week saw Kate more secure with us; there was less anxiety and more spontaneity. The artificial laughter had disappeared. But crying broke out at the slightest frustration and once in tears she found it difficult to stop. Even when cheerful her tears were never far away and she would unexpectedly burst out crying.

Some of the crying was quite out of character; for example, she cried when I would not allow her to cut my hair and again when she wanted to play with an open tube of toothpaste. Reasonable explanations did not get through to her as they had a week earlier. She wanted to control me to an impossible extent and here, too, she could not tolerate restraint.

Deterioration

There was no doubt that a sharp deterioration had occurred around the fourteenth day, and we began to ask ourselves what the explanation was. Was it an internal change in Kate? Could she no longer hold herself together? Had something else happened which had been 'the straw that broke the camel's back'?

Two possible causes came to mind. The first was disillusion with her father. He came regularly to see her but did not answer her requests to take her home. Her greetings became quieter; there was no excitement, just a quiet 'Hello, Daddy.' She had often asked him, 'Take me with you', but he had been unable to do so. During a visit on the twelfth day she said to him, prematurely, 'You go home now', but he did not catch what she said and she would not repeat it.

He missed a day, then visited rather late on the fifteenth. She had already had her bath. She said, 'Hello', then burst into tears, saying, 'I didn't have a bath.' She was less animated than usual and after ten minutes asked me for sweets to give to her father for her mother; shortly after this she said to him, quietly and sadly, 'Kate wants to come in car with Daddy.' Her father answered, 'Not this time, Kate.' She did not repeat the request but turned away and occupied herself. Not long afterwards she told her father to go and offered to get his coat. She helped him on with his coat, pushed him towards the door, then waved him goodbye with absolute composure.

Soon afterwards she went willingly to bed; but when I was half-way down the stairs I heard her crying, 'I want my daddy, I want my daddy.'

THIRD WEEK

Her father missed several visits, which he excused on grounds of having had too much to do. This was so unexpected in a devoted father that we talked about it. What became clear was that he had been so upset by his little daughter's apparent coolness towards him that he could not face it and had stayed away for several days.

At this time Kate turned more to her foster-father, as if in compensation for disappointment with her father. She asked for him when he was out of the house, greeted him warmly when he returned, and wanted him to play with her. This contrasted with the coolness towards her father. Although the wish for him was sometimes intense, she could not enjoy his company as she had done earlier. When he took her out in his car on the eighteenth day she fell asleep. That, together with the general air of dampened affect between them, the cool greetings and the flat, affectless farewells, suggested that the relationship with her father was producing stress for Kate rather than giving support.

She was less sure of him. On the nineteenth day she became distressed. 'I want Kate's daddy. Daddy do want to come. Kate want to talk to Kate's daddy. Daddy do want to come.'

I agreed, 'Yes, your daddy does want to see Kate.' She shouted back, 'Daddy don't want Kate'; and, getting more angry, 'Daddy don't love nice Kate.' Again I tried to correct her, but she continued, 'Daddy doesn't want to come to see Kate.'

The strain Kate was under now showed in her physical appearance. She looked pale and drawn about the eyes and her hair was rarely tidy because she rubbed her hands over it. Her hands were often around her face, sometimes rubbing her forehead, sometimes picking her nose, sometimes sucking her fingers. When she was not actually smiling her mouth had an unhappy droop.

She asked for many bottles and often asked to go 'night-night' during the day; that is, she wanted to be tucked up in blankets on the floor or in a chair. She was less organized. She managed her body less well.

Second Visit to the Hospital

On the seventeenth day I again prepared Kate for a visit to her mother in the hospital by playing out the situation with the doll family. This time Kate listened silently to my story, then said, 'Mummy is not in the hospital. She is better in Kate's house.' Ten minutes later I tried again, but Kate turned a deaf ear and became absorbed in a thimble. She turned my next few remarks into the opposite by adding 'Not'. I asked, 'Are you ready to go to see Mummy?' She answered, 'No, I not ready to go.' I said, 'You are a nice girl', and she answered, 'No. I not a nice girl.'

However, she came willingly enough in the car, and as we neared the hospital she recognized the building. 'Mummy is there. I want to see Mummy.' She walked into the ward smiling and went without hesitation to her mother's bed. She allowed herself to be cuddled, kissed her mother on request and talked of recent happenings. When the visit was over, Kate dutifully kissed her mother goodbye and left without a tear.

She walked along the corridors leading to the exit, not asking for her mother, not holding back.

Displaced Affect

Once outside the hospital and in sight of our car, Kate leaned against a low brick wall and refused to move. 'I want to see the horses,' she said. By moving a yard or so she could have seen the horses in a nearby stable, but she insisted that she had to stand on the boundary wall of the hospital. Once on the wall, with a clear view of the horses, her insistence shifted to wanting her foster-father and me to sit by her.

I had to pick her up and carry her to the car. Kate screamed and kicked and arched her back. She smacked my head and face angrily and when I put up a hand to protect myself she pulled it aside so that she could attack my face. She pinched me with vigour. She clenched her teeth with the effort, demanding all the time to see the horses – not to see her mummy.

Later that day she expressed angry feelings against her mother. Looking at a photograph, she first smiled at it and said, 'Mummy.' Then with a puzzled expression she said, 'That's not my mummy. Where is Kate's mummy?' The sadness in her voice suddenly changed to anger as she threw the photograph on to the floor and stamped on it. 'I don't like Kate's mummy. Kate's mummy is naughty.'

Kate was angry and disappointed at her parents' failure to take her back home, but she still expressed a strong hope and wish that they would do so. I tried to boost her hopes and to give her reality explanations for the delay.

In her play with the family of dolls she showed her feelings clearly. She handled the dolls affectionately as she planned their return home, walking them up the five flights of stairs, tucking them into their beds in the flat she had constructed with bricks. Then a sudden change of feeling overwhelmed her and she scattered her family to the floor. 'Put them away – in the other room.' I took them into the other room and she slammed the door shut. But she could not escape from her thoughts. She cried to have the dolls brought back and again put them together in their flat; but again she threw them from her in distress. 'Throw them in the dustbin,' she cried.

For several days after that incident Kate did not want to play with the dolls, though previously she had asked for them. When I offered the dolls, or photographs of her parents, she shouted, 'Put them away. I don't want to look.'

By the end of the third week, developments in Kate's relationships to the Robertsons were making themselves felt. She began to initiate contact of an intimate kind with her foster-father. She touched him affectionately and asked to sit on his knee. She did little tricks for his benefit and made sure that he really looked at her. She pretended to be fearful so that she could run to him for protection, and she was cross at the slightest rebuff.

To me she was closer than ever, wanting to be with me and able to show her feelings freely. There was now a greater measure of security, and on the street she no longer had to hold on tightly with hand and eyes.

On the twenty-first day an incident occurred which highlighted the change. As she and I walked home from shopping Kate bent down and untied her shoelace, then with a laugh came to me to tie it up. I did so, and a minute later she again untied the lace and wanted it retied. This time I happened to tie it unevenly so that one loop was longer than the other. Still smiling, Kate asked to have it retied. Since we were only fifty yards from home I refused to do it again, whereupon Kate became angry. She cried and hung back from me. I walked on slowly, but the distance between us gradually increased. I turned at intervals and held out my hand to her, but she angrily said, 'No.'

Until this time Kate had not allowed me to get more than a yard away from her on the street; but today the distance stretched to six yards and still Kate said 'No' when I beckoned her. Even when another person came between us Kate still did not run to me. But when I turned into the gate she came quickly, all signs of her bad humour gone.

I was impressed that she could now allow six yards and angry feelings to come between us, even on the street.

That evening she was cross with me at bedtime and was crying when I tucked her in. She told me crossly to go, then called me back to cuddle round my neck and to say good-night.

FOURTH WEEK

The strength of her need for me began to colour her relationship to Jean. It became more sibling-like, jealous one minute, affectionate the next. She deliberately picked quarrels with Jean and smacked her. When reprimanded by Jean, she shouted back a stream of words, her tone and facial expression indicating that she was quarrelling. Jean was amused and did nothing to keep the 'quarrel' going; but Kate went on as though Jean had answered her angrily.

Although Jean did nothing to provoke it, she became the target for Kate's hostility. On one occasion she pulled at Jean's clothing, took mouthfuls of her pullover and tugged at it – nipping flesh as she did so.

After several unsuccessful attempts to control Kate, I took her from the room and told her, once we were outside, that I didn't like this behaviour and neither did Jean. Kate shrieked as though I had hurt her physically, then ran back into the room where Jean was, shouting, 'It's my mummy – not your mummy.'

This possessive attitude was also shown if a child outside came too near me. Kate shouted angrily at a little girl who happened to stop at our gate and look over into the garden. Kate looked very cross and made angry gestures. To another child who looked into our shopping basket, she shouted, 'Not yours.'

The wish to possess sometimes reached her foster-father. On one occasion she and Jean were eating chocolate. Suddenly Kate bent down and bit Jean's leg. She gave the clue to her behaviour a few seconds later. 'Kate did have chocolate. Kate a lucky girl', then turning to Jean she said, 'Your daddy here', pointing to her foster-father. 'That's your daddy.' In another mood she might have insisted that he was Kate's daddy, not Jean's daddy. Jean had something Kate did not have, but wanted.

This situation led to Jean being at the receiving end of much aggression from Kate. On the twenty-fifth day, after Jean had been attacked for looking at me and then for talking to me, I took Kate on my knee and tried to explain to her that she had her very own mummy and daddy and that she would soon go home to her very own flat. She listened quietly, then got down from my knee, climbed on to Jean's knee and stroked her face 'better'. I had the impression that Kate understood. But the following day, when I tried to handle a similar situation in the same way, she shouted me down: 'You are my mummy. You are my mummy.'

At the beginning of this final week the thought occurred to me that, had I been fostering Kate permanently, I would have felt that an important stage had been reached. Kate had found her place in our family, had allocated her affections variously, and was secure enough to express a range of feelings to the three permanent Robertsons. But I was perturbed at what she was in danger of doing – namely turning away from her own parents.

She often looked drawn and sad, sometimes puzzled. She would stand looking into the distance, apparently unaware that she was being spoken to. This subdued and slightly withdrawn element in her behaviour she managed to cover up for most of the time; but she often betrayed the underlying conflict.

Her father's visits during the final week gave neither of them much satisfaction. He was tired of being without his family and tired from the efforts of visiting both his wife and his daughter. Kate was less able to present a happy front to him. When on the twenty-fourth day I told her he would shortly arrive to take her out, she denied the fact. Although she eventually went with him willingly, she told me, 'Kate will see you soon.' She behaved badly while she was out; when they returned she went upstairs and became involved in solitary play and had to be reminded that her father was waiting for her downstairs.

As he prepared to leave she pleaded with him, 'Don't go home. Don't go see Mummy', but let him go without any fuss. Then as she got down from the window seat from which she had waved him goodbye, she cried out as though in panic. She ran to me crying, 'Mummy, Mummy', and wanted a lot of comforting. She said she had bumped herself.

Soon afterwards she became aggressive. She bit her foster-father and she shouted and kicked Jean, saying, 'Don't talk to your mummy. That's my mummy. Kate came back.'

Kate was in some confusion. She wanted her parents, but her disappointment in them and anger against them made her doubt that they wanted her. I did what I could to boost her failing optimism that she would eventually be reunited with loving parents. I knew that Kate would probably go home within the next couple of days, but there was still uncertainty at the hospital. But the imminence of return home was in the air and Kate recovered the doll family that she had rejected a week earlier. She went through the routine of Mummy leaving hospital, Daddy leaving work and Kate leaving the Robertsons. She realized that being reunited with her parents meant losing me and offered me a place in the parental bed. When I declined this, she said, 'Kate will come to see you tomorrow.'

The 'going home' game reactivated the artificial laughter. 'Kate is laughing. Ha-ha,' she said as she had done during her first week with us, and as she was to do later during the preparations for her to leave for home – confirming our impression that the laughter stemmed from anxiety.

During the twenty-sixth day we played out the 'going home' sequence, and, although I could not actually say 'Tomorrow you go home' because of the uncertainty, Kate must have realized that the time of her return home was near. Throughout the night from 1 a.m. to 5 a.m. she vomited.

Twenty-seventh Day: Day of Reunion

Kate looked tired and unwell after the disturbed night; she wanted to be nursed and given bottles. When I settled her on a bed made from chairs, she said she was in bed 'in hospital like Mummy'. Then for a while she brightened and told her teddy-bear that he was going home to Kate's mummy's house. She smiled at the thought of knocking on her front door, Daddy opening it and saying, 'Come in, Kate.'

During the afternoon we were busy collecting Kate's belongings together, packing up her bed, etc. She continued to swing from having a realistic idea of what we were doing to the other extreme of denying that she was going home, or that she wanted to go home. There were also periods of confusion when she talked nonsense.

In a dull, affectless manner she helped pack her toys in a big box, giving nothing away as to her feelings. As she watched the final preparations she was quiet and subdued, even when she got on her hat and coat.

In the car she alternated between singing nonsense songs in a silly high-pitched voice and denying everything we said: she was not going to sleep in her mummy's house; she didn't want to sleep in her mummy's house; she didn't want to walk upstairs to the flat; her mummy was not better, she was going back to the hospital; and Kate wanted to go back to the Robertson house. This continued as we drove right across London, through the bright lights of Christmas Eve.

Just occasionally some affect and understanding of reality broke through. 'Where is Mummy's house?' she asked. 'Told you go to Mummy's house when it's dark,' she exclaimed, remembering that I had explained we were going in the evening.

The breakthrough came when she recognized first the dark outline of the tower block near her home, then, as we rounded the last corner, the shape of her own block. 'There's Mummy's house,' she cried in a robust voice, all the artificiality gone, and made urgent movements to get out of the car.

As we reached the top flight of stairs, she called, 'That's Kate's door. Kate will "Knock-Knock" ', and she did so without hesitation. The door opened immediately, to reveal first her father and then her mother a few feet behind. Kate did not move. She stood and looked, and when her father said, 'Well, come in', she reached for my hand before moving.

Kate looked about the room and smiled at her parents. Her mother felt round Kate's body with both hands as Kate stood with her back to her, and said she was sure Kate was fatter. Neither Kate nor her mother

115

turned the touch into a cuddle. Kate looked at the carry-cot on the settee, and said, 'Where's Kate's baby?' Her mother showed her baby Noël, sleeping next to the Christmas tree.

Kate talked to her mother, getting as many 'Mummys' into the sentence as she could. She reminded her mother, 'You was in hospital and Kate gave you sweeties.' Her mother just answered her adequately and Kate did not demand more.

Her mother bottle-fed the baby. Several times during the feeding Kate went to her mother, seducing her with smiles and sweet-talk. She spoke quickly and excitedly, looking and laughing directly into her mother's face and, as before, saying 'Mummy' many times.

When her mother moved to go to the other side of the room, Kate ran after her and put out a hand which brushed lightly down her mother's skirt, but did not hold on to it.

Kate's artificial laughter and sweet-talk filled the room during this hour, punctuated by many 'Mummys'. She ran with increasing excitement from her father to her mother. She did not address one word to me. A visiting aunt was leaning on the mother's chair. Kate called to her, 'Don't lean on my mummy's chair.'

Her foster-father and Jean joined the group half an hour after Kate had been reunited with her parents. Her foster-father was ignored in much the same way as I was, but Jean was included in the balloon play.

When we prepared to leave, Kate was instructed to kiss us all goodbye, and this she did. She then waved to us vigorously as we went down the stairs.

The most pointed bit of behaviour was the sudden switch from being attached to and dependent on me to completely ignoring me and giving all her attention to her parents. Her entire behaviour during this first hour at home was aimed at pleasing them with her smiles and chatter. The inner somersaults that Kate made during the previous twenty-four hours were highlighted for me when I remembered how aggressive she had been to Jean if Jean reminded her in any way that I was her mother. 'Don't look at Kate's mummy. Don't talk to Kate's mummy. That isn't your mummy. That is Kate's mummy,' she had said fiercely, and showed affection and possessiveness towards me. Yet immediately after being restored to her mother she ignored my presence.

We had completed our mission of caring for Kate, to the end point of facilitating the parents' fantasy that she would first see the aptly named infant Noël under the Christmas tree on Christmas Eve.

Follow-up

For the first week at home Kate showed only slight upset. She slept restlessly and wet her bed on two occasions; she wanted more bottles and cried easily and more often. She warmed up to her father and turned to him for cuddling and play, but was less inclined to be boisterous. She kept close contact with her mother by looking and talking as she did before the separation. On each of my two visits in that week Kate was positive and friendly after an initial shyness.

However, in the weeks following there was increasing evidence of heightened vulnerability.

Relationship to her Mother

At ten days Kate hovered about her mother and was more chatty than previously – an intensification of Kate's known method of keeping contact with her mother. She did not cling physically, but wanted to know where her mother was whenever she went out of sight. She was angry with her father when he spoke crossly to her mother.

Three weeks after the reunion, Kate reacted acutely to being smacked by her mother (smacking was not unusual) and clung to her 'as never before'. From that date she was said to be more cuddly and affectionate.

At six weeks Kate was insisting that her mother hold her hand whenever they left the flat. Her mother was impressed by Kate's insistence and by the tightness of the grip.

Stubborn Resistive Behaviour

At ten days Kate was reported by her parents to be stubborn and resistive. They disapproved strongly. By twenty-nine days this behaviour had lessened considerably. For a while the defiance was replaced by running into a corner, burying her head into a chair and crying. Kate was less willing to wait for help, attention or toys that were out of reach. Her wants were more urgent and more frequent, especially where her father was concerned. She grizzled at slight hurts and wanted more comforting than previously. She had reached a low point, after which she was reported to be improving.

Avoidance of Objects Connected with Separation

Her father said that Kate did not want to be reminded of anything to do with the separation. She passed over toys that she had played with while with the Robertsons, even her favourite red telephone. When the

Robertsons were mentioned she turned a deaf ear and did not spontaneously mention any one of them even briefly until the third week. Not until the fifth week did she talk of them at any length, and then it was of Jean and Joyce to whom she had the strongest attachment.

Vomiting and Anxiety

During the last twenty-four hours with the Robertsons Kate had vomited several times and we had not been sure whether this was anxiety or infection. Later events suggested strongly that it had been anxiety.

Once home Kate appeared well and did not vomit again until ten days later, probably in response to my knocking at the door. Earlier that morning Kate had been separated from her mother for two half-hour periods. On the morning of my visit two weeks later, Kate again vomited, then pleaded with her father not to go to work but to stay with Kate – an unexpected request presumably linked to anticipation of my visit.

Psychosomatic Response

On the sixteenth day after return home Kate became ill and bronchial asthma was diagnosed, the first time ever. The events of the days preceding the onset were suggestive of a young child in a highly vulnerable state being put into situations which stirred up more anxiety than she could cope with.

Kate had few outlets for expression of feeling. Her parents required her to be controlled and unaggressive, and regression was not tolerated. Whatever additional strains the new baby may have put on Kate, the events of this particular week were probably directly linked to fear of a second separation.

Two weeks after her return home Kate had been taken to a local school to enrol for admission two years later. (Places in Catholic schools were in short supply, necessitating very early enrolment.) The waiting-list was full and the headmistress could not 'take' Kate. That night she awoke screaming as though with nightmares. Next day she was taken to a second school where her mother's request was granted. The headmistress would be able to 'take' Kate.

In the night she again awoke screaming. In the morning she was acutely breathless and cried a great deal in a way so unusual for her that she was taken to the family doctor. He diagnosed bronchial asthma and said it was probably a reaction to stress.

It is easy to imagine that the talk about school had created fear of another separation. Kate was 'going' to school. The school was asked to 'take' her. School was where Jean was, and Kate looked for Jean. So 'school' was connected with the Robertsons. School was where Kate would go when she was 'big', and her parents constantly told her she was 'big' and 'must be big'; so going to school must have seemed imminent and not, as it really was, two years hence. The school was full of children without their mothers. Kate was panicked by the fear of again being separated from her mother and, being prevented from expressing feeling, the only outlet for the build-up of anxiety was the psychosomatic one of bronchitis/acute breathlessness. After discussion with us the parents realized that Kate was in a vulnerable state and needed gentler handling.

Kate's Relationship with her Foster-mother

On each visit Kate was positive and friendly to me after an initial brief shyness. In some ways she behaved towards me as she had done during the separation: initiating body contact, asking for attention, showing affection with occasional aggressive outbursts. But her excitement, quick speech and heightened colour sometimes betrayed unease; her anxiety rose when on a few occasions she found herself alone with me.

Seeing me always prompted her to recall episodes and feelings relating to the separation period, though in the days between my visits she refrained from such recollections. Her memories were true ones. Kate recalled her crossness that I had refused to give her a bottle (after she had vomited in the night), the pleasure that I had knitted her a jumper and sadness that her mother had refused sweets Kate had offered her on a hospital visit. She remembered dressing up in Jean's school uniform.

During the separation Kate had called me 'Jean's mummy', or most often 'Mummy', although she had been encouraged to call me 'Joyce'. After her return home she always called me 'Joyce'.

The overall impression during the reunion visits was that I had assumed the role of a favourite aunt. Whenever I saw her, Kate certainly remembered the unpleasant parts of our association but was never overwhelmed by these feelings and could to an unexpected degree keep apart happy and unhappy aspects of the separation period. She remembered that she had 'cried and cried' when her mother washed her hair but that she hadn't cried when I washed it.

Nine Months after Reunion

Kate and her parents came to our home to see a rough cut of the film. It was summer and Kate was smartly turned out in a print dress and hair done up in a large bow. She sat demurely between her parents, then called out in excitement as she recognized people in the film. 'That's Mummy, that's Daddy, that's Jean, that's Joyce'. Then, most strongly, 'That's me, that's me.'

But when she saw the scene outside the hospital in which she smacks my face, the exuberance disappeared. She distanced herself from the scene by asking disapprovingly, 'Why is that girl hitting you?'

12

Film:

Thomas, Aged Two Years Four Months, in Foster Care for Ten Days

THE PARENTS OF THOMAS were in their middle twenties. His father was a craftsman and the family lived in a comfortable flat over his workshop. He was a warm, outgoing man, a keen footballer, family oriented, proud of his son and very ready to consider his needs. There was boisterous affection and quiet understanding in their relationship, with an occasional tinge of irritation when their needs clashed.

Thomas's mother was quietly spoken, gentle and affectionate, with a lot of empathy and understanding for her son; but she was rather more controlling than at first appeared from her quiet, easy manner. She rarely compelled obedience but instead pleaded or disapproved. If Thomas did not comply, she usually withdrew interest with an 'Oh, Thomas!' and this quickly brought him into line with her wishes.

Thomas was a well-developed, sturdy little boy who had a friendly, confident manner and talked well. He was not toilet-trained and had a strong resistance to going to bed. The relationship to his parents was secure and demonstratively affectionate.

The parents had talked a lot to Thomas about the new baby and the coming separation, and were fairly confident that, if well cared for and visited every day by his father, he would be all right.

During several pre-separation visits, mostly at our home, Thomas maintained a friendly but reserved manner towards us. He interacted with all members of our family on the basis of his books and toys and talked of the time when he would come to stay.

121

First Week

Thomas went with his father to take his mother to the hospital, then was brought to us. He solemnly waved goodbye to his father, acknowledging with a quiet nod the promise of a visit later in the day.

Like the other foster-children in the study, Thomas did not break down upon separation, but for the first two days defended against anxiety by over-activity and pseudo-cheerfulness. He was never still. In subsequent days, more appropriate feelings emerged – longing for his parents and home and sadness when his father left after visits. But for most of the time he was in good humour, in friendly contact with his caretakers and able to enjoy the play and activities offered. He ate well and resisted sleep as he had done at home. He did not rest in the day. Each evening he sat on my knee for a long time while I read him a story, strenuously resisting giving way to sleep while his head lolled and his eyes glazed. It was usually 10 p.m. before I carried him to bed.

Thomas asked about his mother and talked spontaneously about her. Mingled among the comments were recollections of times when his mother was angry with him, as though wondering whether she had gone away because he was naughty. Sometimes he cuddled her photograph to him and kissed it. At other times the photograph made him uneasy; he would take a quick glance at it and turn away with pink cheeks. He thought a lot about his parents and momentary sadness often overcame him. He would say, 'Thomas is thinking.'

The highlight of each day was his father's visit, and at first the visits were totally enjoyable with brief tears afterwards. But soon Thomas's grasp of the situation made him unhappily aware that visits were temporary and that a goodbye was inevitable. He pleaded with his father not to go back to work but to 'stay with Thomas', and after a few days the visits were punctuated by tears.

As a reassurance father gave Thomas his pen to look after and Thomas held it tightly. He would not allow us to sit on the chair his father sat on and would not even sit on it himself. 'No! That is my daddy's chair. I want to sit on my daddy's lap.'

His parents had suggested that Thomas would need plenty of activity and this proved to be right. He welcomed every diversion, and unhappiness could always be averted by going shopping or playing in the garden.

On the third day, when tiredness was combined with inactivity, he became unhappy, crying, 'Where's my mummy? I want my daddy.' He refused my comforting, pushing my arms aside and wriggling away from my touch.

Untypically, Thomas had to be protected from careless, abandoned kind of movements. On the stairs he did not walk in his usual adult way, but jumped, and did not hold on to the side-rail. I forgot to warn his father of this change in behaviour and while with his father Thomas almost fell down the stairs. When walking on the road, and in the house, he shuffled his feet and several times almost fell. Sometimes he did fall. At bedtime he ran about excitedly from room to room, bumping into doors in a dangerous way, and had to be stopped.

Several times Thomas was aggressive to me – riding his tricycle into my legs and over my feet or holding on to me with unnecessarily tight fingers. At bathtime the aggression became more direct, nipping my flesh with his teeth and hitting me with clenched fists, grinding his teeth while apparently cuddling me.

His father, too, came in for rough handling amongst the affectionate hugging. Thomas pulled and twisted his father's ears as though being playful, but his father's winces and the colour of his sore ears said otherwise.

Doll Play

I introduced Thomas to the doll family – daddy doll, mummy doll, little boy doll and a baby doll. He listened intently to the story about the daddy doll going to work, mummy doll going to the hospital and Thomas doll going to the Robertsons, but he did not comment. He followed the movements of the dolls, but he refused to handle them. Several times next day he asked for the story to be told again and cuddled the dolls under his arms, saying, 'They're mine.' The following day he showed very little interest in them until I played over the situation of his father taking a sweet in a parcel to his mother in hospital and his father returning to bring a kiss from his mother. Even then his play was half-hearted and confused. After that doll play he punched and scratched me with vicious facial expression. Next day he wanted me to play 'sweet in parcel' again and again and smiled as he listened; but when I suggested he tell the story, he refused, saying, 'You do it.'

On the fifth morning, his voice bold and his mood cheerful, Thomas said, 'My mummy is sitting in the hospital bed. Daddy has gone to work. Daddy has big boots. Thomas has little boots. The baby has bootees.' Letting his hand move over his chair from home, he said, 'This is a nice chair. Mummy bought it.' He stroked my arm and face with gentleness.

'Nice Mrs Robertson.' He cuddled his mother's photo under his arm, then asked to have it pinned on the wall and told us all to look at it. He had a realistic view of the total situation and, although under strain, was coping well.

Thomas fluctuated between wanting my affection and strongly resisting it; his need for mothering, and his growing attachment to me, conflicted increasingly with loyalty to his mother. Late on the sixth day, when he sat on my knee, tired and wanting his parents, he pushed away my encircling arms: 'Don't cuddle me. My mummy cuddles me.' But at other times he lay on the floor near me, chatting in a relaxed way about his parents, what they said and what they did with Thomas.

SECOND WEEK

Thomas began the week looking well and bright. He played in an absorbed way and drew us into his fantasies. He was good-humoured and easy to handle. The evenness of his mood was clear from his play and chatter. He said to himself, when some effort was needed to accomplish a task, 'Let's try again.' And when patience was called for, 'Let's wait a moment.'

Thomas was affectionate to me, but from the sixth day onward the affectionate gestures often changed suddenly to aggression. He would stroke my hair, then twist his fingers in it and pull hard to hurt me. This highlighted the mixed feelings that Thomas was coping with. Sometimes I could avert the aggression by accepting but not returning the affection.

If our daughter Jean was at home, it was usually to her that he turned for comforting after his father's visit. There was no conflict in accepting Jean's affectionate handling; she did not perform the caretaking functions associated with his mother.

On the ninth day Thomas showed more signs that he was less able to contain the strain. He was impatient, slower to respond to my requests; he spoke in a whining voice and chewed his clothing.

In the afternoon of that day he tucked himself into a large cardboard box and played a new game, that of being a baby. 'I a baby. Got no teeth. Can't walk. Want a rattle. I get in a pram.' The game went on and on, and his usual boyish constructive games were set aside.

In interaction with me he was warm, affectionate, demanding and aggressive. Sometimes he sought my care, then angrily pushed it off: 'Not you do it. My mummy do it,' he shouted.

Thomas continued to fight off his growing wish for intimacy. He was rarely affectionate without aggression taking over and rarely aggressive without affection taking over. His kisses began with his lips, then he drew them back and nipped my flesh with his teeth. His hugs and caresses turned into finger-pinching or scratching, and a head that began to nestle into my neck became a butting tool. Likewise, pure aggression did not get expression; the slightest glimmer changed into, or was accompanied by, a smiling 'Hello' or a kiss. Thomas's feelings were running high.

His father's daily visits were very important for Thomas. He anticipated them with longing, experienced them with intense feelings of pleasure and sadness and was tearful for a brief period afterwards. Towards the end of the separation it took Thomas several minutes before he warmed to his father. They then became enveloped in a quiet sadness. His father was himself under stress and very affected by Thomas's tears. On the ninth evening he said, 'We've both had enough.'

Tenth Day

Thomas knew he was to go home this day. He awoke in lively good humour and announced, 'I thinking about my rocking-horse at home. Mummy says, "No, mustn't climb, makes Mummy very cross." ' We all joined in the packing, Thomas busiest of all. With a beaming face he carried possessions across the room and stuffed them into the box.

When his mother arrived, he stood still and for about thirty seconds looked uneasily at her; then he went towards her with gentle affectionate gestures, stroking her hair, touching her face and taking her in with his eyes. His first concern was to rediscover her physical characteristics by looking and touching; his next, that her 'rest' in the hospital was finished.

From various parts of the room be brought little things he had collected during his stay and showed them to her with a gentle 'Look, look.' He made pretend tea for her and several times broke off the game to kiss her. His caresses were tender and his voice soft and affectionate.

When his father arrived ten minutes later, Thomas did not move except to point to his mother and say, 'Look, Daddy.' His mother had to tell Thomas to leave her side and give his father a kiss. This he did dutifully, then quickly returned to his mother. His father noticed the switch from the intensity of Thomas's relationship to him during the separation, but accepted it with a smile. He had brought the new baby in a carry-cot and Thomas gave it a glance in passing.

Thomas's full attention had moved from me to his parents; after bestowing a perfunctory kiss at the suggestion of his mother, he left me with every sign of urgency to get home. There was no backward glance.

AFTER REUNION

Thomas returned to his family in much the same state as he had arrived in the foster home – untrained toiletwise, with a dislike of bedtime and with easy expression of aggression and affection. He had been well supported by me and his father, and returned to parents who continued to handle him with empathy and understanding.

After returning home he was less easy to control than before, and in his relationship to his mother there was a defiant and aggressive element that was new. For instance, during the first week at home Thomas began shouting 'No' when his mother tried to control or frustrate him in any way. She described how, when Thomas had climbed to a shelf where the parents kept their special belongings and she reminded him that he was not allowed to touch these things, he had insisted that he must climb up there. On being stopped he had shouted and cried.

During my visits over the next few weeks he was friendly but cautious and stayed close to his mother. On the third day after reunion, Thomas silently walked past me to his mother with his colour rising visibly. He then walked about the room, saying nothing but not taking his eyes off me. I broke the silence by explaining that I had come to see him and to bring a few things he had left behind in the Robertson house. He looked at what I had brought, but in a flat, silent, cautious way.

He ran out of the room for a few minutes and on return came close to me, looked intently at my face and gently stroked the cheek he had scratched a few days earlier. Thomas had specially liked the daddy doll and I produced it from my pocket just before I left. He looked at it with discomfort and, stepping backwards from it, said, 'No, I don't want the daddy doll. I don't want it.' His parents said afterwards that Thomas spoke spontaneously about Jean and the foster-father, but reluctantly about me.

When I reappeared on the seventh day our meeting was noticeably easier for him than on the third. Again he stroked the cheek he had scratched. When I left, his exclamation 'You are going home' emphasized his relief.

On one of my visits he wanted to eat a yoghurt I brought, but refused to have his bib on and refused to sit at the table. His mother then offered to feed him by spoon as he stood on a chair, but to this, too, he would not agree. 'Not you do it,' he said angrily. This was totally different from

Thomas's amenable pre-separation behaviour. In the home he did not cling to her, but she noticed that on the street he held her hand tightly.

When the observation finished two months later Thomas was still defiant and disobedient, and aggressive both to mother and the new baby.

13

Film:

Lucy, Aged Twenty-one Months, in Foster Care for Nineteen Days

Lucy's parents were in their late twenties, graduates and outgoing. Her father was a business executive, warm and demonstrative to Lucy. Her mother described herself as a pessimist. However, she presented as a gay, lively, untroubled young woman; but some of the liveliness gradually revealed itself as a defence against anxiety about the forthcoming Caesarean birth. (In fact because of complications, she was detained in hospital beyond the expected ten days.) She responded appropriately to Lucy, but did not prolong the contacts. She disliked children who clamoured, she said, and added that Lucy had never been a cuddly child.

Lucy's early developmental history was normal. At twenty-one months her body control was excellent and she played intelligently and constructively. But there were some less satisfactory features. Lucy did not talk, slept a great deal, had an eating problem and tended to withdraw when frustrated. There were patches of eczema on her cheeks and forehead, her expression was sombre and she dribbled. Some of these features possibly related to a withdrawal of cathexis by her mother during the latter stages of pregnancy.

During the first few familiarizing visits, Lucy was often glum, her face puckered and her brows drawn together to give a disgruntled expression. Even when she had warmed up, there remained a great deal of reserve and caution. On later visits she became quietly friendly, using her toys to make contact. She showed little variation in mood.

First Week

We collected Lucy from home in the morning an hour before her mother went into hospital. The parting of mother and child was as undemonstrative as if Lucy had been going for an outing to the park. That first day in the foster home she interacted quietly with all of us, singling me out as the most familiar. She played contentedly in our house and garden and ate a small tea with pleasure. She watched us carefully and sometimes stood just touching me or directing me to go wherever she wanted. She looked for me whenever I left the room.

Father's Visit

Two hours after Lucy arrived, her father made his first visit and for half an hour Lucy played happily with him. Then she took his hand and tried to direct him to take her out of the house. When he left she tried to go with him and did not realize for some minutes that he had gone without her. She then began to cry and could not settle to play. Now and again she recovered, then whimpered and went to the door obviously looking for her father. She had a disturbed night – no desperate crying but some whimpering.

On the second day Lucy was more animated than we had ever seen her, gay at one moment, protesting crossly at another, and at bathtime affectionate. She cried several times, never in distress but mainly in protest at any interference.

There was no behaviour we could interpret as asking for her parents, but her many attempts to get out of the house suggested she was trying to get away from us. This was the day of the birth, so her father did not visit. Lucy settled quickly at bedtime, but again whimpered in her sleep during the night.

On the third and fourth days Lucy was mainly active and cheerful. But her father said that Lucy's laughter had a new quality about it, that it sounded hysterical and artificial. This artificial gaiety readily gave way to turbulent behaviour. Any frustration, for instance when I tried to stop her tearing a book, sent her into a tantrum. She reacted to ordinary routines in much the same way: she refused to sit in her feeding chair for tea and protested when put down to rest. There seemed to be a great deal of anger in her crying, not distress. But compared to our pre-separation impression of Lucy, she was a child come alive in all directions. Her facial expression had lost its flatness and now reflected a variety of feelings.

Lucy was increasingly affectionate, running to me and burying her head in my lap; but she drew away if I attempted to touch her with a caress when she had not asked for it.

Lucy smiled when she was shown her mother's photograph, then became extremely cross and threw it away.

By the fifth day Lucy presented a very different picture from the pre-separation one. There was a marked improvement, contrary to what is commonly expected of young children during separation from the mother. She looked bright and happy and only occasionally withdrew. There were fewer tantrums, less resistance to routine handling and less crying. She was eating proper meals and the dribbling had stopped. Solitary play had given way to interaction with me.

Her father's daily visit was a pleasure to them both, and Lucy cried when he left. Her father commented on her improved physical appearance and on her greater animation and responsiveness.

We wondered at this point whether the change was the result of heightened activity to deal with the new anxiety-provoking situation, or whether the change was the result of stimulation and cathexis which had been missing in the weeks before the separation.

SECOND WEEK

On the eighth morning Lucy awoke early after a restless night. There was a marked deterioration in her appearance and behaviour. She looked tired and blue around the eyes, grizzled at the slightest thing and reacted aggressively when I offered comfort. This abated a little when I took her out to the shops. At rest time she would not have even her favourite animals in her cot; she threw them out angrily. When she got up after her rest she had tantrum after tantrum.

The feeding disturbance which had been troublesome at home was transferred to me with all its anger and provocation. She refused to have her bib on and refused to sit in her chair although she was certainly hungry. I eventually fed her on my knee.

She hurt herself several times as she threw herself about and sometimes pinched herself. She walked around aimlessly, not settling to play, not giving anyone peace. She interacted with me continually, often aggressively.

The disturbed behaviour continued for two days. On the tenth day she looked tired but did not complain. Tears rose quickly and there was a new sadness in place of the crossness of the previous few days. Sometimes she sought my comfort, but at other times she isolated herself by crawling under a table or behind the furniture out of reach. Ultimately she came to recover in my arms.

In the afternoon of that day Lucy's father took her to a park within sight of her home, where she had often been with her mother. On return she was unsettled and aggressive towards me, crying and scratching.

As the range of feeling became more richly expressed within the foster-family, Lucy interacted less with her father during his visits. On the eleventh day he was unhappy that she was distant towards him and they could not get into their former warm relationship. That night Lucy slept badly.

By the end of the second week Lucy seemed to be emerging from the unhappiness of the previous three or four days. There were fewer upsets, more spells of concentrated play, more affection, less negative hostile behaviour. She was less aggressive and, more important, turned none of the aggression on herself. She looked prettier and more animated than any of us had ever seen her; not even her father, he said.

Lucy's relationship to me was now all-embracing. She could accept a prohibition without offence, could allow me to comfort her and was secure enough to withdraw from me for short periods to play alone in a purposeful way.

THIRD WEEK

Friendly distance continued to characterize Lucy's attitude to her attentive father, but within our family she was now usually relaxed and responsive. She sought more attention from the foster-father. To me she was affectionate; she could tolerate my prohibitions, could accept comforting and could play quietly apart while remaining in contact. But without warning she would for a few hours be negative and defiant. Lucy was in a highly sensitive state.

On the seventeenth day her father again took Lucy to the park near her home. She returned in a good mood and greeted me affectionately. But at parting she averted her face to avoid father's goodbye kiss, looking up at me with a little smile as she did so. After he had gone she threw herself on the floor and rolled about in misery refusing comfort. After a while she allowed herself to be picked up, and at bedtime she clung tearfully to me and could not be put down.

On the eighteenth day there was no doubt that Lucy was still in a touchy state and in need of careful handling. To cope with her restlessness I ordered the day so as to give her plenty of change – upstairs, downstairs, in the garden and to the shops. Lucy looked well physically, her skin clear of the eczema she had come to us with, her body plumper. She ate well and with pleasure, and at more usual intervals. There were no tantrums. She played well, her language had increased from two to eight words ('bye, down, all gone, shoes, doggy, choo-choo [train], Daddy' and, we thought, 'Joyce').

On the Day of Reunion

Lucy's mother came to collect her. The reunion was accomplished smoothly and pleasantly. With only a few seconds' hesitation, while twitching fingers plucked at the hem of her dress, Lucy responded with affectionate overtures and withdrew from me. She looked intently at her mother from top to toe, then smiled and went towards her. She looked searchingly into her mother's face, listened intently to what she was saying, fingered the fabric and buttons of her dress, then when her mother touched noses she smiled radiantly in remembered play. Recognition was complete.

She collected as many of her belongings as she could find and piled them on to her mother's lap, then climbed on top with a pleased expression. Without words Lucy showed where she and they belonged. But before leaving for home she ran affectionately to me and sat for a moment on my knee.

AFTER REUNION

Lucy's mother reported on the telephone that the first thirty-six hours had gone without a hitch, except for some distress at bedtime on the first evening. Throughout the day Lucy had been sweet-tempered, happy to be with her mother, yet in no way clinging. But several times she seemed 'a little withdrawn'. She stared at her mother 'strangely and thoughtfully'. At bed-time, when mother bent to kiss her good-night, Lucy burst into 'a torrent of hysterical sobbing' and clung to her very tightly.

My first visit on the third day after reunion was an unhappy one. When Lucy saw me she burst into tears, then sat on her mother's knee sucking, clinging and whimpering for most of the time. Occasionally she interacted with me in a friendly way, but when I responded she became hostile and rejecting. When I left the room to go home she ran crying after me, then slammed the door shut between us. When the door was opened and she saw me she smacked a toy penguin that stood near by, then threw herself on the floor in tears.

As soon as I left her home Lucy was put to rest. When she awoke she screamed and could not be comforted. She refused to allow her mother to touch her, refusing to have her in the same room. She attacked her mother, then scratched and tore at her own face and hair as she rolled about kicking and screaming. It was one and a half hours before she recovered. A similar but less severe scene occurred later in the day.

Her mother told me this on the telephone and we agreed that I should visit again the following day. We shared the view that Lucy's reaction to the visit was so intense and so unresolved that she should have another opportunity to work through her confusion and to experience again her positive feelings for me.

(Lucy was in a very painful situation. She had been separated from her mother for nineteen days, and in her need for mothering care had formed a strong attachment to her foster-mother. This relationship supported her through the separation and enabled her to cope with the separation without intense distress. It seemed that, because she had not the means to recall and talk about her mother, or to show specific need of her, the mother had lost importance and the foster-mother had taken her place. But, although she did not have the capacity for spontaneous recall of the mother, on reunion attachment to the mother reasserted itself, alongside competing attachment to the foster-mother. The child was put into a turmoil of conflicting emotions – love for both mothers and intense anger about her plight which was directed against us both. She wanted the foster-mother, yet feared her as associated with the pain of separation from her mother. The nature of her distress was beyond the child's comprehension and she needed help to be freed from the pain of these conflicting attachments.)

When I arrived the next day, Lucy silently got her hat and coat and indicated that she wanted me to take her out of the house. This I did, as we had done many times from the foster home. We walked along the road to the shops and, when I invited her to go back and see Mummy, she readily turned towards home and greeted her mother warmly. She seemed to enjoy my visit and, according to her mother, was more relaxed during the next few days.

Her mother said, 'Although all is well for most of the time, Lucy does show flashes of confusion and distress. But she is sleeping and eating well.' The next two weeks were difficult. Lucy was sweet and charming as long as her mother did as she wanted, when she wanted; but if her mother failed to do so there was an instant violent temper tantrum. Lucy also engineered situations in order to create such scenes. She showed clinging behaviour, from mild clinging to lengthy spells of excessive clinging.

(Several visits over these few weeks were needed to help Lucy wean from her substitute mother and re-establish the relationship to her true mother.)

THIRD WEEK OF REUNION

The parents reported that Lucy's mood swings continued – the sweet affectionate communicative one and the screaming provoking demanding one. For two or three days she maintained a mainly good mood, then changed to the bad mood for the next few days.

During the good days she was happy and active, responsive to her mother's wishes and spontaneously affectionate. During the bad days she whined her wants, but her mother could never satisfy them. She rejected everything that was offered. In these moods she was aggressive towards her mother, the baby and herself. From that point the bad moods gradually decreased in frequency and intensity and the good periods became longer.

During the third week we met Lucy and her mother in the park near their home. Lucy initiated a game which played out the separation experience. Taking my hand she walked with me away from her mother, turning occasionally to look at her, then dropping my hand she ran back ahead of me to greet her mother affectionately. She then left mother, sought me out, pulled at my hand to walk with her away from mother again. At a distance of about fifteen yards she again ran back to throw herself into her mother's arms. This game of separation and reunion was repeated seven or eight times.

The game then changed. Lucy took her mother's hand and led her away, leaving me sitting on the grass. When they had gone about fifteen yards, Lucy turned, let go of her mother's hand, and ran towards me as though going to play the game in reverse. But she swerved away, ignoring my outstretched arms. This was repeated several times. She never returned to me.

Later she invented another game. She sat in the arms of one of us, stretched her arms to the other, and made the transfers with smiles. But she finished nestled into her mother, showing that although now friendly to me she was her mother's girl again.

The game became too much for Lucy. She went to her pram and indicated that she wanted to go home.

14

Film:

Jane, Aged Seventeen Months, in Foster Care for Ten Days

JANE was a lively, attractive child of young parents. They lived in the same block as ourselves, but the two families were on no more than smiling terms before they were brought together by the research project.

Jane had lived a quiet life with a minimum of outside contacts. Her mother was entirely devoted to the child's care and provided activities in an imaginative way. Fussing and crying were discouraged and high standards of obedience set. At seventeen months Jane understood many of her parents' prohibitions. For instance, when tempted to pull the heads from flowers in the garden, she could be deterred by a clap of the hands or a call – 'No.' She had reached the stage of development where she would sometimes deter herself by clapping her own hands and shaking her head.

Familiarizing Jane with the foster home and family was more difficult than with the older children in the study. While mother was available, Jane had only fleeting interest in the foster-mother. It was therefore several weeks before the rudiments of a relationship were established.

There were unexpected difficulties in acquainting Jane with the layout of our home, mainly because she transferred her parents' prohibitions to the new setting; she would not, for instance, enter the bathroom because it contained a washing-machine like her mother's which she had been painfully taught not to touch. However, by the time the separation began, Jane was fairly at ease and had briefly visited us without her mother.

Jane was awake when her parents went to the hospital in the middle of the night. But I, by then a familiar figure, was in their home before they left. After lying awake for an hour in her cot Jane fell asleep. I stayed until she awoke at 8 a.m., showed her round the empty rooms, then carried her up to the foster home. She ran with pleasure to the box of toys.

FIRST WEEK OF SEPARATION

Jane immediately accepted full mothering care from me and entered into a warm and pleasurable relationship. During the first few days she functioned well, feeding herself, sleeping and playing well, and did not cry.

She was gay and lively and directed intense, purposeful smiles at her caretakers. These grimaces were clearly intended to elicit answering smiles from those about her and in this she was successful. (Some of the laughing, grimacing episodes are in the film and the mask-like artificiality is most apparent.) The gay over-activity and the intense smiling were understood as defensive, a means of combating anxiety. When a smile stopped, it was often replaced by a blank, tense expression.

After the first few days the smiling behaviour lessened and was then only seen immediately after sleep, as though at each awakening Jane had to assure herself that this was a friendly and safe place. (Her mother, on seeing the film record, commented, 'Jane smiles a lot like that after I have been angry with her and she is trying to placate me.')

By the fourth day gaiety had given way to restlessness and lowered frustration tolerance; more appropriate cross, negative behaviour appeared. Jane played less well, sucked her thumb more and wanted to be nursed. None of these changes were very marked, but they combined to give an impression of a child who was under stress and at times bewildered. There was no crying, but increasingly she wanted attention and company.

On the fifth day there was less smiling and some irritable crying. She wanted to be held more and resisted routine handling. For the first four days she had played in the communal garden without going to her own garden gate, not even appearing to notice it, although the setting was very familiar to her. On that morning she went to the gate and tried to open it but could not undo the catch. She looked over the low wall into the empty garden where she had played with her mother, shook her head in a negative gesture, then turned away with a wide, disarming smile filling her face. She ran a few yards into the communal garden, then stood as if uncertain which way to go.

On the sixth day Jane again went to her garden gate and this time it pushed open. She ran down the path and tried the handle of the door into her home. Then she turned and hurried back to the garden gate with a distorted expression on her face. She closed the gate very carefully, but for some minutes hovered nearby, peering through the bars of the gate and straining to look over the low garden wall at the empty house.

Then, for the first time, she resisted going into the foster home; and for the first time during the separation she spoke the word 'Mama'.

Jane's father visited for an hour each day. At first she played happily with him and cried when he left, sometimes trying to go with him. Then, as her general frustration tolerance declined, she got angry with him. Later in the week she pointedly ignored him throughout a visit, but clung and cried when he made to leave.

SECOND WEEK

In the second week Jane continued to relate warmly to all members of our family. She sought to be picked up by her foster-father and would take comfort from him after minor hurts. When foster-sister Jean came home from school Jane loved to play with her.

She had gained a new word, 'f-flower', pointing to the flowers on my apron. Although she was quieter and ready to cry at minor frustrations, she continued to eat and sleep well. On a visit to a weekly playgroup run by me she was completely at ease, interacting competently with the other children.

By the tenth day (the day of reunion) Jane was warmly attached to me, and called me 'f-flower'. That morning she was lacking in energy, wanted nursing and became upset when I moved away from her. When her mother came to take her home, Jane recognized and responded to her with only slight hesitation. Initially there was some uncertainty and shyness; then sweet, smiling, placating behaviour came to the fore – a remembered way of getting her mother's attention and approval. Mutely she invited her mother to take over: first she wanted her potty, then she fetched her hairbrush, then her dress needed attention.

When her mother arrived, Jane and I had been playing a favourite game of putting pennies into a purse. But she transferred the game to her mother and in a teasing way avoided me with whom she had been so intimate a few minutes earlier.

AFTER REUNION

During the first two days at home the placating behaviour towards both parents alternated with its opposite – doing what she knew would bring their disapproval. Smacks and frustrations now led to outbursts of severe crying, which was a new feature. This was very different from the sunny obedient Jane who at a clap of the hands or a sharp call would heed their prohibitions.

It was several weeks before there was a lessening of the provocation towards her parents. But the easy obedience did not return. 'No' now went unheeded. Forbidden activities, which previously she had held herself back from, she now performed without a backward glance. She picked her mother's flowers and her father's cabbage plants and, although her parents tried as before to curb her with stern voices and smacks, Jane was not deterred. Formerly an obedient, non-crying child, smacks and frustration now led to severe crying outbursts. This was still true four months after reunion.

Although Jane had responded to her mother with recognition and pleasure, she was reluctant to give the foster-mother up.

In order that she should not suffer the sudden ending of a good substitute relationship, I visited several times in the next few weeks. I was at first warmly welcomed by Jane and not willingly parted from. Then, as the relationship to her mother became more established, Jane hovered uncomfortably between the two mother figures. A week after the return home she ran towards me, but the mother put out an inviting hand which caused her to change course. She reached neither mother nor substitute mother, but fell between us and cut her mouth.

Two weeks later Jane had weaned herself from me, but there was no avoidance. Although the foster relationship had lost importance, it remained friendly and warm. When we met in the street Jane was always pleased to see me.

15
Young Children in Brief Separation: Reception and Implications

A LL FOUR FILMS gained awards from the British Medical Association which recommended them for teaching. Audiences enjoyed the innocent charm of these very young children, empathized with their plight and discussed appreciatively the subtleties of their behaviour. Some viewers were brought to tears by the poignancy of the reunion of mother and child, and quotes from two reviews illustrated these favourable reactions:

> One of the world's outstanding series of documentary films is 'Young Children in Brief Separation'. The Robertsons have made remarkable research data on child behaviour available; the films have been universally successful as training materials at all levels of professional experience. (*Audiovisuals in Mental Health Education: A Quantum Leap*)

> James Robertson records the entire period of each child's experience with sensitivity, and Joyce's narration is as good as a textbook on the emotional needs of young children. Each of these five films is a miniature work of art. Not to know them is to miss a rare treat. Indispensable for child study classes, and very informative for all who work with young children. (*Mental Health Films*, USA, 1979)

The four films extended and refined the observations by James Robertson (1953a, 1958b) on which his concept of the phases of Protest, Despair and Denial (now called Detachment) were based. These phases were explicitly linked with separation from the mother when aggravated by strange environment, confinement to cot, multiple caretakers and other stress factors associated with institutional care. Let us review all

139

these variables, initially by focusing on the contrast between John and the fostered children.

John, who in addition to loss of the mother was subjected to the inadequacies of residential nursery care, displayed the acute distress and despair commonly described of institutionalized children. (He was not long enough in the depriving situation to reach Detachment.) None of the four fostered children (Kate, Thomas, Lucy, Jane), by contrast, responded with acute distress and despair. In our view, the difference between their responses and those of children observed in institutional settings was qualitative and not merely of degree. They showed some upset, but the relationship with the foster-mother gave comfort and an emotional anchor which prevented them from deteriorating and held them safely until they were reunited with the mother – very different from the behaviour of unsupported young children in institutions who, like John, go downhill into Despair; and, if the institutional experience is sufficiently extended, into Detachment.

LACK OF SUBSTITUTE MOTHERING, MULTIPLE CARETAKERS

In ordinary family life there is always some awareness of the changing needs and moods of a younger member. There is a measure of certainty that unhappiness, hunger, tiredness, playfulness, will be answered more or less appropriately and without too much delay. For the very young child in a family there are some known and expected responses, because the same one or two people will be tending him. Even if his first cry is not taken too seriously, a real need is unlikely to go unanswered.

This is not so in the majority of institutions with their changing caretakers. These respond in varying ways to what they see, if and when they see it. They are unlikely to see or understand the subtleties of the new young child's gestures, language, needs and anxieties. Just when he most needs to be understood, protected and reassured, he is most likely to be overlooked or handled without empathy and understanding. Several unfamiliar people will deal with him, one after another, and no one of them will share his anxieties or support him through the maze of new experiences.

John, accustomed to turning with confidence to his mother or father, found no consistency of response from his many caretakers in the nursery. He tried again and again to get a response, to relate to them at first by asking for play, by giving gifts, then by asking for comfort by tears. But to little avail. No one person was sufficiently aware of what he was experiencing; the nurses came and went according to their duties, not according to his need of them.

Multiple caretaking meant for John that his previous methods of communicating his needs and of getting a response did not bring results. He tried, but withdrew eventually in the face of repeated failures. It was not just that he was cared for by many people, but that the many people all failed to meet his needs. His confusion and despair were partly a result of this.

In contrast, the fostered children continued to use their usual methods of communication and demand and were answered in ways which approximated the responses they were accustomed to receive from their parents.

STRANGE ENVIRONMENT

'Strange environment' is a vague term which is commonly used in the literature with a facility that conceals how complex and gross the factor may be. It is perhaps thought of as having to do with change of building, colour scheme, furniture.

But for the very young child a strange institutional environment is a multitude of harsh experiences, deprivations and demands, which place a great burden on him. He will be offered strange foods and strange implements with which to eat. He may be helped too much, or too little. The noise and movement during mealtimes are likely to impose strain.

His toileting will be fitted into the institution's routines, not geared to his particular rhythm as happens at home. His special signs or calls will probably not be seen or heard. Toileting accidents will happen, recent gains be lost. The child who is toilet-trained may be put back into nappies, or the child used to nappies find himself without them; this happens because information about individual children is not shared among caretakers efficiently and to make the child fit into the group. Had we not intervened, John, an untrained child, would have been toilet-trained by strangers at a time of stress.

'Strange environment' may mean the sudden withdrawal of a dummy or bottle, just when the child has most need of its comfort. It may mean the unavailability of his special cuddly blanket or toy, not deliberately but by the accidents of institution life.

The child used to sleeping for several hours in the morning and having a late lunch, may find himself too tired to eat, wakeful when

141

others sleep and ready for sleep just as the rest wake up. His sleeping rhythm will be disturbed.

In the literature, insufficient attention has been given to 'strange environment' and lack of substitute mothering. It has been implied, for instance, that if a young child is not upset by a strange environment while his mother is present, the strange environment can have little significance if he shows distress in her absence (Bowlby, 1973, pp. 29ff). This illogical assumption overlooks the fact that in a strange setting the mother helps to mediate the environment, to keep it within his limits of tolerance; and that if she is absent and there is no familiar substitute he not only loses her but is totally exposed to the impingements of the environment from which she had protected him.

LEVEL OF DEVELOPMENT AND MATURITY OF RELATIONSHIPS

Kate, Thomas, Lucy, Jane, who were observed while in foster care, showed with a clarity not previously reported the influence of variations in level of development and maturity of relationships. This can be illustrated by comparing the over-two-year-olds (Thomas and Kate) with the under-two-year-olds (Lucy and Jane).

Thomas (two years and four months) had a good understanding of why he was with us and sought to co-operate in what his parents wanted of him. He knew that he was only temporarily in foster care and recalled his mother with affection and in confident expectation that he would return home. At first he talked about life at home and cherished a photograph of his mother and himself. It was only as time went on that longing to go home occasionally roused sad and angry feelings; but although he needed mothering by the foster-mother, his level of development and the maturity of his relationship to his mother enabled him to sustain unweakened the strong attachment to her, so that he returned home after ten days without hint of regret at leaving the foster-mother.

Kate (two years five months) could also remember and talk about her home and parents. She spoke of the preparations she and her mother had made for the new baby and how she was going to help her mother look after it. She compared her mother's domestic equipment with that of the foster-mother, noting what was like and what was unlike.

She asked often, 'Where is my mummy?' She explained to herself that the foster-mother was Jean's mummy and not Kate's mummy. But as the separation became extended into a third week, there were times when her hold on reality weakened and she said loudly and with emphasis to the foster-mother, 'You are my mummy', and prefaced every remark with 'Mummy'.

Both Kate and Thomas were reserved during the first few days and kept the foster-mother at a distance because the relationship to their own mother was vivid and real. Then their growing attachment to the foster-mother sometimes brought conflict of loyalty and provoked negative or aggressive episodes with the foster-mother.

Because these two-year-olds had clear memories of their mothers and home they could be helped to maintain these memories and to anticipate eventual reunion. When Kate in unhappy spells said, 'My mummy doesn't love me, she won't come to take me home', it was possible to help her separate fantasy from reality. This reduced the build-up of hostility against the mother and kept alive the memories of a mother who cared.

There was no doubt that Kate and Thomas missed their mothers and were under stress; but there were many hours of relaxed play and no desperate unhappiness like that of John in the residential nursery. Memories of the absent mother, their understanding of the reality situation reinforced by the ability to play out their preoccupations through the doll family, the support they got from their fathers and the emotional interaction and ego support provided by the foster-mother, combined to enable them to weather the experience without being overwhelmed.

Both Thomas and Kate were able to drop the foster relationship as soon as the real mother returned.

Jane (one year five months) and Lucy (one year nine months), the younger children, did not have the sophistication in ego development of Kate and Thomas; nor had they reached the older children's level of object constancy. Their understanding of what was happening was more limited and they did not have the language to enable them to talk about it. They were more dependent on the adults for physical survival, and their needs were more urgent.

Jane and Lucy could therefore not be helped to the same extent as the two older children to keep the absent mother in mind. Because of this, and the intensity of their physical and emotional needs, these two younger children accepted the foster-mother without the loyalty conflict of the two older children. Almost immediately they related warmly and whole-heartedly to her.

At their level of development the two younger ones did not carry a clear image of the absent mother and did not have the older children's ability of spontaneous recall. Specific reminders were needed to bring the mother into mind and for simultaneous resistance to the foster-mother to be felt. For instance, when on the fifth day Jane saw her own garden gate, and Lucy on the tenth day had been taken by her father to the park near her home, both children said 'Mummy' for the first time and for a brief period pulled away from the foster-mother.

But these explicit feelings for the absent mother, and the related resistance to handling by the foster-mother, could not be sustained; Jane and Lucy had not reached the level of object constancy that Thomas and Kate had achieved. This made the fostering of the younger ones easier and the reunions more difficult.

At reunion Jane and Lucy greeted their mothers with spontaneous pleasure; but they had more difficulty than did the older ones in disengaging from the foster-mother and re-establishing the relationship with the mother.

COPING WITH ANXIETY

Kate and Thomas were very different from each other in their ability to control and express feeling, and their separation behaviour reflected this.

Kate (two years five months), during the first week, was obedient, reasonable and very easy to handle. She recalled vividly her parents' disciplines and instructions: 'Kate must be a good girl, mustn't make a mess. Kate mustn't touch your books. Must eat my potatoes first.' She recalled that her mother smacked her when she was naughty.

Kate was indeed a 'good girl' who did not cry and who always did as she was asked. Her upbringing had been strict; angry feelings had to be controlled; crying was 'naughty'.

Kate was over-active and over-cheerful, making tremendous efforts to maintain herself without her parents. 'Look, I'm a good girl, I'm laughing,' she said repeatedly to the foster-parents, laughing artificially. She kept herself busy, cleaning windows and sweeping floors, activities she had shared with her mother.

For five days this defensive behaviour kept anxiety at bay. But when on the sixth day she was taken for an hour into a strange setting amongst strange people, a precarious balance was lost and she cried for the first time since leaving her mother.

For most of the first week Kate behaved in line with her parents' expectations. Then she found it difficult to maintain that standard of behaviour without their support and demands. Her defensive behaviour fell away and she became more openly anxious and clinging.

144

Thomas (two years four months) for the first two days also coped with anxiety by being over-active. It was well nigh impossible to keep him in the house. He needed to run, jump and kick balls about non-stop. But by the third day the over-activity had passed and he was expressing sadness and anxiety with mature understanding of the situation.

Thomas showed his feelings more freely than any of the other children. He was more overtly aggressive and affectionate. This was in line with his pre-separation behaviour and with his parents' expectations of him.

Jane (one year five months) was expected by her parents to be a smiling child, and crying was discouraged. To smile was to be 'good'. Mother reported that Jane always smiled more when she had been naughty and wanted to placate her mother.

During the first three days Jane smiled a great deal, in obvious need to get the reassurance of answering smiles from her caretakers. The smiles gradually took on an intense grimacing quality which would suddenly disappear and leave her with a confused, unhappy expression. This lessened after the first three days, but for some further days the soliciting smiles were seen immediately after sleep.

LENGTH OF SEPARATION

This topic has been largely covered by the discussion on level of development and maturity of relationships on pp. 142–143.

Level of development and maturity of relationships, combined with length of separation, determined the extent to which the children were able to remain firmly attached to the absent mother. Although stable and responsive foster care enabled them to cope with the separation as well as they did, it was clear to us that the longer the separation lasted and the stronger the child's attachment to the foster-mother became, the greater was the danger that attachment to the mother would be undermined.

Thomas (two years four months) at the end of ten days, returned to his mother whole-heartedly, without a backward glance at the foster-mother whom he discarded as someone who had fulfilled a function for him.

But Jane (one year five months), by the end of her ten days, had such strong feeling for the foster-mother that although she returned gladly to her mother she continued for some days to try to get back to the foster home.

Lucy and Kate had lengthier separations.

Lucy (one year nine months) by the end of the nineteen days had moved into a strong attachment to the foster-mother. On her return home she showed disturbances of behaviour which were clearly linked to ambivalent longing for the foster-mother from whom she had now been separated and to fear of again losing her mother. Much time and effort had to be given to enabling her to wean from the foster-mother and become firmly re-attached to her mother.

Kate (two years five months), on the other hand, at the end of the longer twenty-seven days' separation still yearned for her mother and, although fond of her foster-mother, had no difficulty in separating from her. But indications were that had Kate's separation continued the attachment to the foster-mother could have become greater than to her mother, resulting in conflict of attachments at ultimate reunion like those which endangered Lucy.

A danger of foster placement for very young children is that in a very short while they become the *de facto* children of their foster-parents and are in grave difficulties when returned to natural parents to whom they are no longer attached and who have lost feeling for their child. This is the basis of serious problems in social work which are still not always recognized.

As always happens in research, questions answered discover still more questions to be asked. Kate, Thomas, Lucy and Jane did not show acute distress and despair, and in the third and fourth weeks Kate and Lucy even appeared to be adapting and finding secure niches in the foster-family. But what would have happened had the separations gone on indefinitely?

Would the two younger children, Jane and Lucy, with their slender object constancy and ego immaturity, have merged the memory traces of the mother with the person of the foster-mother and have achieved the transfer with no more manifest upset than had been shown during this study? Our data suggest that this would have happened.

But even if Jane and Lucy had changed mothers without extreme upset, what might have been the consequences for their subsequent development? From birth, internal structures including precursors to object relationships are in the process of increasingly refined development. These are endangered by interference with or interruptions of the affective interactions unique to the particular mother–infant couple. Infants from birth to about two years may show less upset than those over two, but the level of overt upset is not a true indicator of the damage that may be occurring. We would expect that in a new relationship following transfer a child would be more anxious and less trusting.

This study 'Young Children in Brief Separation: A Fresh Look' extended and refined James Robertson's original observations. We have shown that variables do play a large part in determining the young child's responses to separation.

When given a substitute mother who cared for them with concern and empathy, none of our fostered children was acutely distressed, as were the children James Robertson had observed in hospitals and other institutions many years earlier.

These variables were initially dismissed by John Bowlby as of no importance, but in a change of attitude some years later Bowlby said: 'Study of the Robertson findings has led to some modification of [my] views expressed in earlier publications' (1973).

However, of more importance than differences over the detail of research findings are, to our mind, the implications of our work for social policy and practice which will be illustrated in Part 4.

PART 3

The Emotional Needs
of the Very Young

Joyce Robertson

Introduction

IN 1957 Joyce Robertson returned to the Anna Freud Centre to work in the Well Baby Clinic where she observed mothers and babies who came for routine health checks and guidance, and to become consultant to a residential nursery where she observed infant development under institution conditions.

Three papers resulted from this work and are reprinted here as Chapters 16, 17 and 18.

'Mothering as an Influence on Early Development' was first published in 1962 in *Psychoanalytic Study of the Child*; 'Infants in Institutional Care' was written in 1966 and is first published here; 'Mother–Infant Interaction from Birth to Twelve Months' originally appeared in *Determinants of Infant Behaviour* in 1965.

16

Mothering as an Influence on Early Development: A Study of Well Baby Clinic Records

VARIATIONS IN DEVELOPMENT IN THE FIRST YEAR

WHEN A MOTHER swells with pride as she recounts her baby's achievements, or complains that he is not as accomplished as another, we tend to listen indulgently. We know that despite variations *en route* all normal babies will eventually smile, sit up, crawl, walk and talk. The fact that babies develop at varying rates during the first year is commonly regarded as unimportant in itself.

It is well known that babies reared in institutions develop unfavourably and slowly in the first year as compared to family babies, even where the institution has made the best possible efforts to provide substitute mothering. Thus Dorothy Burlingham and Anna Freud say in *Infants Without Families* (1944):

> Whenever we have an opportunity to compare our five- to twelve-month-old babies with family babies out of average homes we are struck by the greater liveliness and better social response of the family child. The latter is usually more advanced in reaching out for objects and in active play. He is more active in watching the movements of people in the room and more responsive to their leaving or entering, since whoever comes and goes is known to him and concerns him in some way. A child of that age is, of course, unable to take in and differentiate between all the changing personalities in a baby ward or big nursery. For the same reason the baby's emotional response to changing expression, face or voice, of the grown-up person may be slower to develop. His ability to imitate which he develops from the eighth month onward is stimulated in a lesser degree where contact

with the grown-up is less frequent, or less close, or has to be divided between several grown-ups as is inevitable in a nursery. Even where our residential babies are stronger and healthier, these differences in intellectual and emotional development are sufficient to make the private baby appear more 'advanced' and therefore more satisfactory. The comparative backwardness of the residential baby at this stage is due to the comparative unfulfilment of his emotional needs which at this age equal in importance the various needs of the body. (p. 13)

It is now common knowledge that the failure of institutions to meet the emotional needs of a young child arises mainly from the number of people participating in his care. But it is not possible to make a simple antithesis between multiple care and the care of a mother. In this paper I wish to show:

(1) Even when the child is in the sole care of a devoted mother, defects in the quality of her mothering can result in emotional needs being unfulfilled.

(2) Deficient mothering in the first year causes poor general development which can look similar to, but is not to be confused with, retardation due to organic defect.*

(3) The impairment resulting from the experience of deficient mothering will persist after the first year, but may become partially obscured by neurotic features.

The importance of this concept is that since subtle deficiencies inimical to the good development of the infant may exist in women who otherwise function adequately, these defects may easily go unnoticed; and since they are particularly difficult to detect in retrospective case histories, their contribution to faulty development may be overlooked.

A Study of Well Baby Clinic Records

The Well Baby Clinic of the Hampstead Child Therapy Clinic has been in existence since 1957. Children who were then in the first year of life are now between three and five years of age. In addition to continuing under the care of the Well Baby Clinic, many of them attend our nursery school where they can be seen as a group.

---

* Points 1 and 2 have been stressed by Coleman and Provence (1957).

Watching these children play together I became interested in the differences in muscular tone – the strong sturdiness of some as contrasted to the flabby limpness of others, the directed and skilful movements of some and the clumsy uncoordination of others. I noticed that the clumsy ones were those whose mothering during the first year had been recorded as unsatisfactory, and formed the hypothesis that there is a connection between deficient mothering and disturbed motor development.

To test this hypothesis I have studied the observations on these children and their mothers which I had recorded during the previous four years of the clinic's existence. These records describe the physical and emotional development of these children, and the observable features of the mothers' handling, but the records were not designed to throw light on any specific aspect.

Areas of Development Observed

Although my intention was to study muscular development, it soon became clear that this could not be isolated from the rest of development. In observing and assessing the normality of development in the first year, I have therefore considered the following areas: bodily tonus, muscular activity and achievements, quality and quantity of responsiveness to the mother and to the wider environment, communication and expression of feeling.

For the purpose of this study little notice is taken of fluctuations which occur during illness or holidays, or of isolated areas of late development.

Correlation of Mothering Quality and Infant Development

There are twenty-five mother–infant pairs whom I observed from the babies' first months of life.* A simple analysis of the children's status at twelve months of age shows the following:

(1)　There was a group of five babies whose development, in comparison with the other twenty, was poor in the following areas: bodily tonus, muscular development, responsiveness both to the mother and to the wider environment, ability to communicate,

---

* There are in fact twenty-three mothers with twenty-five children. For purposes of this communication these are dealt with as twenty-five separate mother–infant pairs.

expression of feeling. Paradoxically, alongside the general dull-ness and the lower developmental levels, there was in four of the five babies a heightened visual perception (James, 1960).

(2) Very early in the lives of these five babies, the maternal res-ponses had been recorded as unsatisfactory because they were lacking in meaningful affect. Some of the mothers made a normal impression in social situations. The deficiency of their mothering responses could be detected only when they and their infants were seen together. Furthermore, a mother who was deficient in relation to the infant under observation might be completely adequate in relation to another of her children, or to this infant at a later stage of development.

(3) Some of the mothers of the remaining twenty babies had perso-nality and character traits which by common standards would be regarded as unsatisfactory, but each of them was able to answer adequately to the emotional needs of her baby.

(4) None of the twenty adequately mothered babies was poorly developed at twelve months.

(5) None of the five inadequately mothered babies was satisfactorily developed at twelve months.

Inadequate Mothering

Interrelation between Deficient Mothering and Disturbed Infant Development
From clinic records I will now describe the nature of the defective response in the mothers of the five babies, and the interrelationship between the quality of the mothering and disturbed infant development. At the end of the first year the babies were behind their peers on every level, but there was no doubt as to their potential normality. From the early months our concern was directed toward bringing about a change in the way the mothers responded toward them. But though in some minor ways improvements were effected, these did not alter the main trend of development.

Peter When first seen at a few weeks old Peter was a picture-book baby, contented and round, delicately coloured and presenting no problems. His mother handled him competently but appeared harassed and depressed. She was conscientious, devoted to her son and pleased with his development. But she was an unhappy woman, seriously inhi-bited in her ability to express feeling or to witness it in others.

Peter first smiled at about six weeks, but did not progress to the free smiling which is typical of babies between two and three months. When talked to he would listen and look, move his limbs and head and lips, but only rarely would the expected smile appear. His mother did not try to elicit smiles from him and she became uneasy when I tried to do so. When he wriggled in response to my talking to him, she said, 'He is embarrassed', and thereby gave the first clue to her inhibition. We were to become very familiar with this inability to elicit or to answer to an emotional response.

She did not talk to her baby or play with him. In the waiting-room mother and child would sit silent and still like two wooden figures. By the time Peter was seven months old his lack of facial expression, lack of bodily movement and lack of expression of feeling were conspicuous.

When he cried she would hold his shoulder as one might do a strange school child found crying in the street. Inadequate comforting led in his case to the gradual development of an exceptional ability to control his tears when in pain. He would tremble, flush, screw up his eyes and swallow his tears. By the time he was a year old this meagre response had gone; even injections did not make him cry.

He was slow in attaining the usual developmental steps: he sat up, crawled and pulled himself into a standing position just before his first birthday. He walked at sixteen months and said his first words at two years.

It became clear that subdued unresponsiveness was what his mother wanted. The attention and stimulation that came his way during illness, or on one of the frequent family holidays spent in hotels, brought about more demanding behaviour. In our judgement, this behaviour was more normal, but it invariably caused his mother to complain.

Peter always looked healthy, but there was no animation or pleasure in his body movements or in his facial expression. In the consulting-room he sat silently on his mother's knee, intently watching whatever was going on but rarely responding. His watching sometimes had a self-protective quality, like that of a petrified animal – eyes staring, body tense and stiff – waiting and watching for danger. When a therapist first observed him at eighteen months of age his unwillingness to respond to stimuli made her ask: 'Is he psychotic?'

At three years he sucks his thumb a great deal, and his play is hindered by it. He is passive – watching rather than doing or responding. When he is excited he has a disturbing habit of standing rigid, trembling and making unusual hand and finger movements.

He is now in the nursery group, where the following was recorded after his first week:

He takes little notice of the other children and his teachers, tending to ignore grown-ups who speak to him. He makes no spontaneous move to amuse himself, but stands rather near his mother looking about in a dazed, inhibited way, not really watching anything, not looking for anything to play with.

Peter makes a queer impression with his rapid alternations of joyous excitement and inhibition. Even his expressions of joy seem somehow unnatural and inappropriate to his age or to the occasion, for instance, when he names objects. He does not seem to know how to communicate with his mother, to express his wishes verbally, or to be aware of what to expect from her, the way one would expect at his age. His closeness to his mother is not simply like that of a younger child.

Beatrice Her mother was conscientious but lacking in intuition, warmth and identification with her baby. The work with her consisted largely in trying to make her aware of the baby's needs. In a limited and unintuitive way she did much of what was suggested to her, but it was impossible to invest her care with feeling.

At three months mother and baby made a curious impression of dullness. They would look at each other silently, with expressionless faces, and there was little evidence of contact between them. Beatrice had less bodily movement, less expression and was less responsive than is normal for babies of her age.

At six months she was serious and her looking had a staring, intense and apprehensive quality. She looked with interest at toys and was aware of the person offering them, but she showed no pleasure and rarely made any movement toward them. A glimmer of a smile appeared very occasionally.

At seven and half months she had not attempted to turn over. Mrs A reported that as Beatrice was happiest when left alone in her cot or pram, she never took her shopping or for walks. She left the child unsupervised in the garden for long periods, even while she went to the hairdresser or the dentist.

This mother did not fulfil the role of comforter. When her child cried, for instance, after an injection, it called out no response. She would look away from Beatrice and continue talking. When Beatrice wanted attention – wanted to be lifted from the floor, for instance – she would again look away to avoid responding. It was painful to witness a baby trying to get protection and response from a mother who defended herself by being blind to these demands.

The reason for this mother's looking away was not difficult to understand, but it was one which reassurances were unable to touch, and it held the key to the original inhibition and to the improvement which we saw later. Her own mother had for many years suffered from disseminated sclerosis and Mrs A had been much affected by her erratic movements. She remembered as a school child being ashamed and afraid that her mother would behave badly in front of her friends. When she was faced with the jerky, uncoordinated movements characteristic of babies, all her old feelings were revived – hence, the need to look away.

But when toward the end of the first year the baby's movements became more co-ordinated, the mother was able to respond more adequately. Beatrice showed some improvement too, though she was still tense and lacking in animation. A tight-lipped little smile was the only sign of pleasure.*

Maurice and Gordon   These two boys were siblings. Both showed the effects of deficient mothering – with due allowance for other factors.

Maurice was a baby who cried from birth. Breast-feeding was never established. At three months he was in a hospital for twenty-four hours, accompanied by his mother, to have a hernia repaired. It may be that bodily discomfort added its weight to the usual run of difficulties experienced in the early weeks. By five months he was overwhelmed by anxiety, screaming at everything and everybody, and this typified his behaviour for the rest of the first year.

It was difficult to assess his normality at this time because of the all-pervading apprehension. Much of his energy seemed to go into being alert for danger or into crying in fear. He did not make contact. To offer a toy or even to look at him was to risk provoking the most excruciating screams.

At nine months he could grasp and put things to his mouth, but was flabby and moved his limbs very little. He did not attempt to sit or crawl.

---

* Observation ceased at one year, because the family left the country.

To strengthen his flabby muscles and to encourage movements, exercises were suggested; but his mother did not do them. When he eventually walked and talked there was a noticeable peculiarity about both activities. His movements were slow, stiff and overcautious, and he held his head and shoulders in an abnormally tense way. His movements lacked pleasure and spontaneity. Though his vocabulary was good, he spoke in a high-pitched staccato manner which never failed to draw comment. Over his whole being there was an air of diffuse anxiety.

The behaviour which characterized this mother was her imperturbability and the detached way in which she could discuss Maurice's difficulties. Initially her control of anxiety and the calm way in which she handled this very difficult first child appeared to be positive features, though it was puzzling that she could not give him the comfort he so badly needed. It seemed reasonable that she expressed no pleasure in a child who did nothing to elicit it.

Gordon was born when Maurice was twenty-one months old, and though small he thrived. The mother's imperturbability, which had seemed an admirable quality in relation to a screaming and apprehensive baby, was now recognized as remoteness and excessive control of feeling when directed to a more normal baby.[*]

After four months this baby began to show a lack of bodily movement, a dulled responsiveness, and a deceptive state of contentment. He could be left alone for long periods without demanding attention. At nine months of age he was still and quiet and showed little animation. He smiled in response to attention, but made no attempt to reach out to people or to things. Again, exercises were suggested to stimulate the baby; but again the mother did not do them. When talking about it, she was well aware of her resistance to doing exercises with her babies. It was noticeable that she did not fondle or kiss them. Bodily contact did not come easily to her and was kept at a minimum. Maurice, who had the hernia, may well have been in special need of body contact – one of the things his mother could not give.

Remoteness and lack of empathy affected her ability to answer even the physical needs of her babies. On one occasion she was waiting with her two children for a car lift home. The younger child, then six months old, began to cry and the cry soon mounted to a scream – enough to cause comment from the rest of the clinic. The mother was less concerned than everyone else and, explaining that he was tired, put the baby

* See Marianne Kris's description of a similar case (1957).

into his carry-cot in the corner of the room. But the baby did not sleep; he went on screaming. Since in principle we try to adhere to 'Mother knows best', no comment was made. But when the screaming went on and became more desperate, I eventually intervened and suggested I get a drink of milk because he might be hungry. The mother counted up the hours and came to the conclusion that he was due for a feeding. She thereupon opened her blouse and fed the baby.

Her aloofness, her rigid control of feeling, her avoidance of body contact and lack of empathy meant that she was unable to meet the needs of her children on many levels. To know why this was so one would have to know the nature of the feeling which she was so rigidly controlling.

Remoteness and lack of empathy were reported by the nursery observers when Maurice was two and a half years old:

Maurice is quiet and subdued, even sad, but is quite trusting. He often asks his mother questions: 'What's that for, Mummy?' but his mother tends to give replies like: 'I must tell you honestly I don't know' – conscientious replies that are a bit too grown-up or intellectual for Maurice. After which she returns to her knitting and must seem rather distant to Maurice. Though kindly, she does not seem much inclined to leave the adult world and enter into his childish enjoyments. One day Maurice played with the balls and slide with wonder and delight. But every time he tried to call his mother's attention to his game saying, 'Look, look', she replied without grasping what Maurice was showing her.

[When Maurice was three years two months, they said:] Maurice speaks in a monotonous, affectless way, and says inappropriate things as though repeating what he has heard an adult say. His movements are stiff and tense and lack spontaneity and he walks with his knees rubbing together. Maurice does not initiate any activity for himself. It is very pronounced that he never takes the active role in play, e.g. never initiates a new step, develops any fantasy, or starts any conversation. When the teachers do not engage him in play he just walks around seemingly quiet and interested.

Mary and Norman These two siblings developed in completely different ways. Mary, the first child, was breast-fed for two and a half months, but it was not a success. The mother reported that she disliked feeding the baby and the baby did not enjoy it either. Toward the end of the third month Mary refused the breast and the bottle that was offered in its stead. A period of chaos followed during which Mary was fed entirely on solids, until at four and a half months satisfactory bottle-feeding was established.

Mary was a beautiful baby, but at seven months her large, watchful eyes were expressionless and her mouth drooped unhappily; she showed no pleasure in anything. Her development was slow and dull, but she seemed more sensitive and perceptive than a baby should be, too aware of the changing mood and expression of the adult. She sat at eleven months, crawled at thirteen months, walked at seventeen months, and said her first words at eighteen months. She was undemanding and was left alone for long periods of time.

From the very beginning the mother was aware that she was dissatisfied and unhappy with Mary and got no pleasure from her. Though there were times when the closeness of their relationship was obvious, this closeness came in flashes and was not maintained.

By the time Mary was a year old the mother was comparing her unfavourably with every other baby she saw and rejecting her by word and gesture. Our efforts to help her to stimulate and cathect the baby she sabotaged by the way she carried out the advice. For instance, when it was suggested that Mary needed company, the mother put her for long periods in the front garden where she could see passers-by; and later when Mary needed scope for free movement the mother emptied a room of furniture and left her there by herself. Thus she succeeded in protecting herself from entering into a closer relationship with the child.

When Mary was two and a half years of age the mother complained of Mary's lack of pleasure, her inability to concentrate or to bear frustration and her greedy demandingness. She was sucking, masturbating and rocking a lot. The relationship between mother and child was so bad and the child's misery so acute that early entry into nursery school seemed the only solution.

A colleague seeing Mary for the first time at three years of age described her as a 'not very bright little girl a little below average in intelligence'. The nursery staff consistently recorded a similar impression:

Mary is appealing and evokes a protective attitude in the adults. She makes affectionate relationships. She does not speak a great deal and has poor co-ordination, and in all other areas she lags behind. She is inclined to be greedy and has no idea of sharing with other children. She masturbates in an uninhibited way. She has a short concentration span.

They asked: 'Is this a case of organic mental retardation?' But when at four and a half years school entrance had to be arranged, an intelligence test revealed an above average IQ of 116.

When Mary was three years old a second child was born and in contrast to her he developed well. He was communicative and full of life and movement. The mother was aware of a difference between her feelings for this child and the first. She said, 'This time I feel like a real mother.'

It is to be noted that soon after Mary's birth the mother went into analysis. Perhaps because of this she could respond with positive affect by the time Norman was born three years later, and could enjoy mother-hood. Perhaps also because this second child was a boy she could give him what she could not give to a girl. Some of this improved mothering ability overflowed on to Mary, but it was still not consistently available to her and was perhaps too late.

This mother maintains a satisfactory marriage and has good social relationships. It is therefore not surprising that some colleagues, impressed by Mary's general demeanour, were of the opinion that the defect lay in the child's inheritance. But to those of us who witnessed the interplay between mother and daughter in the first year it seemed clear that inadequate mothering played the primary part in bringing about Mary's unsatisfactory development.

There are no set rules to mothering. To decipher and adequately meet the needs of her baby a mother must be able to have empathy with him. If she cannot empathize, then she must fail as these mothers failed.

In each of the instances described, the mother was conscientious and concerned. The object tie was, at the manifest level, intact; but its quality was in question. The babies showed a heightened perception – a special quality of looking, as though taking over part of the mother's proper role of protector. This activity of looking took precedence over doing or responding.

At first glance it might appear that development was retarded, but a closer look reveals that the behaviour would not be normal even in a younger child. Development was not retarded but faulty.

In the first year, subtle faults in development may be mistakenly regarded as slight and transient deviations from the norm. It may seem unimportant whether a child focuses his eyes at three weeks or six weeks, smiles at four weeks or at seven weeks, grasps at twenty weeks or at twenty-eight weeks, crawls at nine months or at twelve months, walks at twelve months or at seventeen months. Yet our material shows that these first ego activities are helped on, or not helped on, according to the quality of the emotional interplay between mother and child; and that delayed achievement appears to correlate with poor quality performance. When crawling and walking are eventually achieved the increased activity may conceal temporarily the lack of integrated development. It was the poor performance still evident in the third and fourth year that prompted this study.

Early Clues to Inadequate Mothering

It will be asked on what grounds assessments are made on mothers who are seen for only half an hour each week, and even then only in a limited situation. My answer is that although mothers differ greatly in the degree to which in the presence of a third party they openly demonstrate their attitude to their babies, *any* mother who on a clinic visit sits for half an hour or more with her new-born baby reveals a great deal to the trained observer.

There are the changing expressions on the face of a mother who is in contact with the baby, her body movements in response to the baby's stirrings, her hands as they steady the stretching limbs, the moments when in answer to a whimper she withdraws from the conversation, the way in which she strokes and kisses the top of the baby's head or curls and uncurls his fingers and toes are evidence enough. Similarly revealing is the behaviour of the mother who puts her baby in the far corner of the room out of sight and reach, who shows neither pleasure nor anxiety.

One such mother walked into the consulting room, put her five-week-old baby on the couch as if he was a parcel, and then sat some yards away to discuss him. The baby was as though still *in utero*, unmoving and with eyes closed. During the medical examination of her baby she stood aside from him, described him as 'ghastly' because he had spots on his face and was offended by the colour of his hair. She was nauseated by the sight of his dirty napkin and grumbled at him for spitting on his nightie. There was no point of positive contact between them.

When the baby was nine weeks old the lack of closeness between them could be seen in the way she handled him. When she lifted him she did it awkwardly and jerkily, without supporting his head. She sat with the baby on her knee, but held at arm's length in a sitting position. He was a crumpled bundle, with head and eyes rolling about alarmingly. He was held in such a way that the mother could not see his face, and when at one time she caught sight of his rolling eyes she put her hand over his whole face and told him to 'find your eyes'. With his eyes as crossed as ever, and his head lolling about drunkenly, he smiled and gurgled – not at his mother's face and voice, because these were not available to him – but at a brightly coloured scarf at her neck.

She had no idea how to make contact with him and her efforts were sometimes incongruous; for example, she lifted his foot and squashed his nose with his big toe, and though this amused her it startled the baby and made him wince.

Confirmation of this mother's attitudes came from her accounts of happenings elsewhere. For instance, she told how during weekends spent at the family country house he had from birth been handed over to a nanny who put him to sleep in a room out of everyone's hearing, explaining that if it was not intended to answer the night cries of a baby then he should not be heard. He was fed at 10 p.m. then put back into his cot until 6 a.m. The mother knew from his behaviour during the week that he awoke at 5 a.m. and cried until he was fed. But she voiced no anxiety that during the weekend his night cries would not be heard, no sadness or concern that he would certainly cry with hunger for one hour in the morning and no wish to take action to relieve the situation for him.

Another clue is a mother's readiness to separate from her young infant. One mother weaned her baby at two weeks of age, because 'it is such a nuisance if one wants to go out', and went on a skiing holiday when the baby was seven weeks old. She showed neither anxiety nor regret at parting from the baby. On return her only comment was: 'Everything was fine, just fine. Nobody missed anybody.'

I suggest that although it may be appropriate that a mother can separate from an older child without anxiety, this is biologically inappropriate in the mother of a young infant and may be a bad prognosis for the relationship.

A baby mothered in this way, without warmth or empathy, will develop broadly along the same lines as other babies. He will focus his eyes, smile, babble, find his limbs; but he will do it largely alone. There will be no fusion between the baby's achievements and the mother's pleasure and support; and for lack of mother as intermediary there will be less reaching out to the environment. His pleasures will be those he can find for himself, and they will most easily be found in his own body. The balance between sufficient stimulation and potentially overwhelming experiences will not be maintained, and the baby may attempt to take over part of his own protection.

As early as eight to ten weeks the consequences are low quality and quantity of body movement, slow responses, serious facial expression, with eyes incongruously alert and watchful. The mother will say, 'But he is so contented', meaning that he is undemanding; or 'He is happiest when alone in his cot', unaware that her baby may be withdrawing. With the passage of time these deficiencies become more gross. The uncomforted baby who swallows his tears at seven months may not cry at twelve months.

CRITERIA FOR ASSESSING MOTHERING

The post-natal period from birth to eight weeks is one of adaptation. The mother adjusts to the new demands made upon her, to the reality of this baby, and there is a reshuffle of relationships within the family to permit the integration of the new member.

The baby has been created out of a complicated marriage relationship. Will the father's reaction to the baby be the kind wanted and expected by the mother? What kind of baby did each of them hope for in size, sex and appearance? How did the mother experience her pregnancy and confinement? Was the baby planned? If not, did she come to terms during pregnancy with the idea of motherhood?

The baby himself will be adjusting to life outside the womb, initially demanding little more than that his physical comforts be maintained. He sleeps or feeds or cries, his awareness stretching no further than to feel discomfort or lack of discomfort.

Sometimes mother and baby come to terms quickly and easily, and before the first month is out their response to each other contains positive and pleasurable elements; but physical difficulties common to the postnatal period may hinder adaptation. It remains an open question to what extent the degree of difficulty experienced in these first weeks influences the eventual quality of the relationship. The records of the Well Baby Clinic are not sufficiently detailed to give a definite answer, but indications are that a warm relationship is often established despite considerable early difficulties; conversely, a beginning free of physical difficulty does not necessarily signify a satisfactory first year.

The outcome of the adaptive period is successful when, on balance, the mother feels and expresses pleasure not only in owning her baby but in the activities of mothering; is aware of her baby's affective states and able to respond to them; uses the heightened anxiety which is normal

165

during this period in the service of her baby (lack of anxiety at this time may be an ominous sign).

When by the end of the second month a mother is still not fulfilling these three criteria, there appear to be four possible reasons for her failure:

(1) It may be caused by a prolonged post-natal state that will pass.
(2) It may be caused by current stress in the mother's personal life, for example, the death of a near relation.
(3) It may indicate a neurotic response to this particular child or to this phase in his development.
(4) It may reflect a feature of the mother's basic personality which will be similarly evident in her other relationships, including to her other children.

In the weeks that follow birth a baby's needs are not always easy to understand. His crying can be dealt with in various ways. It can be stopped by food, by body contact, by cuddling and rocking; or he can be left to cry until he exhausts himself and sleeps. Already in the first weeks the personality and the background of the mother will determine which method she chooses and which balance she achieves. If, for instance, she is a woman to whom body contact does not come easily, she may stop the crying by giving extra food. To some extent the baby will accept this. Another mother, following the older methods of child rearing, may leave the baby to cry. A baby will adjust to almost any condition and survive – but at a cost.

During the first few weeks of life the experiences of babies will therefore differ greatly. In bodily discomfort they may be soothed by being nursed or fed. When restless they may be sung to or fondled, or they may be left to cry. Their needs may be understood correctly and answered appropriately, or not. They may get food when they are restless and fondling when they are hungry. They may be handled lovingly or impersonally, or even with hostility.

This early time is like the beginning of a children's spelling game, when the letters are dealt. From then on the play of each partner answers and in turn affects the play of the other, with neither wholly responsible for the outcome – the final word.

THE NATURE AND FUNCTION OF ADEQUATE MOTHERING

Although in the few days after birth the baby shows only discomfort or lack of discomfort, gradually a third state is added in which the baby responds in a minute way to the human voice and tries to focus on the human face. The way in which the environment, mainly the mother, responds to these minute responses and those which follow, appears to set the tone for the first year's development.

Although Gesell (1946) says that a baby stares vacantly until the twelve tiny eye muscles begin to co-ordinate at about six weeks, it is common experience that a well-mothered baby responds and smiles much earlier.

One mother demonstrated how she evoked a response very near to smiling when her baby was two and a half weeks old. She held the baby's foot, sat very still in such a way that her face was in the baby's line of vision, and spoke quietly to her. After a minute or so of lip, eye and nostril movements the baby looked directly at the mother and dimples appeared in her cheeks. At two and a half weeks it was not a smile, but it was a response. When she was a month old this baby was focusing and unmistakably smiling.

Another mother sat with her third baby, then nearly six weeks old. As she spoke the baby turned, looked at the mother's face, and smiled with rich facial expression and accompanying limb movements. When the richness of the baby's response was commented on, the mother said, 'We play and talk to our babies, but some mothers don't.'

A baby can hear earlier than he can focus. Anyone who has talked to a very young infant of about ten days knows that in response his lips, eyes and nostrils move, and then his head swivels. It is not inconceivable that the making of these early movements promotes early focusing and smiling and that the lack of such stimulation delays the mastering of them.

By two and a half to three months the well-mothered baby has a repertoire of accomplishments. He will have mastered them with his mother's participation. In the early weeks most babies have difficulty in getting and keeping their thumbs in their mouths. Mothers often lend assistance by steadying the jerking hand, gradually withdrawing help as the baby becomes more proficient.

A very young infant conveys awareness to the mother by eye movements when she talks to him. She gives him the opportunity to focus by putting her face in his line of vision while she talks or sings to him. She steadies the rolling head until he can hold it himself. She gives him her fingers to play with until such time as he can play with his own fingers and hands.

The mother values and encourages these minute responses. By her own libidinal involvement she libidinizes the various areas in the child where the early achievements take place. Although his early achievements will culminate during the third month in a general responsiveness to anyone who smiles or talks to him, this is usually short-lived. By the fourth month the well-mothered baby differentiates between the mother and all other people, and withdraws to some extent even from other members of the family. It is therefore again in the close relationship to the mother that the development of the next few months proceeds.

The communication already begun in eliciting and answering the first minute responses is gradually added to. Once the baby can clasp and unclasp his fingers he will be given the opportunity to grasp his mother's fingers and then a toy. Babbling and laughing is accompanied by stronger and more varied body movements. He will be assisted in his first fumblings; and the play, the learning to manipulate, the communication, his mother's pleasure and affection will be fused into one experience. Each new function that appears will be used by them in their moments of play. The baby of four or five months pushes when he feels a surface under his feet. His mother holds him in such a way that his feet wedge against her body, and together they will play with this latest muscular movement.

A mother reported that her baby had pulled on the cot bars and lifted head and shoulders off the pillow. She added, 'Now he loves it if I give him two fingers so that he can pull himself into a sitting position.' This movement was mastered, and with the increase of muscular strength which it gave the next followed – that of pulling himself into a kneeling position.

In brief:

(1) New movements, initiated by the baby or elicited by the mother, are perfected with her support and encouragement.
(2) Because the acquisition of new skills is all part of his play with his mother, he gets special pleasure and satisfaction from them.
(3) The skills are directed outward, and become at first part of his communication with his mother and then via her to the environment.

Alongside this handling of his bodily activities runs the mother's empathic response to his emotional states. She keeps a balance between adequate stimulation and potentially overwhelming new experiences, giving and withdrawing support as necessary.

The baby whose responses are answered, who is helped from the very beginning to get pleasure from his early strivings and eventually to master them, progresses smoothly from one achievement to the next. He is not content to babble to himself or to play for very long with his own fingers and feet. The baby who has been given attention, whose responses have been answered, continues to demand these responses. He cries when hurt or unhappy and expects comfort: he expresses his happiness too and wants to share it.

Not all the Well Baby Clinic mothers are able to have such an intimate life with their infants. Those who have done so have produced babies who are alert, active, communicative and expressive, on tiptoe for new experiences. Being mothered adequately does not guarantee development free of neurosis, but it promotes a sturdy ego with which to meet conflicts (Winnicott, 1960).

CONCLUSION

Indications of deficient mothering which seriously threatens the overall development of an infant can be detected early in the first year. Of the five inadequately mothered children in this study, the fate of one is not known because the family left the country before he was one year old. But by their fourth year the remaining four children were so disturbed that they needed psychoanalytic treatment.

One's spontaneous wish is to provide adequate substitute mothering for infants endangered in this way. But the mothers reported here would not have understood any reason for handing them over to anyone else. They wanted their babies and loved them. Psychoanalysis for the mother would not bring results quickly enough, even if she had the insight and were willing to be analysed.

Therefore the question remains: is there any form of intervention that would be effective?

I offer this paper in an attempt to subtract a little from the unknown boundaries of endowment, believing as I do that the factors I have described are important influences in the development of all normal infants, and to draw attention to a serious problem in preventive mental health.

17
Infants in
Institutional Care

THE FAMILIAR IMAGE of the small child reared in an institution is of someone who, for lack of stimulation and stable relationships, is impoverished in mental and emotional development – functioning together with his institutional fellows at a lower level of intelligence than his peers in the community, lacking in concentration, with attachments which are slender or non-existent and with a limited range of emotional response.

So generally true is this and so appropriate to the conditions of care, that when the occasional exception is discovered – the child who appears to have weathered conditions which have taken toll of his fellows – we are somewhat puzzled. For most children the generalization is unfortunately true; but there are varying degrees of exception which, whatever the contribution of endowment, can be related to experiential factors not immediately apparent when taking an overall view of the institution and its population.

Thus it may matter enormously for later development whether an infant is taken into institutional care at birth or after a few weeks or months of family care, though the differences in age at entry may appear so trivial as to be insignificant. Even in an institution in which staff are in constant rotation and opportunities for object relationships almost negligible, it can happen that a fortuitous circumstance gives an infant a significant relationship to one person, not perceived or understood within the institution but again a factor influencing development in a way different from the run of his peers; and whether a first relationship with a chance continuity is sustained or broken will bring another variation to

170

the kinds of development that can occur within an apparently consistent system of care.

Thus at one end of the scale there is the generality of small, institutionalized children who fit the classical image, and at the other end the occasional child for whom there has been a fortuitously consistent relationship with one person – and whose experience and level of development are therefore nearer to that of the family-reared child than to the institutional one. Between the extremes there are a few children whose more complex development can, on close examination, be related to special features in their individual experience.

In this report I shall present summary accounts of a series of children in the order in which they would be placed on this crude scale – ranging from Jack and Jim, who typify the classical institutional child, through Mary and Thelma, whose unique blend of good and bad experience has led to outcomes which are complex and very different from each other, to Eddy who throughout his six years in the institution has had a consistent relationship to one person with clear implications in his development.

All these children except Thelma had a visiting mother, but these mothers visited so rarely that for the first two years at least their children could not distinguish them from other visiting strangers. After that time the children began to understand that the mothers were personal to them, but visits continued infrequent and the name 'Mummy' was without much meaning. By the time the children were three years old a special significance began to attach to having a 'Mummy' visitor, but it had little in common with a family child's conception of a mother.

Eddy and Mary are now visited perhaps once a month by their mothers; Jack had a grandmother to whom he went for an occasional stay; Jim's mother and siblings come to see him once a month; Thelma's mother has not visited.

THE CHILDREN

Jim

Jim is a typical institution-reared infant – slow in motor development, indiscriminately smiling in his social behaviour and silent. He came to the nursery a few days after his birth and from the beginning was handled by many nannies – as many as six in one day. Some or all could then change every two weeks – some with no experience, some with a little, some who liked infants and some who were afraid of them. By three months he was still like a new-born – unmoving, with poor tonus and silent. No one was attracted to him. By eight and a half months he smiled and babbled, but there was no variation in his response. He lay on his back, unmoving. When put on to his tummy on the floor for playtime he let his head fall and often slept. He was dull and unappealing. It was a year before he could sit, and then he had to be propped up. Some months later he was moved to the toddler department in the hope that the extra stimulation would help him on, but it made little difference.

His body co-ordination was extremely poor; at eighteen months he was crawling but still could not lift a biscuit to his mouth.

By twenty months he was feeding himself and by twenty-three months he was walking round the furniture. He babbled but had no words.

For most of the day Jim was content to amuse himself. He did not demand attention from the adults and was rarely seen sitting on a nanny's knee. He interacted more with the other children than with the nannies. But the other side of the picture was the screaming attacks from which he could not be rescued and in which he could not be comforted. In these fits he would throw himself about in complete disregard for his own safety, and these often resulted in bruises and bumps. These screaming fits, which were a feature of some of his peers, too, were a most worrying feature.

Staff were not proud of Jim; they explained to me that his parentage was poor and went on quickly to point out that he was improving.

Jim is not yet two years old and the chances are that he will be moved in the next year as many infants have before him; no one will follow his development and link its defects to his early experience.

There is so much change and movement among the child population of the nursery that permanent staff do not get confronted with the 'final' results of their methods of care. This, plus the low level of understanding, results in wrong inferences being constantly made.

For instance, when at five years of age a child is noted to have relatively good development, it tends to be assumed that this is to the credit of the institution and not understood that this is usually a child who was admitted at a relatively late age (perhaps twelve to eighteen months) and who brought with him some good development which was not completely lost despite the inadequacies of institutional care. On the other hand, if a child is admitted in the second or third year from a severely disturbed home, and at five years of age is himself disturbed and difficult, the staff not unreasonably do not blame themselves. But they tend to generalize that all of the children who are in difficulty must be so

172

either because of poor endowment or because of bad experience antecedent to their coming into the nursery.

Even if staff had the knowledge and competence to consider the possibility that total care in the institution is damaging, there are few children who are admitted at birth and stay for the years necessary to show that their impaired development is attributable to the institutional experience and not to other causes. But such a demonstration child is Jack.

Jack

Jack was admitted to the nursery at a few weeks old, and apart from an occasional holiday with his grandmother remained there until he was five and a half years old. When I first saw him in the nursery, Jack was three and a half years old – a tall and physically strong boy. He was a disruptive influence everywhere; he was aggressive and noisy and threw temper tantrums whenever he did not get what he wanted. He could not be disciplined. By the time he was four and a half years old Jack's strength, plus his lack of control, made him the terror of the nursery and the student nurses were helpless to deal with him. The matron had frequently to be called to handle him, especially at bath and bed time. It often took three nurses to hold him down to avoid his hurting himself and others. The screaming that went on with these scenes was blood-curdling. These aggressive outbursts became worse and worse and in them he would attack anyone and anything in his path – people and furniture alike.

At infant school he was difficult and aggressive and began to steal.

Everyone asked why Jack was like that, and the explanations arrived at were varied but did not cause anyone to look at the regime under which he had been reared; staff reasoned that if all children were not behaving like him the fault could not be theirs but must be inherently in Jack.

Some said he needed bigger boys to play with, some that he needed a man to discipline him, some that he came from bad stock; but no one thought of him as being the product of a regime that had not provided him with stable affectionate relationships.

Jack had come through the nursery rather as Jim is doing now, without becoming anyone's favourite. These two children are typical of the worst products of institutions; they show low functioning, poor control and an inability to relate.

But staff were right. All children reared in the nursery are not like Jim and Jack. There are some children who come into residential care when they are a few months old, to stay for several years. This is commonly due to sudden illness or death in the family, or the breakdown of a fostering arrangement. The common factor is that for the first few months of life these infants have experienced family-type care.

When they arrive the good development of such infants startles staff because it highlights the difference between a family infant and an institutional one. A few years later they may well be described as having always been in residential care, but they have to be differentiated from infants who have never known any individual care. In my experience infants who have had some weeks or months of family care before admission never entirely lose the lead they have on the totally residential ones, even though their development slows up. Their forwardness also initially attracts the attention of staff and for a while brings extra stimulation their way.

In the institution these infants continue to get good physical care and fairly adequate stimulation, but no provision for a stable relationship.

Thelma is such a child.

Thelma

Thelma came into the nursery at ten weeks of age. She had been well fostered from birth, but when her real mother saw the affection which the foster-mother was developing towards the infant she removed Thelma to the nursery.

Thelma was a minute baby who weighed four and a half pounds at birth; her lively responsiveness and varied facial expression, her strong body movements and loud vocalization when she arrived, indicated the combination of good potential and good care. But by sixteen weeks of age Thelma was quickly losing her ability to babble; her noises were less intense, had less variation and were harder to elicit. Her plain little face, which had been attractive because of its vitality, now looked plain and ugly. Her body movements were still strong, but she had lost ground in other areas. From this time on, Thelma gave trouble to staff because she wanted so little food. They were not allowed to let her take small feeds, so every mealtime became a battle. Thelma's strong body movements came into play as she fought and struggled. To the nannies' eyes she was a small ugly baby who made trouble for them becuse she would not finish her bottles. She became no one's favourite. Several times a new staff member or a new nanny was attracted by the challenge of a bad feeder and took Thelma over. But each one in turn left her for an easier baby who brought them praise from their superiors and not grumbles. Thelma continued to fight off unwanted food. During the next few months she lost her babbling ability and her muscular development slowed up; but at nine months the babbling started again and surprised everyone by its richness, variety and volume.

At ten months Thelma was moved to the next department. Her eating improved. She ate with interest, but made clear signs when she had had sufficient. Staff called her a 'madam' and a 'horror' and were unable to get the better of her, but still they fought and struggled and often made her cry. She got quite a lot of attention through her feeding behaviour but still was nobody's favourite.

Her muscular development was slower than a family child's, but was not bad. At ten months she could sit securely and her tonus was quite good. By twelve months she was walking around her cot and saying the odd word. She was not an under-stimulated child, but she was an unloved one.

Thelma continued her progression through the junior toddler department, the senior toddler department, to the nursery school group. She took every move without upset, impressing staff by the easy manner she took changes of room, routine and caretakers. She also impressed staff with what they described as her strong character; she could not be made to do what she didn't want to do, nor be made to eat what she did not want. She was strong-willed and fought off interference with her wishes; she fought for what she wanted, whether from adults or children. She became an alert, highly verbal, cheekily attractive two-year-old.

Thelma was taken up by one student nurse after another for varying periods of time according to the student's whims or duties, and was dropped as often. But she showed no upset. She took what the nannies offered, played them up, was often taken home to their families, but was never conquered by any one of them.

Many tried to discipline Thelma and I often saw her in an angry tearful tantrum with a nurse standing over her, having removed Thelma from the group for some misdemeanour or other; but these disciplinary episodes had no good effect. Thelma remained incorrigible. This alert, rather plain but attractive child was one of the naughtiest but one of the liveliest children in the nursery. She greeted every visitor, had lots to say and said it well.

Her liveliness and chatter and lack of depression made Thelma immediately noticeable in her group. When the daughter of a long-standing staff member wanted a bridesmaid for her wedding, she chose this child knowing that Thelma would not be awed by the goings-on in church and the many strange people. As it happened, the choice was not a good one because Thelma could not be controlled in the church; everyone would have been glad of a little healthy awe on Thelma's part.

At nursery school she does not cause much trouble; she is happy to wander about playing with one and then another, but she is restless and does not become involved in play. She is liked by her teachers, but she slides through their fingers as she does through everyone's. The mother of a local child who attends the nursery school invited Thelma to a birthday party when she was about three years old. The mother commented on her behaviour which at first seemed untypically but comfortably unshy and easy but which was gradually seen to be shallow and superficial.

At three years Thelma was tested by Miss P, the clinic psychologist, and she reported as follows: 'The attempt to give Thelma the Merrill Palmer test was unsuccessful. She did a few items and these plus her fairly good speech suggest there need not be any concern about the level of her intelligence. She was hyper-active, uncooperative and controlling. She did not make a sufficiently good relationship with me to carry us through the test, nor did she respond very well to Mrs Robertson. It was not possible to hold her attention for more than one or two minutes at a time. She was quite aggressive as, for instance, when she threw the towel at me or pinched Mrs Robertson's throat quite hard. When she found a rubber she bit it and when I tried to take it from her she went on biting on to my finger. One feels the child's development is quite endangered, as she is impulsive, aggressive, lacking in concentration and shows difficulty in relating to others.'

For my part, I found Thelma impossible to control. She was demanding, constantly chattering provocatively, and needed physically restraining for much of the time. She showed no concern that she was in a strange place with strangers and no acknowledgement that I was her link with the nursery. I was most relieved when she was out of my custody. Thelma is an institutional product, but differs from Jim and Jack because she has good functioning; this is due, I think, to the better start she had, but she shares their fate of having no relationship to hold her.

Occasionally, and quite fortuitously, it happens that an infant achieves an attachment even under these same institutional conditions. Two such children are Mary and Eddy.

Mary

Mary was conceived in a mental hospital by two patients and was sent to the nursery when a week old with no expectation of being visited or cared for by her mother. She was a dark African child, well shaped, compact. She arrived on the same day as a new staff nurse who was to take over the department. Both Mary and Nurse W stayed together in this department for ten months. Nurse W was an outgoing, warm, very lively young woman who within a few weeks could walk into a room of six babies and have them all gurgling and responding to her voice or her touch or her smiling face. Mary had a special place in Nurse W's affections for several reasons; she was the youngest infant in the group of eight babies under her care, she was an appealing infant and she and Nurse W were arrivals together. Mary was specialled by her, cuddled, talked to and taken out by the nurse in her off-duty time. Mary thrived under the warmth and stimulation of Nurse W's care, even though she was handled by other nurses when Nurse W was not available. The care given by Nurse W was quantitatively and qualitatively more than Mary received from other caretakers. She was often bathed by Nurse W and was given two or three feeds of the day by her. Although she was often changed by another nurse, sometimes fed by another and had night feeds given by night staff, it was mainly Nurse W who escaped to the infant room between feeds to cuddle and talk to her.

At three weeks of age Mary had better tonus than institutional babies usually have; she had a steady gaze, listened when talked to and was very near to smiling. This good development reinforced the relationship that was already developing between Nurse W and Mary and also brought her attention from other staff. By the fourth week Mary was in all respects as mature and responsive as a family-reared infant. Her tonus was good and when laid on her tummy she lifted her head. She smiled and cooed and later stopped crying when touched and talked to. I noted at the time that Nurse W was a warm, spontaneous young woman who gave all the babies a lot of physical handling; and that it was she who mainly handled Mary, because there happened to be no student experienced enough to handle so young an infant.

At six and a half weeks Mary was still being specialled by Nurse W and one student during the daytime. Mary's smiling and cooing was more pronounced and easier to elicit, so much so that it was difficult to be sure who was doing the eliciting – baby or nurse.

At eleven weeks Mary gurgled in high-pitched, pleasurable screams which elicited smiles from the adults. She could take her weight on her legs. (These two features – vocalization and leg muscle development – are usually missing in inadequately mothered babies, whether in family or institution.)

At three and a half months Mary was moved to the second department (also under Nurse W) to join five other babies under one year. When I visited the department Mary was babbling and kicking and was the only infant awake. The staff nurse reported with concern that Mary was smiling less than she had done a month earlier. In my notes at the time I speculated that this infant was showing the falling-off in general responsiveness that a family-reared infant does at about four months when the infant becomes specific to the mothering person. This seemed to be the case; at five months Mary was smiling less freely than we have come to expect from nursery-reared babies. She also sucked two fingers.

At six months she could hold a sitting position and could turn from back to tummy. She babbled in a great variety of sounds including a clear 'Dada'. Her smiles were kept mainly for Nurse W and were certainly richer in response to her. When she saw Nurse W in the room she refused a meal offered by another nurse and immediately ate when Nurse W took over. She responded in an anticipatory way when I played a repetitive game with her – waiting for the climax of the game. Mary recognized and greeted with special vocal sounds and animated movements a small soft teddy-bear. (These are missing features in most institutional babies, and in my view were seen in Mary because of the good experience with Nurse W from the first week of life.) At seven months she was the pride of the department.

At nine months Mary was taken out of Nurse W's care by being moved to the next department, though Nurse W continued to visit her several times a day and often took her out during off times. I visited Mary in her new department on the fourth day after the move. She was subdued, silent and sad-looking. She sat sucking her fingers and I could not get the usual friendly response from her. Nurse W, who had been away for the weekend, visited her while I was there. Mary was at first responsive, then she covered her eyes and cried – not attempting to get to her. Nurse W picked Mary up and after a few minutes she recovered and became playful and affectionate. The nurse commented on Mary's loss of babbling and increased sucking. During this first week Mary caused concern to everyone because of her subdued sadness. The matron told me that she had gone in to see Mary every day and tried hard to cheer her up, but without success. On the eighth day Mary was taken back to her old department by Nurse W for a play session. She was a delight to watch, her face brightened, her eyes shone and she smiled and babbled as she looked around at her familiar home.

A month later Mary had still not recovered from the move and the loss of her nurse. Her development had come to a standstill. Her facial expression was still sad, she moved little and did not babble. She just sat where she was put and came to life only when her nurse visited her – reverting to depressed behaviour when Nurse W left.

This was the pattern of Mary's behaviour for another month. There was much discussion among staff and criticism of the nurse who, by specialling her, had caused so much unhappiness which the other children did not show. Other babies who had suffered a similar change did not react as Mary had done. Their development did not come to a halt as hers did. Eventually she adjusted to the change and to the different nature of the contact she had with Nurse W and her development went ahead again.

By thirteen months Mary was no longer depressed or withdrawn; she could walk freely and was trying to feed herself. She made good contact with other nurses who cared for her and could become absorbed in play. The contact she now had with Nurse W was a different one; she often played near the nurse in the staff-room as she got on with her administrative duties, quietly occupied but happy to be in the vicinity of her nurse. Her physical care was taken over by several nannies. Nurse W continued to come under fire because Mary was easier to handle when she was out of the way and often made a fuss when she caught sight of her or heard her voice. In a typical instance, I saw Mary contentedly trying to feed herself, but throw down her spoon and cry when she heard Nurse W's voice outside the room. She then would continue her meal only when fed by Nurse W.

During this time I had visited Mary regularly each week and had become a known figure – but not in the same class as her favourite nurse.

At sixteen months two things happened. Mary was moved to the next department and Nurse W announced that she was engaged to be married. The plan was that Nurse W would begin to withdraw from Mary in favour of another nanny who was fond of her, so that when Nurse W left a substitute relationship would have been established.

This did not go smoothly; the substitute relationship was nothing like so good as the original one, but it did help to carry Mary over. Nevertheless she again went into a depressed state, became inactive and sucked a great deal – was subdued and sad. By the time Nurse W left Mary was eighteen months old; she had adjusted to the change, had widened her circle of known and liked nannies and was a favourite with several. Mary was a warm, appealing, cuddly child who responded well to the adults and who called out a positive response from them.

At nineteen months I was impressed by her state. She could use about thirty to thirty-six words spontaneously, which for a nursery-reared child was unusual. Her play was organized and concentrated. She looked bright and happy and was active. She ran freely about, greeting and being greeted warmly by the nannies as they went about their work. She looked intently at people before she committed herself, but having decided to respond did so with warmth and humour, though with some reserve. She continued to be discriminating in her social relationships, although she widened them considerably. But she still sucked a great deal and at times showed more sadness than the other nursery children.

When at two years she went to nursery school the teacher commented on Mary's adequate frustration tolerance, her concentration and how she came to life when she could interact with one person; but expressed concern about her tendency to become depressed. Then she said Mary would sit and suck her fingers until someone came to her aid.

Not long after she started nursery school there was great consternation because Mary became very tearful; it was reported to me that she burst into tears when she heard her new nanny's name mentioned. She was inconsolable. This had been going on for some days. The usual discussion followed and the usual recriminations were made against the current nanny who, it was said, was 'spoiling' Mary. Whoever became involved with Mary laid herself open to such criticisms because it was impossible to have a superficial relationship with her. Mary demanded more and gave more.

This current unhappiness was a puzzle to the staff; but the matron, in asking me about it, reminded me that Mary came from 'bad stock' and was probably going the same way as her parents.

To me it seemed more likely that Mary had suffered some object loss and was reacting with depression as she always did. A few inquiries brought the answer. Mary's new nanny had been on night duty and had spent a lot of time with Mary during the evenings before Mary went to sleep, and during the nights when she woke up. During the afternoons she had been taken out by the nanny before she went on duty. This had been a tremendous increase in contact between the two.

Then had come the let-down. After the period of night duty the nanny had gone on holiday for several days before returning to day duty. So Mary suddenly lost her nanny. When the nanny returned from holiday she was not posted back to the same department, so Mary only heard her name, heard her voice and caught glimpses of her – sufficient explanation for the depression.

But staff found this hard to put up with because most other children do not behave like this.* They take the comings and goings of staff without much concern.

Miss P tested Mary in the clinic and reported: 'Mary shows high average ability; within the test situation she knew very well what she wanted and what she did not, but her co-operation and concentration were quite adequate. She showed good hand–eye co-ordination and space perception. Her speech was well on the way. Mary was cautious, but appropriately so, and was more at ease with Mrs Robertson than with me.'

Though Mary knew me quite well from the nursery she had never been out with me before. She was rather anxious and asked me several times on the way to the clinic where her nanny was. I explained that nanny was in the nursery getting lunch ready and that I would take her back in time for lunch. Mary asked from time to time, 'Has Nanny got my lunch ready yet?' She clung tightly to my hand on the road and in the strange clinic building. She responded quietly to Miss P and co-operated well in the test, coming to me for a reassuring cuddle between times. When the test was over she looked out of the clinic window to the garden. 'Where are Grace and Tania and my Nanny? I want to see them.'

In discussions about Mary, the matron was as critical as any other staff member of the nurse who had 'spoiled' the child. This was extraordinary, because the other child who has managed an attachment under these conditions, who presents similar problems and who shows similar relatively good development, is Eddy who has been specialled by none

---

* I recall another child David who developed similarly to Mary and for identical reasons. He showed similar good development, and the same tendency to depression. He also had an excellent, warm, outgoing nanny from his birth who left to get married when he was eighteen months of age. I did not, however, record enough detail to present him; but my notes put him in a similar category, the main features being a constant search for a love object and depression at each let-down. Staff were upset by David as they were by Mary because both showed an untypical sadness and longing for people. These children did not take life as easily and as superficially as others in the nursery. They did not chat to and amuse visitors. Their sadness made staff feel uneasy.

other than the matron herself. Because of him the matron comes under fire from her entire staff.

Eddy

Eddy, now aged six years, has been in the nursery since birth. The matron became interested in him at about three months when he was not thriving as well as she thought he ought to be. Nobody knows anything about him before that.

Eddy has not had to shift his main attachment as Mary did. He never got enough of the matron, but he has never lost her. In a way she has been an ever-growing attachment – he now demands and gets more of her attention than he did as an infant and toddler when he had to wait for her to come to him.

He is discriminating, does not have temper tantrums at the drop of a hat as so many do, is manageable in school, can concentrate, has good, co-ordinated movement and is not a bed-wetter. His speech is not as good as his other development; though he talked quite early his pronunciation has always been extremely poor. He is sad when matron is away, wants to be with her when she is in the house, manages to join her for breakfast, watches television in her sitting-room and insists that she collects him from school and sees his school work. Eddy's relationship to the matron has always caused a great deal of jealousy and Eddy has not had an easy time. Much less sympathy came his way when he was unhappy because matron was unavailable, and he was less inclined to take comfort from anyone else – especially as he became older.

Even his peer relationships were complicated, because some of the other children soon realized that to be Eddy's friend meant advantages all round – the odd lollipops, the outings, the bus rides, the evening walk to the sweet shop to buy the paper. But Eddy stuck to his main object – the matron; and she has remained absolutely true to him. Even now when his mother has come on the scene the matron has done her best to facilitate their relationship without withdrawing from him at all.

CONCLUSION

It has been known for a long time that children need a warm, continuous relationship for healthy development, yet our institutions are full of children who, although well fed, well clothed and adequately stimulated, are cared for by a rotation of staff. This is particularly true in the care of infants under eighteen months when the emphasis is still largely on physical well-being.

But emotionally deprived infants are notably uncomplaining and contented. They do not draw attention to themselves and a superficial look does not show up their deficiency. Their bonny, smiling exteriors hide the early stages of faulty development which by nursery and school age will be manifest and irreparable.

This difficult problem has not been faced up to in our institutions. Unless ways are found to meet the emotional needs of infants in care our institutions will go on producing maladjusted children.

18
Mother–Infant Interaction from Birth to Twelve Months: Two Case Studies*

INFANTS AT BIRTH are different from one another. Their potential, their birth experience, their physical health and the intensity of their needs constitute some of these differences. For reasons of nature and nurture they develop into as many different personalities; but during the first year their development follows a common maturational path. They focus their eyes, smile, babble, grasp, find their limbs, distinguish the mothering figure, sit up, stand up and walk, search for lost toys and so on. Nature and nurture combine to ensure that most infants develop along these lines and within weeks of a maturational timetable. As students of child development we are concerned to evaluate the relative importance of environment and endowment.

In recent years the influence of environment has been increasingly understood. Many studies have shown that the inadequacies of institutional care can cause in all areas of development gross deviations which might appear to be constitutionally determined. But as yet little investigation has been made into the differences between children who are reared not in institutions but in ordinary families (Kris, 1962; Joyce Robertson, 1962; Sander, 1962).

I have the impression that, in accounting for the deviations and differences which occur in babies who are reared in their own families,

* My contact with these two mother–infant pairs originated in the Well Baby Clinic of the Hampstead Child Therapy Course and Clinic (Paediatrician Dr J. Stross). This Well Baby Clinic, which is one of the Service Departments of the whole organization, is maintained by the Grant Foundation, Inc., New York.

undue weight is sometimes given to the concept of endowment and insufficient to the infant's earliest experience.

My work in a Well Baby Clinic has led me to the belief that the quality of mothering, and of the interaction which develops between a mother and her infant in the earliest weeks of life, plays a substantial part in determining whether development in the first year follows closely on established maturational stages; and that the infant's status at twelve months is of prognostic importance. My belief derives from clinical experience and not from systematic study. I realize that this is a complex area in which definitive findings will require techniques which are outside my competence.

In an earlier paper (Joyce Robertson, 1962) which was based on a study of twenty-five mother–infant pairs, I instanced five extreme cases where the mother's lack of empathetic interaction with her infant, and her failure to protect him against potentially overwhelming experience, had resulted in deviant development. At twelve months the infants were poor in bodily tonus, in responsiveness both to the mother and to the wider environment, in ability to communicate and to express feeling. By five years of age four out of the five had been deemed in need of analytic treatment; the fate of the fifth was not known.

In this paper I take up another aspect by seeking to show that what might appear to be minor and transient disturbances occurring at an early stage in the mother–infant relationship can influence the course of an infant's development. The material is derived from my direct observation of two mother–infant pairs.

Summary

John and Peter were born in the same week, and each had a sibling of two years plus.

In the second month both families went through a crisis which caused each mother to become acutely anxious and to withdraw from her infant for a period of just under two weeks.

During her period of emotional withdrawal the first mother was able to maintain the physical comforts of her infant, including the feeding. On recovery from her upset she found him slower and quieter and less responsive than formerly. He demanded less and thenceforward she mothered him at this lower level.

The second mother was unable to maintain satisfactory physical care of her infant. He became desperate and had to struggle to find the perfunctorily offered breast. On recovery from her upset this mother found herself with a very alert, precocious infant. She responded to this with satisfaction and answered his new-found alertness with stimulation and reward.

At twelve months there was a marked disparity between these two infants. John was slow, undemanding, placid and lacking in outward investigatory behaviour. Peter was precociously forward, unrelaxed and relentless in his demands; he showed extreme mood swings and was unusually aware of the sights and sounds of his environment.

I believe that these differences were substantially determined by the way in which each mother responded to the stressful event in the second month of her infant's life; and by the repercussions this had on the infant and on subsequent mother–infant interaction.

John

Mrs H was young, rather unsure of herself but warm and sensitive and spontaneous in her relationships. She had a good relationship with her first child, Andrew, and his development was most satisfactory. When baby John was born, Andrew was a lively, intelligent and spontaneous child and a delight to his parents.

John was born normally at home, weighing six pounds six ounces. He was a healthy, hungry infant and four-hourly cow's milk feeds were started on the first day to tide him over until the breast milk came in on the third day.

Breast-feeding was established easily and he gained a pound in his first week. The mother quickly became sensitively in contact with him – answering his needs without delay. She found pleasure in holding and looking at him.

At ten days I watched them together after a feed. The baby lay on his mother's lap, wide awake, moving his head and eyes and mouth and sometimes his limbs. She was relaxed and happy as she caressed him, watched his movements, and spoke to him in a soft voice. Then after a while she reluctantly put him back into his cot, saying, 'I could sit all day with him.'

At two weeks she was adapting well to the rhythm of the new baby, fitting easily into his pattern of feeding and sleeping. When he looked with open, steady eyes she tried to convince me that he was looking at her. He was 'a real baby', she said. By three and half weeks she was becoming impatient for him to smile.

186

Her handling was warm and sensitive. He was peaceful, feeding well, putting on weight. His movements were gentle and flowing, and when one talked to him he listened and his gaze became steady. The mother was ready and waiting for the first sign that the infant was aware of her.

She tried to balance the needs of both children, but found it difficult to delay attending to the baby. If the baby cried when she was doing something for Andrew, she felt impelled to turn from Andrew and give immediate attention to the baby. She said, 'If he cries and no one comes he must feel deserted and unloved'; and added, 'He can't think, he can only feel.'

She realized, she said, that she felt at peace as long as she was able to follow the baby's rhythm, pick him up when he cried, feed him when hungry; but when conflicting demands were made on her her anxiety rose and she behaved in a confused way.

Her mood and that of her infant were closely interlocked. Every success in her mothering added to her contentment; every failure made her anxious.

At morning bathtime she usually contrived to have Andrew entertained downstairs by the daily help, so that she could play and talk freely with baby John. As I saw on a visit during the seventh week, this was a mutually satisfying time. John was active and responsive throughout the bath, babbled and exchanged smiles with his mother during the dressing, listened when she talked to him. He fed well. He looked peaceful, his skin was clear and delicately tinted, his chin rounded, his eyes clear and bright, and his limbs relaxed. The mother looked prettier and happier than at any other time over the four years I had known her.*

During this period the father supported and protected her, and she was able to accept his help. When, like many babies of this age, John did not settle after the 6 p.m. feed and needed extra comfort, they shared in his care – nursing him, giving him a dummy or an extra feed.

It looked as though the family was emerging satisfactorily from the adaptive period. The parents were pleased with their new son. They had reallocated their affections to include baby John, and the family was

---

* Applying my own critera for assessing the adequacy of early mothering (1962), this mother was adequate because:

   she felt and expressed pleasure in the activities of mothering;

   she showed awareness of her baby's affective states and a willingness to respond to them;

   she used the heightened anxiety normal to this period in the service of her baby.

settling in its new constellation. John was developing satisfactorily – feeding well and putting on weight, bodily active, lively and responsive. But a week later, when he was eight weeks old, the serenity of his environment was suddenly disrupted.

The father became ill and malignancy was suspected. On visiting the home next day, I found the mother shocked and confused. It was lunch-time but she was still in her dressing-gown. She could not eat and had to be persuaded to have coffee. She was withdrawn and sat for long periods silently sighing. The baby was awake and a feed was due, but she could not decide whether or not to feed him. Throughout my visit, which stretched to four hours, she was slow, dreamy, indecisive, and near to tears.

The feed I then observed went peacefully, but in her withdrawn subdued state she fed the infant mechanically and without interaction. John remained wide awake throughout. Instead of finishing in his usual drowsy and sated state he was still alert when put into his pram.

During the next week the mother continued in a state of extreme anxiety and withdrawal from her baby. She managed to keep the breast-feeding going, and he suffered no physical neglect. But she was not in her former warm, responsive relationship with him.

Throughout a lengthy visit on the third day of the mother's upset I saw that he was not cuddled and talked to, kissed and caressed. His smiles and cooing failed to bring her answering voice and smile. Looking into her eyes did not bring him her answering look and touch. His limb movements were not answered by her caresses.

Within a week a marked setback to his development could be clearly observed. His bodily activity had decreased and his smiles were fewer and harder to elicit – not only by the mother but by the father and me, to whom he had earlier reacted with animation.

A few days later a more hopeful statement about the father's prospects lessened the mother's anxiety; and when after another week it was confirmed that there was no malignancy, both parents gradually reco-vered much of their equilibrium. The mother was ready to resume her former relationship with John, but she complained that he was sombre and unresponsive.

At ten weeks I watched her bathe and feed him. Her handling was as tender and intuitive as before, and she was eager to be playful with him. But although John listened and looked intently as she cuddled and kissed him, his responses were slower and his face serious and unsmiling. She shrugged off her disappointment and said in mock crossness, 'Don't look so serious!' I saw that she was mirroring his serious expression, as two weeks earlier she had mirrored his smiling one.

This was an instance where a mother's readiness to interact with her infant was inhibited by the infant's lack of response. No longer withdrawn, she was ready to mother her infant sensitively as before; but John had not made the same spontaneous recovery. He now smiled only after much stimulation, more like a younger infant of six or seven weeks. Recalling the lively interactions they had enjoyed only two weeks before, the mother complained, 'Smile at your mother' – as if he had been deliberately withholding.

By the end of the third month most infants begin to discriminate between the mother and other people, and a phase of intense interaction develops between them in which the infant plays an increasingly active part in the mounting sequence of cues and responses which stimulate and draw them closer together.

In John the onset of discrimination was timely. By the thirteenth week he smiled more readily to his mother than to anyone else, and watched her as she moved about the room. But he did not develop outgoing, actively seeking behaviour. They did not enter upon the sequence of intense and mounting interaction which is characteristic of the phase, and which I have little doubt would have occurred had not the mother's temporary withdrawal of affect inhibited his responses.

Throughout his third month John had recurrent bronchitis and was made miserable by the troublesome cough. During this illness, it was notable that when he was restless and fretful the mother responded adequately to meet his increased need of her. To comfort him she breast-fed him often and carried him around day and night. But when he recovered from the illness and reverted to his quiet, undemanding behaviour her attention subsided; she gave him no more than he demanded.

In the sense that she responded appropriately to the varying cues given by her son in health and sickness, this was an adequate mother who could not be faulted in her care. She met his needs at the level at which they were expressed. But I had no doubt that the level of interaction between them was too low to facilitate optimum development. At four and a half months his muscular development was not satisfactory. His back muscles were limp, his head not firmly held and his limb movements few and poor. From this point I became increasingly uneasy about his general development, with its constellation of physical and emotional retardation.

As I saw it, the lowered interaction between them was an important causative factor. The mother had made a substantial recovery from her anxiety state and had tried to resume the relationship with John at its former level. But John had not responded, and after meeting failure in her attempts to restore their lively interchange the mother's activity had dropped to the level that was no more than sufficient to meet his lessened demands. I therefore suggested to the mother that she should stimulate John beyond the extent called for by his meagre demands, that she should play and handle him more than she was doing.

I was surprised by the success of her efforts along these lines after only one week. He held his back and head more firmly, his movements were stronger and he was generally more outgoing. He did not lie passively in his pram but cried until taken on to his mother's knee where he watched the play of older children with lively interest.

But a week later this improvement had disappeared. John was again passive, limp and undemanding. I was puzzled, but the mother had the answer – 'I couldn't go on doing it. It seemed so unnatural deliberately to upset his contentment by playing with him – and into the bargain rob myself of a peaceful hour.' This mother, who did not hesitate to answer the demands of her baby, could not or would not give him what he did not ask for.

After the fifth month my visits to the home were reduced to once a month, but I also had weekly contact when the mother brought both children to my mother–toddler playgroup. I continued trying to persuade her to play with and stimulate her undemanding baby. Now and again, usually in the days immediately after a visit, she followed the advice and it always resulted in increased liveliness in John. But she did not persevere and John seemed unable to hold on to his livelier behaviour. Looking at her placid baby she would say despondently but affectionately, 'Well, he may be slow but he is very sweet.'

During the next month his slowness became more and more apparent. At eight months he was more like a five- or six-month baby. He did not use his shoulders, neck and limbs in an age-adequate way. This may sound relatively unimportant, but it threw out of gear his pulling and clutching, held back his sitting and crawling and thus inhibited the exploration of his surroundings. Furthermore, because he did not try to move, he did not get himself into the awkward positions from which babies often have to be rescued. He thereby missed this contact with his mother.

At nine months John would not settle to sleep in the evenings and his parents brought him down to join them in the sitting-room. Once downstairs he stopped crying and smiled and babbled to them. They played unreservedly with him, glad that Andrew, safely asleep upstairs, was not there to be made jealous.

These evening playtimes went on for eight weeks. Whereas he had formerly been content to lie quietly alone, his only attainment being to turn on to his tummy, within two weeks of the onset of the sleeping disturbance and of the heightened attention of his parents, he was much more lively and outgoing. He moved more, held his back and head more firmly and his muscles generally were less flabby. He complained when left alone. The mother answered to this new level of demand and John was brought more into the active life of the family. But although this surge forward lessened the gap between him and his peers, his development still fell substantially short of the normal.

At twelve months a normal baby can sit securely at play for long periods, can crawl efficiently and swiftly in pursuit of his interests, and can pull himself up and lower himself at will; he can walk around a room with the aid of furniture, can balance for a few seconds and is almost ready to take his first faltering steps; he will be able to indicate 'No!' and his resistance will be tinged with aggression; he will show sustained interest in play activities. But when John sat, he slumped forward with a rounded back; he could not crawl, but still moved around the floor like a lumbering sea-lion; he did not try to pull himself up on furniture or the cot bars, and if put into a standing position he was reluctant to take his weight and flopped into a sitting position. He was passive, undemanding and perhaps depressed; he babbled but did not attempt to say syllables.

He was at least two months behind his peers and in some functions still more retarded. (He did not walk until nineteen months.) It is an open question whether more, or more skilfully applied, stimulation would have narrowed the gap still further.

To the uncritical eye John was a placid, good-natured, compliant and undemanding child. He looked healthy and bonny and responded benignly to attention.

Peter

Mrs O was an intelligent, unemotional young woman; although for much of the time in good contact with her family, she sometimes lapsed into a rather cold efficiency. Betty, the two-year-old, a serious, depressed little girl, was the apple of her father's eye.

Peter was born normally at home and weighed six pounds six ounces. During the second day he was restless and the doctor ordered three-hourly bottle-feeding until the breast milk came in.

Breast-feeding was established fairly easily, but supplementary bottle-feeding continued as precaution against loss of weight. He sucked well but was a drowsy baby and fell asleep several times during each feed. By the end of the second week the time between feeds was extended from three hours to four hours.

For a month the breast-feeding was satisfactory and Peter gained weight. But the mother was unable to withdraw sufficiently from Betty, the older child, to be fully committed to Peter during feeding times. She contrived to feed him and at the same time to play games with Betty. Though she was skilful in the way she did this, Peter showed by restlessness at the breast that the situation was disturbing for him.

During the third and fourth weeks he was less sleepy and fed better. His movements were strong and his development generally satisfactory. He slept well and was not easily awakened, but during feeding he continued to show sensitivity to noise.

In these weeks the mother did not adequately adjust to her infant's feeding needs; but she was still in the process of adaptation, and there were episodes of gentleness and affection which showed that she could emphathize with her infant. However, between the fifth and seventh weeks two events occurred which put further stress on their relationship.

The first was that both the father and Betty caught influenza and were ill for several days. The mother became overburdened by looking after the two patients; her breast milk decreased and the baby became restless. She reacted characteristically to these stresses, managing to keep going but in a dull and affectless way.

A week later, just as the family were recovering from the influenza, the mother's brother became involved in a serious situation which did not begin to resolve itself for more than a week – during which time the mother was in a state of acute anxiety. Again there was a flattening of affect. She became automatic and wooden and said she could cope only if she 'held tight' to herself.

Whereas John's mother had managed to maintain the physical comforts of her baby despite her anxieties, Peter's mother failed to do so during these two weeks. At seven weeks I saw them together after a bath and just before a feed. The baby screamed to the point of going blue and losing his breath, but the mother completed his dressing in an automatic and affectless way, down to the last button and ribbon; she stopped only to pinch the baby to make him breathe again, as if quite unaware of his intense distress. His genitals were blistered and raw but she neglected to apply medication.

Her apathy extended into the feeding situation, which was character-ized by the baby's fights and struggles to get food. She went through the motions of breast-feeding, but in a perfunctory and inefficient way which was intensely frustrating to the baby. She held him awkwardly with head too high for the breast, so that her slightest move caused him to lose the nipple. She bent about – attending to Betty, reaching for her coffee, trying awkwardly to light a cigarette – with no concern for the baby who was struggling desperately to get food. Throughout half an hour he wriggled and whimpered, choked and cried. When given a bottle he quietened and sucked peacefully.

The baby was then put on to the floor and the mother, freed from the difficulties of the feeding situation, talked to him and elicited smiles. He was very responsive, gurgling and smiling with much bodily activity and lively facial expression. I was impressed by the extent of the mood variation – from desperate crying to extreme responsiveness.

Earlier there had been nothing to suggest that Peter was a specially active or forward baby. But when at eight weeks he was put on to his tummy he held up his head and looked around; when his eyes caught a bright object about eighteen inches away he babbled and smiled at it. This behaviour was certainly much earlier than usual.

At nine weeks he reached for his bottle and directed it to his mouth. He was extremely alert to sounds and would turn in the direction of a voice. I recorded the possibility that his unusual awareness of the environment had been accelerated by the struggle for survival that had been forced on him during the difficult feeding situation. This inference is in line with James's theory of precocious ego-development (1960).

At nine weeks the mother resolved the feeding difficulty by transfer-ring the baby on to the bottle. Her brother was no longer in such acute trouble. Family life became more peaceful except for the minor upsets caused by a series of bronchial infections common to infants in winter time – and from which John was suffering more or less simultaneously.

Peter's 'forwardness' was welcomed by the family, with its high regard for intelligence and forward development. The parents recalled high intelligence in various relatives and believed that Peter was showing the benefits of a favourable endowment. His displays of precocity gave further incentive to the mother's trait of courting her children when lively and vivacious and of withdrawing when they were in trouble. His lively smiling phases were usually rewarded by play and stimulation, and with his strong directed movements he would try to get still more. Often his mother withheld her responses and thus provoked him into still more energetic displays.

Following these two stressful weeks, the extremes of Peter's behaviour were more and more marked – on the one hand, his desperation when hungry and unhappy and, on the other, his exaggerated responsiveness and gaiety. He was extremely alert in a high-pitched brittle way and rarely relaxed; a dummy was bought to help bridge the gap between wakefulness and sleep, because for him there was no in between stage of quietness.

Peter was continually pushed forward in his development. For example, on a visit to the playgroup when he was six months old he was brought in from the garden to lie on the nursery floor. There were three other toddlers in the room, so there was considerable noise; in addition, the room was strange to him. The mother immediately put him on to the floor with toys. He was frightened and cried. Another mother would not in these circumstances have put her infant down, and most mothers would have responded to his crying by picking him up; but Mrs O rattled toys in front of him, gave him a biscuit and talked to him until his crying stopped. He was then left on the floor to play while she sat proudly near by, basking in the comments on his 'forwardness' which came from the other mothers.

The intense interaction between mother and baby continued, in which she stimulated him by a combination of response which pleased him and withholding which drove him to still greater efforts. The more forward Peter became, the greater was her pleasure in him. But in the ensuing months his demands became so insistent that the mother was forced into answering them at his pace in order to get peace.

By seven and a half months he was beginning to crawl; by nine and a half months he could stand up and walk around his cot; and by eleven and a half months he walked freely and could say five words appropriately. Before his first birthday he tried to lift the telephone when it rang and went to the window to look for an airplane when the adults in the room had hardly registered the noise.

He was then an attractive, vivacious child, but he could not relax to be cuddled. His alertness had a brittle quality, with an undercurrent of irritation which broke through at the slightest frustration. He was continually trying to do things that were outside his competence.

CONCLUSION

This presentation is open to the instant criticism that it cannot be known what would have happened had the infants been differently endowed or had the crises not occurred.

I do not know what would have happened had the infants been differently endowed, and I doubt if much is to be gained from speculating about this. These two cases are insufficient to prove anything, but they are consistent with my view that in the early weeks of life innate differences between normal infants are less important than are the similarities of their needs and their responses when these needs are not met.

I suggest that the disparity between the development of John and Peter at one year is to be understood less in terms of inherited constitution than of 'acquired' constitution (James, 1960); that infants as young as were John and Peter when these major upsets occurred are immature organisms, not capable of selective response and able to react only on the basis of primitive adaptation; and that these primitive adaptations become 'acquired' constitution and influence subsequent development.

As to what would have happened had the crises not occurred, this question perhaps implies firstly that the maternal withdrawals may have been of little or no significance; and second, that in so far as environmental influences can affect early development these may in both instances be accounted for by the type of family in which the infant was reared.

It is true that Peter's family had a tendency to hasten the development of their infants, and that he was therefore likely in any case to have been forward. But as early as nine weeks of age, when most infants do little more than cry when they feel hungry, Peter reached for his bottle. That was ego development disproportionate to the phase. I suggest that inner stimulation, created by the struggle for food, led to precocious development which reinforced his mother's tendency to overstimulate and greatly exacerbated the demands that were made on him for yet more precocious activity.

John, without the early disruption, would have had every chance of a phase-appropriate development. His mother, though neurotic, was warm and intuitive, and adequate in meeting his needs. But just as he was entering upon the phase in which mother and infant stimulate and respond to each other, she suddenly stopped playing her part and his attempts to elicit a response from her were unsuccessful. During his mother's withdrawal he adapted to what was available; and she, consistent with her general tendency to meet demands at the level asked of her, on recovery responded only to the lower demands that he made. As a direct consequence of her temporary withdrawal in the third month, his ability to elicit a response from his mother became inhibited and from that point the interaction between them proceeded at a lower level. This had consequences for his subsequent development.

The ability to interact, to demand or to elicit a response from the environment, is initially experienced in relation to the mother. This capacity, a forerunner of a more general cathexis and mastery of the environment, was inhibited in John. It is probable that had the withdrawal occurred a few months later, in the phase where the ability to make demands is more established, John would have fared better because he would by then have been able to maintain loud and insistent pressure on his mother.

I suggest that the differences in the motor development of these two children can be understood in the same terms. At twelve months Peter was in respect of motor development a 'forward' child; his functions, accelerated by the withdrawal in the second month, had been consistently overstimulated by the mother and by his need to get appreciative response. John, on the other hand, did not exploit functions as they developed; he did not have the incentive to perfect and practise his skills or to explore his surroundings.

I have tried to show that an event which occurred in the second month of life significantly affected the infant and altered the quality of mother–infant interaction, and in consequence affected in a fundamental way development throughout the first year. At the time of writing both children are two years of age. John is placid and undemanding, with insufficient drive and cathexis of the environment; Peter has low toleration of frustration, a marked inability to relax or regress and an ego which is perhaps too strong to allow instinctual development fully to emerge. I suggest that this reflects the trends given to their development during the first few months in the ways that I have described, and that these are likely to persist.

PART 4

The Robertson Centre

James and Joyce Robertson

Introduction

IN 1975 we retired from the Tavistock Institute of Human Relations and established the Robertson Centre, whose purpose was 'to promote understanding of the emotional needs of infants and young children'; in other words, to apply knowledge we had gained over many years. Our founding members were all people with whom we had long been associated. They included Dr Anna Freud and Dorothy Burlingham, psychoanalysts, with whom we had worked since 1940 in the Hampstead Wartime Nurseries and subsequently in the Anna Freud Centre; Dr Dermod MacCarthy, consultant paediatrician, and Dr Mary Lindsay, child psychiatrist, whom we had known since 1952 and whose work is featured in our film *Going to Hospital With Mother*; Katherine McGilly, psychologist, our elder daughter, a pre-school playgroup course tutor; the Right Honourable the Baroness Serota, JP, formerly Minister of Health; Ruth Thomas, psychoanalyst, and Clare Winnicott, psychoanalyst, formerly Head of Training, Home Office Children's Department (at the time when the film *John* was released). The founding members shared our concerns and were active in support of our aims.

We had become painfully aware that in whichever area relating to young children we had worked – paediatrics, social work, foster care, day care and the law (as it related to custody) – we had found there to be insufficient knowledge of early emotional development. This in our opinion had led to wrong assessments being made, wrong decisions taken and harm caused to young children. Many people professionally responsible for young children talked superficially about the importance of early relationships – it was in their training – without the conviction that would have caused them to apply such knowledge. Although there were many books on infancy, none, we thought, spelled out emotional development, the emergence of relationships and the vulnerability of infants, as we attempted to do.

Using our films, and slides of our first grandchildren, we conducted seminars and were key speakers at conferences for professionals and parents in Britain, Europe, the United States, Canada, Australia and New Zealand. The focus of our presentations was on emotional development in the first three years of life. We had previously had experience of conferences, nominally on the under-fives, in which discussion invariably strayed up the age-scale and overlooked the under-threes. The Robertson conferences were explicitly on the period from birth to three. With some concern about sounding too soft and sentimental, we nevertheless began to emphasize the importance of the intimacy between the infant and its mother or main caretaker.

As we travelled and lectured, the world seemed to divide into two groups – those who welcomed our approach because it confirmed their own intuitive beliefs and practices, and those who thought that in stressing that the very young develop best in care of one person, preferably the mother, we were attacking women's rights. That was not true, though we realized that what we said was felt as a threat by some women. Our sights were always set on presenting the needs of infants and young children, which it seemed to us did not change – had not changed – over the years, even though the aspirations and social conditions of some women had changed. We felt young parents needed to know about infants' emotional needs if they were going to make the right decisions about child-care.

Some people thought we were implying that mothers and young children had to be together undiluted for twenty-four hours a day for seven days a week until the child went to school. We had never said this and have always approved and encouraged the use of one o'clock clubs, mother–toddler clubs and (for the over-threes) pre-school playgroups and nursery schools.

What we are against is changing caretakers and group care of any kind for infants and young children of under about three years. Many of the features shown in our film *John* are present in day care and impinge detrimentally on young children and on the mother–child relationship.

We believed and still believe there is a serious danger that both women and infants will lose out unless the emotional needs of infants are met and women are alerted to the satisfaction and enjoyment they can get from caring for them.

Some women fear that if they allow a very close relationship to develop between them and their infants they will never escape from that level of closeness. But this is not true. An infant who experiences closeness at the appropriate time (that is, in the early months and years) becomes ready to let go and achieve independence naturally without being pressed to do so. The woman who can forego her own career or work interests for a few years, and who can give this level of whole-hearted commitment to the infant, gives them both a good experience which will have a profound effect on family life and will repercuss down the years. Society needs to play its part by making it easier for women to return to careers.

It has been put forward that a woman who has pursued her career until her early or mid-thirties is then able to set it aside and meet the needs of her infant more willingly than the younger woman just starting on a career. This sounds likely and is perhaps the answer for one group of women.

Much more difficult is the situation where a woman is in conflict about career and children – where the eventual solution arrived at meets the woman's needs leaving the infant's needs unmet either because they are not understood or because they get overshadowed by the strength of the woman's needs and wishes.

There are situations where money could solve the problem, where a woman has to work and has no choice but to put her infant into care outside the family. In that situation everyone is a loser – the child, the parents and the country. What a pity some far-sighted government minister does not fight for adequate financial support for parents so that mothers (or, in some cases, fathers) of infants and young children who want to stay home and rear their families can do so.

Yet another group of mothers do not specifically want to work but come under pressure from friends, family and colleagues to return to work.

Each of these situations results in infants not getting the care that we think is essential for their adequate emotional development and therefore some of the essential tools of life – a sense of identity, self-esteem, trust in themselves and others, a sense of right and wrong and the ability to make lasting relationships.

One thing seemed essential to us – some knowledge of what happens in the early weeks and months between infants and their parents; to spell out what the various behaviours mean and why they are important; to show what part the parents play; to emphasize that infants don't just grow like Topsy but are influenced by the hour by hour interaction with those around them.

We hope the reader, both professional and lay, will bear with the detail of the next chapter describing the interaction between child and caretaker. It is a description of stages of development when things go right – it provides a base line from which any infant's development can be viewed. It was because we were frequently surprised by how little the phenomena of bonding and attachment were understood, even by professional agencies, that we set the material down in such detail. We think it will help parents and the child-care professions to make better decisions for the care of infants and young children.

It used to be said that the first five years are the most important – we think the first three years are, with the first year, most crucial of all.

With these thoughts in mind we set down how we understand early emotional development and the emergence of relationships. Chapter 19 is an extract from *A Baby in the Family* (1982), written for a general readership. Chapter 20, 'The Psychological Parent', is based partly on a paper of the same title published in *Adoption and Fostering* (1977).

19

Bonding and Attachment

THERE ARE TWO separate parts to the parent–child relationship. 'Bonding' refers to the feelings parents have for their children and 'attachment' to the feelings children have for their parents. Although they run in parallel, bonding and attachment begin at different times, have different qualities and different outcomes. To see them in this way aids our understanding of family relationships.

BONDING: THE FEELINGS OF PARENTS FOR THEIR CHILDREN

Parents feel their own children to be special and make allowances for their shortcomings, make special efforts for them, share their experiences, are sad for them, are happy with them. They even find their naughtiness has a curious appeal and they reserve the sole right to be angry with them.

Parents' preference for their own children is quite irrational, having little to do with their actual qualities. This irrational love has to be experienced to be appreciated. When seen in others it can irritate.

Before having their first baby a young couple can be puzzled by the behaviour of friends who have a child. These friends may have been level-headed and interesting to talk to, but after having a baby they seem to talk too much about their offspring and to plan their lives too much around him. They may appear over-anxious, over-protective, possessive, besotted, indulgent.

Not until the couple have a baby of their own can they understand the behaviour of their friends. They then find themselves caught up in similar feelings which they could not have anticipated. They begin to be 'bonded'.

'Bonding' is increasingly recognized as a major force in keeping families intact, in safeguarding children from parental abuse and abandonment.

Mother and Baby

The bonding of mother to baby occurs most easily when conditions during and after the birth are right – when mother and baby are kept together, when the mother can see and touch the baby and answer to his needs, when there is the intimacy of breast-feeding and when she has the love and support of her husband or partner.

It is not only because she is the principal caretaker that the mother becomes deeply bonded. Within a day or two after giving birth, most mothers experience an upsurge of anxiety and tearfulness. The intensity varies from one woman to another. The anxiety springs mainly from hormonal changes, triggered off by the birth; it serves natures's purpose of safeguarding the baby by keeping the mother's attention focused on him.

The mother is specially alert to the baby; she cannot ignore his cry, which she feels as much as she hears. Each time she answers the baby's need for attention, each time she comforts or feeds him, each time she holds him – has him look into her eyes, has him curl his fingers around hers – she feels more necessary to him. The baby's survival depends upon the mother's care and this knowledge adds to her anxiety and to the tightening of the bond.

In the early days and weeks, the more opportunity she has of being the person who answers the baby's needs, who knows him better than anyone else, who is the one he depends upon more than any other, the quicker and stronger the bond will develop.

If breast-feeding is established this brings mother and baby closer still, partly because of the intimacy and partly because of the hours that are spent in feeding.

If hospital provisions, and family support have kept the mother–baby couple together, then by the time the heightened anxiety lessens (at around eight weeks) the mother is unreservedly 'in love' with her baby.

The Appeal of the Baby

At first the baby's contribution to the bonding of the mother is his appealing helplessness, but he soon has other means of drawing her to

204

him. By about the third or fourth week (often even earlier) he begins to smile, then to gurgle and coo. Few adults can resist a smiling, babbling baby – least of all the one who has waited nine months to give birth to him.

As the bonding deepens the mother is more and more convinced that hers is indeed a very special baby. Her pleasure and pride in caring for and 'owning' him, in sharing and facilitating his development, help to compensate for the disturbed nights and the setting aside of her own wishes in favour of the baby's needs.

Need for Early Contact

The foregoing account presumes a mother who has had a good confinement, early access to her baby and a ready response to him. But bonding also occurs when the mother has had a bad confinement, perhaps coupled with a delayed response, or when the baby is ill or handicapped, provided contact between mother and baby is begun without too much delay.

Bonding of the mother will be interfered with if the baby is left in hospital without her. The better special-care maternity units recognize that delay in getting parents and baby together can be detrimental to the baby's development and to the quality of the parents' relationship to him. For this reason they encourage mothers to stay with their premature, sick or small babies and to feed and handle them. Mothers who cannot stay visit frequently.

Father

Many a modern young father is in close contact with his baby. He shares in the baby's care and becomes deeply bonded. But the father's bondedness is unlikely to be as compelling as the mother's, because much of his day is spent away from home and his involvement with the baby is therefore less.

Where this is so, it is just as well that fathers do not become quite as bonded as mothers, since fathers have to go to work. If the mother is the breadwinner, the process is reversed. They must be able to resist the baby's cry, and later the toddler who pleads, 'Don't go to work. Stay home with me.' But when necessary, for instance, if the mother is ill, the father who has helped in the care of his baby is usually the best substitute for her.

Grandparents

The grandparents become bonded to a degree reflecting the amount and quality of their involvement. But except when they are the child's caretakers (for example, during a mother's prolonged illness or when a mother is in full-time work) the bondedness of grandparents will be much less than that of parents. A degree of grandparent bonding is useful in providing a safety net for the young family.

ATTACHMENT: THE BABY'S FEELINGS FOR HIS PARENTS

Birth to about Six Months: Everybody's Friend

The new-born baby cannot at first make sense of the world. But as his mother handles him day after day in familiar ways the pattern begins to emerge. Each time she picks him up he recognizes the smell and touch and voice, and soon learns that feeding or comforting follows.

Within the small world she thus creates for him the baby 'knows' the mother in these primitive ways and in time she becomes the person he can distinguish from the more fleeting people who come and go.

At about three months he recognizes her face clearly, where previously he sensed only her familiarity, and he responds to her with greater animation than to others. But throughout most of the first six months the baby is friendly and smiling to everyone and allows himself to be held by almost anyone.

It is part of the parents' pleasure in their baby at this time that his friendliness draws appreciative comments from acquaintances. But, generally friendly though he is, the baby is gradually developing a specially intense response to his mother.

About Six Months: Fear of Strangers

At about six months his behaviour changes quite dramatically. He clings to his mother: he wants her and her alone and cries when strangers approach him. She has become his haven of safety. Father and grandparents may find themselves shunned and avoided. Father can feel a pang of hurt that his baby is unwilling to stay with him, and the grandparents may be puzzled and even impatient that the cherub will no longer sit beaming on their knee. The baby dislikes being apart from the mother and cries if she goes from him.

This is not a step backwards and the baby has not been 'spoiled'. The recognition of strangers is an important step in the baby's development.

During the previous months his mother had shared his pleasures and anxieties, tended him during illness, aided him in the gradual mastery of his body, understood his non-verbal communications. This and their physical closeness has established her as the most familiar person in his life, the person he most enjoys being with.

Now he is aware of the world beyond his mother, and for a time he is fearful of it and cannot cope. He therefore turns for safety to the person to whom he has become powerfully attached. Everyone else is for a time unwelcome.

This phase of 'stranger recognition' can be embarrassing and tiresome for the parents, but it is normal and necesary for good social and emotional development. It is a first step towards the child's ability to discriminate between strangers and those he loves, an ability to enter into enduring relationships in later life.

After about Nine Months: Making Real Relationships

The fear of strangers lasts from two to eight weeks, during which time the baby may have withdrawn even from the father. But by eight to nine months he will return to him again in a more mature way of relating. The strength of the baby's attachment to him reflects the extent of the father's availability and involvement. The father is known and enjoyed but is as yet less important than the mother because his role as a breadwinner usually means that he has the smaller part in the ongoing care. But the father becomes increasingly important as the months and years go by.

Gradually the baby makes a few other relationships to close family members, and perhaps to family friends, but always according to the extent of their involvement with him. His behaviour towards people outside the family is reserved. He is now acutely aware of the difference between intimate family, friendly acquaintances and strangers. The blood tie has no meaning for him. His relationship to a near neighbour may be closer than to a distant grandmother.

By the end of the first year the baby is crawling and perhaps walking, curious about the world around him; bravely moving a few yards away from the mother or father but speedily getting back to one of them as a place of safety if danger threatens, or if he is tired or hurt; friendly to familiar people outside the family but not indiscriminately so as when he was four or five months old.

After the First Year

During the second and third years the importance of the child's attachment to his parents becomes clearer. In his relationship to them he begins to show 'giving' aspects of loving. He wants to share – even if it is only a corner of his sticky bun; he shows concern if he thinks a parent is hurt or unhappy and wants to kiss them better. He is beginning to love.

As he moves out of babyhood his parents begin to expect more grown-up behaviour, and because he loves them he tries to do what they ask of him. He is gradually expected to tolerate frustrations, to be toilet-trained and to substitute language for impulsive action.

The child can accept these curbs because it is his parents who want this behaviour from him. He loves and wants to please them – wants to be in harmony with them, wants to be like them. The parents, because they are bonded to him, sympathize with the struggle within the child and give him time to comply; they are patient with backsliding and give constant encouragement to his efforts.

At first he does what they ask of him only while they are there to remind him; but in time these codes of behaviour become his own and form the basis of his social behaviour outside the family.

What Happens to Bonding and Attachment?

There are many degrees of bonding, depending mainly upon the amount of the parents' involvement in the care of their child during the early years from birth. Some parents are unable to commit themselves deeply for personality reasons related to their own unsatisfactory childhood experiences; but here we are writing about the majority of ordinary parents who are capable of bonding fully to their children.

Children of families where there is unemployment, poverty or only one parent may still have bonded parents but only in so far as they are together during the early months and years. If as so often happens the children are in day nurseries or with childminders, then bonding will be adversely affected.

Parents who are bonded rarely act selfishly towards the child. His well-being takes priority and whatever is in the child's interest feels right to them. They accept his love, tolerate his demands and failings, share his pain and pleasure – and get satisfaction from doing so. They may be sorely tried at times, but more than anyone else they are able to tolerate his growing pains.

The child knows he is special to them, whether he is pleasing or not, well or ill, succeeding or failing. He unhesitatingly turns to them with his pleasures and miseries, confident that they will be there. He knows they are likely to see his point of view and give him the benefit of doubt before voicing critical comments.

They become the brick wall he can safely kick against. Impatient or angry though they may sometimes be, he recognizes that these are often signs of their concern for him.

His feelings about himself reflect his parents' feelings about him. The child whose parents value him values himself.

Parents usually carry these strong feelings throughout their lives – the love, the anxiety for their children's welfare and happiness. In a modified form these extend to their grandchildren. Bonding is a mature form of loving.

But the attachment of child to parents is an immature form of loving – unstable in the early months and years, with dependency as its main ingredient.

At adolescence, as the child achieves independence and moves towards adulthood, attachment to his parents lessens. His feelings for his parents lose some of the earlier traits, and a caring attitude towards them eventually replaces the former dependency.

Having learned to love in his relationship with his parents, he marries or forms a long-term partnership and in due course bonds as deeply to his own children and becomes the object of their attachment.

So bonding progresses down the generations to promote the well-being of each new batch of babies.

The reverse side of the coin is that in families where the parents are not bonded to the children, the children are put at risk. Family life is never without stresses but when parents are not bonded there is insufficient positive protective feeling to mitigate the negatives. Lack of bondedness may well be a factor in child abuse – both sexual and physical. In some of the cases which have reached the headlines in recent years there has been an unbonded step-parent and a period of time when the child has been out of the parents' care.

20

The Psychological Parent

THE CONCEPT of the psychological parent (Goldstein, Freud and Solnit, 1973) is a useful one. Whoever loves and looks after a young child in the early years, whether she is the blood mother, adoptive mother or foster-mother, becomes the object of the child's deepest feelings, his psychological parent. There are of course usually two parents, but during early childhood it is usually the woman who is the main psychological parent. This is the person the child cannot imagine being without – whom he loves and wants to be with, whom he calls for when hurt or unhappy, whom he feels most secure with, whom he can most safely be angry with. It is she who shares the child's joys and sorrows, is glad when he is happy, is angry when he displeases her, helps him to control his aggression and to tolerate frustration, from whom he learns to give and take within a love relationship. When this relationship is established it promotes, as time passes, his social, intellectual and emotional development.

THE BLOOD MOTHER AS PSYCHOLOGICAL PARENT

Normally it is the blood mother who becomes the primary psychological parent. The child's choice of psychological parent occurs alongside the parent becoming bonded to him within a context of care. But, paradoxically, a young child's attachment does not depend upon the quality of care he receives.

He may progress emotionally, even within a relationship to an impoverished and unstable personality. If the psychological parent is

210

incapable of making a stable, warm relationship, and by reason of her personality is a harmful influence, then in extreme circumstances the relationship may have to be broken. Yet however necessary the break may be it cannot be done without distress and probable damage to the child.

THE ADOPTIVE MOTHER AS PSYCHOLOGICAL PARENT

An infant adopted in the first few weeks of life stimulates in the adoptive mother feelings comparable to those of a mother who has given birth. The necessary anxiety is aroused by the infant's helplessness and her responsibility for keeping him safe and well. Care-giving, at a time when every cry and gesture of the baby is genetically designed to elicit pangs of love and concern, sweeps the adoptive mother into the process of bonding. Thereafter the course of attaching and bonding will be similar to that in blood relationships.

If the infant is taken over later in the first year the bonding is likely to develop more slowly; and because the adoptive mother has not been exposed to the seductiveness of the infant's behaviour in the first few months the bonding may lack something of the fullest commitment. Adoption still later, after the first year, is unlikely to result in bonding of the intensity of a very early adoption. But the relationship can be deep and satisfying, with the adoptive mother ultimately becoming the psychological parent, especially if the infant's experience in the first year has been good and he transfers from one loving person to another. However, if the infant has made and lost a number of relationships his attachment to the adoptive parent may be marred initially at least by his lack of trust.

THE FOSTER-MOTHER AS PSYCHOLOGICAL PARENT

The phenomenon of attachment and bonding, which society welcomes for its binding effect in early adoption, is inconvenient in foster care. In recent years we have been made painfully aware that foster-parents can become psychological parents and the objects of the foster-child's deepest attachment.

Foster-parents have long been expected to keep in mind that their function is only temporary, that they should remain clear about their role and not become 'possessive'. But no matter how conscientiously restrained a foster-mother may try to be, if the child is very young he will

211

become attached to her and the absent mother will gradually slip into unimportance.

If the foster-mother gives the quality of care needed and demanded by the very young child, she, like the adoptive mother, may be swept into a deeply bonded relationship. But, whereas society welcomes this when it occurs in adoptive relationships, attachment and bonding are not welcomed when equally irresistibly they occur in foster care. Social work and the law have been in painful confusion over the way in which these inevitable processes can interfere with plans for the child and his blood parents. There has been a struggle to find compromise solutions which take full account of the conflicting claims of blood parents and foster-parents. Insufficient attention has been given to the consequences of severing the child's established relationships, whether they are in the blood family or in the foster-family.

Only a few years ago press and television showed children being wrenched with all the authority of police and social service departments from the foster-parents in whom all their expectations of love and security had been vested.

MARIA COLWELL

Maria Colwell was one such child. (In this discussion we are relying mainly on the official report into the case.) She had been with foster-parents since she was a baby, for as long as she could remember. She knew they loved her and she loved them more than anyone else and wanted to be with them. But when her legal parents claimed her, the social services decided to make the transfer. Maria resisted with the small voice of a six-year-old. Her wishes were ignored. Nobody except the foster-parents seemed to understand that for Maria the relationships to them were the only ones that mattered. The social workers who understood kept quiet, because they thought the law as it then stood would not uphold the relationships.

The social services department encouraged and expected Maria to change her allegiances, but of course she could not since the blood mother and stepfather meant little to her. Nevertheless, she was removed to their home. She escaped and tried to get back to her foster-parents, but she was forcibly returned to the blood mother and stepfather.

The running away, the unhappiness, the rejection of them and other difficult behaviour typical of a child separated from those she loved were highly provocative to the blood mother and stepfather. They had not

212

shared in Maria's growing up, had not looked after her, were not bonded to her. They had not become the recipients of her love. Maria's trust and security were not vested in them.

The plight of this hounded child does not bear thinking about. Only death at the hands of her stepfather released six-year-old Maria from intense unhappiness and from a society which would not listen to her. With hindsight we can be shocked that so little understanding was shown of the child's need to stay with her psychological parents.

We hoped it would never happen again. But we know that even today young foster-children can be put into states of comparable distress and danger when they are moved with insufficient regard for their attachments. It can too readily be overlooked that the feelings of a loved and attached very young foster-child are no different from those of a child living in the family into which he was born.

It can also be overlooked that it is being bonded to a child through the intimacies of day by day care that enables adults to love him and tolerate his behaviour and his demands (Robertson and Robertson, 1982). The prolonged absence of a child in a foster home and lack of involvement in his care can cause the parents' feeling for him to become shallow. Furthermore, if there is a stepfather who has not had the experience of becoming bonded, he may be specially intolerant of the difficult behaviour of a newly returned child who is fretting for his foster-parents. If the stepfather is immature and prone to bad temper or violence the child will be at risk of being ill-treated.

The public are shocked and horrified when young children are killed in such circumstances (Blom-Cooper, 1985). But these are the tip of the iceberg. Other children similarly removed from loved foster-parents are in danger of abuse and ill-treatment which may go unnoticed because they do not result in death.

Foster care undoubtedly offers better possibility of stable relationships than institutional care, but there are hazards. Foster placements can result in young children being subjected to repeated changes of care-takers which are as painful and damaging as institutional care. These risks can only be minimized if foster care is used with greater knowledge of the development of early relationships.

21
A Delayed Infant Adoption

In 1977 a group of social workers and their solicitors were rebuked by a judge because of confusion amongst themselves about the nature and needs of an infant. The judge urged the necessity for expert guidance, and the social services department telephoned the Robertson Centre for urgent consultations. Several such requests followed as one area learned from another of the service we could give. In all instances what we did was to help staff who had been in dispute with each other to greater understanding of early relationships and emotional needs of very young children.

These consultations, and our experiences as expert witnesses, confirmed our views on social services departments gathered over the years. However competent they might be in dealing with older children, social workers had very limited understanding of the under-threes.

Not enough about the under-threes is taught in social work trainings, even at university level, and their nature and needs tend to be glossed over in generalizations and clichés which do not create the depth of conviction that the social worker needs. The newly qualified social worker therefore fits readily into the framework of the average department with all the potential for inadequate and harmful social work practice.

This is not to doubt the concern and commitment of social workers but to question the level of their knowledge and training. In earlier years social workers could specialize in work with children, but now they are commonly expected to carry case loads which cover from early childhood to old age. The demands on them are too varied and too great.

This chapter and Chapter 22 set down some of our experiences of social work

*practice as it affected infants and very young children up to 1980. They cover the
first five years after the 1975 Children Act.*

The 1975 Children Act laid down a duty that:

*In reaching any decision relating to the adoption of a child, a court or
adoption agency shall have regard to all the circumstances, first consideration
being given to the need to safeguard and promote the welfare of the child
throughout his childhood . . .*

*The persons qualified to apply for a custodianship order are a . . . b . . . c
any person with whom the child has had his home for a period or periods
before the making of the application which amounts to at least three years
. . .*

*In any proceedings under sections 2(5) or 4(3) or 4A of this act, a juvenile
court or the high court may, where it considers it necessary in order to
safeguard the interests of the child to whom the proceedings relate, by order
make the child a party to the proceedings and appoint, subject to rules of
court, a guardian* ad litem *of the child for the purposes of the proceedings.*

*These were welcome steps forward, but our experience was that this benefited
older children more than the very young, who are our concern.*

*In many local authorities it is now considered bad practice to place children
with long-term (more than three months) foster-parents unless there are exceptional circumstances, e.g. a wardship case that is unavoidably protracted. But
three months for an infant is very different from three months in the life of a
school child, or in the diaries of the social worker, or the busy court. Furthermore, precise knowledge of infant development and conviction of its importance is
essential, because without that knowledge and conviction the best interests of the
infant and young child cannot be established.*

EVERYONE in the caring professions is taught that the infant and his
parents should be together from birth, in order that the infant shall
experience their care and the subtleties of interaction with them from the
beginning of life; and in order that the bonding of parents to their infant
will begin and develop from the earliest possible moment.

Lack of involvement in the early care of their infant which impairs the
bonding of parents, can lower their threshold of tolerance for the
demands normal infants make. Parental impatience can then erupt more
readily than if the bonding has had a satisfactory beginning. So one
ground for having parents close to their infant from the beginning of life
is that this establishes concern and commitment to him and a readiness

215

to put the infant's needs before their own.

Adoption societies and social services departments are expected to act on this knowledge. Some try to place new-born infants directly with adoptive parents. But this is far from being usual practice.

Some social services departments used to put infants awaiting adoption into residential nurseries where they could languish for months in conditions of care which run contrary to all that is known of developmental needs, and which was to the detriment of the infants in their functioning and future relationships. Many authorities now seek to avoid the dangers of institutional care by placing infants with short-term foster-parents until adoption is arranged. This, although much better than institutional care, is less good than placing the infant direct from hospital into the adoptive home. It exposes the infant to the possibility of procedural delays within the social services department.

Final placement can, however, be unnecessarily delayed, with dangers for the infant's attachments and for the bondedness of the adoptive parents, as in the following case.

'JUST A CLERICAL ERROR'

A foster-mother wrote to the Robertson Centre:

We had been short-term fostering for a year when we decided to try pre-adoptive fostering. On Monday, 3 December we were asked to foster an eight-day-old baby for six to eight weeks. We had twenty-four hours' notice. Although Christmas was approaching and we had three school-age children, we accepted the challenge.

The baby was a tiny boy weighing six and a half pounds. He settled in very quickly without any problems, and we were soon into our new routine. The children enjoyed the experience of a new baby in the house. We were very pleased that they were not disturbed by the night feeds.

The social worker visited us a few days later to see that all was well, and then again about three weeks later just after Christmas. The social worker visited us later in January and told us that the papers had not gone before the panel in January (no reason given for this delay) but would go through in February.

Our baby was now nearing two months old and started to notice his surroundings. His social worker called on 14 February to say that the date of the panel meeting had been changed and she had not been informed. So the baby's adoption papers had missed that meeting. Now the baby would have to wait until the beginning of March for the next panel to meet to agree his adoption.

Our baby was growing fast and showing that he recognized the children and me. We were being rewarded by his first tears and smiles and gurgles. Everyone was becoming emotionally involved and charmed by this little baby. The children were beginning to say, 'We want to keep him' and 'You can't give him to strangers.'

Telephone calls to the social services to ask what was happening got us nowhere. No one seemed to be worried that this little baby was becoming attached to us and we to him. It appeared that until this meeting was held nothing else could be done. Prospective parents hadn't even been matched.

At last it was March. The baby was over three months old – awake most of the day and very much part of our family. He was very aware of the children's company and quite accustomed to being in a noisy atmosphere. We now felt strongly that it would be disturbing for him to go to another kind of family. We told the social worker how we felt about this.

On 5 March the panel met. The baby was cleared for adoption. But now the matching panel had to meet, but not the next week as his social worker was on holiday, and not the following one because her senior was on holiday.

Our baby was now four months old. He was very alert and very knowing and beginning to get fussy about wanting only me to feed him. At the end of March prospective parents were selected. They already had a two-and-a-half-year-old adopted child and did not need to be vetted, but they were not contacted until 2 April as their social worker was on holiday and someone else had to be found to take her place.

We were very attached to our baby. Watching this tiny baby develop into a contented little boy had drawn us very close to him.

On 8 April the prospective parents came to meet our baby. The children were restless. The couple were delighted because a second son was what they longed for. They had received their first adopted son at six weeks of age. They wondered if there was something wrong with out baby, but were told by the social worker that the delay was 'just a clerical error'.

We had discussed with the social worker a lengthy hand-over period so that the baby could get to know his new family, but we found

217

it was too much of an emotional strain on all of our family to carry on the visits for more than a week.

We all cried during the week we knew he was leaving, but we could talk together about why and where he was going. Not so our baby. He was too young for explanations. His world was going to change from one hour to the next. I knew he would miss me and the children. It would have been so much better for everyone had he gone to his new family at six to eight weeks – for him, for us and for his new family.

But it was 'just a clerical error'. How many other clerical errors are there? Dare we try again?

They did try again and again and met with similar delays and apparent lack of concern with this authority and with others.

The Implications

This story must ring true to many. It was the foster-mother, not the social worker, who became concerned that she and not the adoptive parents was becoming bonded to the baby. It was the foster-mother who was troubled that the baby was becoming more deeply attached to her with every week that passed. She knew that she would find it difficult to part with the baby but was more concerned that the baby would have to lose her – his first love, his haven of trust and security.

It was the foster-mother who tried to push the social worker to act more quickly. Her call to the senior social worker was neither welcome nor effective in cutting through delays caused by staff holidays, team meetings cancelled or missed, and the waiting for signatures within the department. The social worker's colleagues on relevant committees must have been aware of the delay, but as insensitive as she appeared to be to the hazards.

The Association of British Adoption and Fostering Agencies (ABAFA) was sympathetic, but infants in foster care while awaiting adoption were not an urgent concern of theirs. They suggested that the foster-mother put pressure on the senior social worker. This she did and the senior social worker promised action. But it was a further six weeks before the baby was removed to the adoptive parents. He was then nearly five months old.

The delay was dismissed lightly by the social worker as 'just a clerical error'. All the foster-mother got for her pains was a rebuke for having gone over the head of the social worker to her senior.

It sometimes appears that a fostered baby, or a baby awaiting adoption, is thought to be a different kind of baby from yours or mine. But his needs are the same. The social services department did not show awareness of this. Only the foster-mother understood the baby's plight.

For the baby, time is not the same as for the establishment. In the life of a social worker a few weeks matter little; a holiday break or a missed meeting goes unnoticed. But a few weeks in the life of a young baby are vital for his emotional development. One stage of development gives way to the next with great speed, and once gone cannot be recovered. So this baby became attached to the wrong person, and the wrong person became bonded to him.

The consequence is that his emotional development has been knocked askew. He has gone to adoptive parents who, however suitable, have missed five months of bonding that may never be fully recaptured. This loss to the infant and adoptive parents did not occur because the infant had failed to pass a medical test, nor because the mother delayed giving permission, nor because there were no suitable adopters.

The loss occurred because a social work department was, for whatever reason, inefficient or uncaring or ignorant. Whatever knowledge there might be presumed to have been at the top was not expressed in procedures reflecting a due sense of the urgency of early placement. As the social worker revealed, this was not the only baby to miss the meetings. Mishandling which ignores the importance of time and continuity of care for infants and young children is not uncommon. A blood mother who, acting in the best interests of her baby, had given permission for adoption from birth could feel betrayed that procedural delays had put the baby's well-being at risk.

In 1980 the Health Service Ombudsman investigated a complaint that a special care baby unit had not allowed sufficient contact between parents and their baby. He restated the importance of early contact and requested the Area Health Authority to review its practices (HMSO, 1980).

22

Custody and Access

Iᴺ ᴛʜᴇ ᴄᴏᴜɴᴛʏ ᴄᴏᴜʀᴛs particularly, the position of court welfare officer, adviser to magistrates and judges, was commonly held by a social worker linked to the local social services department and thereby mistakenly regarded as expert on families and children. Her advice could influence the findings of the court and, being unsupported by specialized knowledge, could sometimes be injurious to the welfare of very young children in custody and access hearings.

The cases we report here are more complex than can be shown, partly for reasons of confidentiality, but also to highlight what we consider to be their chief features.

SHARED CUSTODY

A young father, worried by the deterioration of his three-year-old daughter following a shared custody order made by the court after a divorce, wanted to have the order changed. His solicitor asked us to investigate and make recommendations to the court.

Some months earlier, on the advice of the court welfare officer, the child's mother had been awarded two days overnight custody each weekend and visiting access on two days each week. This meant that the child's life was divided between the two parents and between the radically different regimes provided in the homes of the two sets of grandparents, one relaxed and the other strict.

We found a disturbed, withdrawn child who could not attach herself securely anywhere. The mother was unreliable and not bonded to her child although for other reasons she clung to the custody and access award.

We interviewed the court welfare officer who had advised the court and was supervising the shared custody and access. She had no insight into the damage that the court order was doing to this three-year-old and made no concession to our views. She thought the court order was 'fair' to both parties. She admitted that there had been episodes of protest by the child at the movement between the two homes but said the child had now settled to the arrangements. (The erroneous notion of the 'settled child' was familiar to us.)

Our report included a description of the behaviours of the child which caused us to be deeply concerned about her future development unless she were put securely into the care and control of the father who worked at home.

We strongly recommended that, in order to eliminate stress and confusion for the child, and in order to establish security and continuity of care, shared custody should be stopped; and that visiting by the mother should be restricted to once or twice a week within the security of the paternal home, with the father in easy reach of the child.

This we thought would lift the main pressures off the child and halt the deterioration. The relationship to the mother might then become more like that of aunt and niece, which the child would enjoy but place less dependence on. When this was suggested to the father's solicitor he was sceptical of the judge agreeing to what would in effect be to deprive the mother of her parental 'rights'.

In the event the judge did agree with our recommendations. Our expectation that the mother would find this arrangement acceptable proved justified. This unstable and only slightly bonded mother slipped smoothly into the role of friendly visiting aunt, and the child's state improved greatly. The divorce was made absolute and the father awarded full custody.

But had the judge been given more appropriate guidance initially, this child would have been spared an unhappy and potentially damaging experience.

CONTESTED ACCESS

A mother wished to have her ex-husband denied access to their young children because his violent behaviour frightened her and the children and frustrated her wish to build a secure home for them. She was obstructed by her solicitor, who insisted that fathers had rights of access which the courts would uphold; and by the court welfare officer who over several months firmly counselled the mother along the same lines.

Ultimately the solicitor gave way to the mother's insistence and grudgingly allowed us to be called as expert witnesses on her behalf.

Discussion with the court welfare officer revealed that she was holding to the traditional view that fathers had incontestable rights of access, but her stance was not rigid. She agreed that the children were afraid of their father and that because of his aggressive interference the mother was being prevented from establishing a secure home for herself and the children. In reasonable discussion she agreed that 'in the best interests' of the children the father should be denied access. In the court she supported us in that recommendation. The insight of the social worker/court welfare officer had been extended.

Access by father to the children was withdrawn. The judge had been given expert evidence which had not been available to him at the original hearing.

Neglect of Attachment

The Children Act 1975 allowed foster-parents who had care of a child for three years to contest a social services department decision to remove the child from their care. Despite a barrister's advice that they had little chance of winning against the authority of a social services department, a working-class couple insisted on opposing the intention to remove a four-year-old child who had been in their foster care since infancy. We appeared as expert witnesses on behalf of the foster-parents.

The local authority conceded that the natural mother was unsuitable to care for the child and that no fault had been found in the foster-mother, but argued that, in order to placate a violent stepfather who had taken a dislike to the foster-parents, the child should be removed from the foster home and placed with other foster-parents. This plan might have had some justification had the contest been over the custody of an inanimate piece of furniture; but the plan was not appropriate for a four-year-old child who was deeply attached to her foster-family.

Another sign of the insensitivity of the social workers towards the vulnerability of a very young child was that for the four months preceding the beginning of the hearing she had been placed in what their spokesman called 'the neutral situation of a children's home. Our primary concern is for the child, but we are considering the feelings of the adults.'

There is no 'neutral situation' for a young child parted from those she loves. Feelings and needs do not go into suspension. That this child was removed from adequate substitute mothering indicated failure to recognize that she was emotionally a child of the foster-parents, with the certainty of acute distress and probable damage through being separated from them. Furthermore, that the social workers failed to keep in mind the primary importance of the child's best interests is shown by their readiness to manipulate her situation in order to placate an adult.

As expert witnesses we spelled out as we had done in other cases the emotional needs of young children and the consequences for this child if her existing relationships were broken. The foster-parents were clearly the psychological parents and the erratically visiting blood mother was no more important than a visitor might be to any family child. The plan to place the child with other caretakers would abandon the basic principle of stable relationships and continuity of mothering-type care in favour of an expedient which would be harmful. Already damage had been done through the placement in a children's home.

In the light of our evidence the social services department withdrew their submission and the child was restored to the foster-parents from whom she should never have been removed.

Experience in the courts confirmed us in our view that serious mishandlings occur because of social workers' lack of knowledge of early child development and family dynamics. The main shortcomings are: lack of conviction about the importance of stable early relationships; lack of understanding of the nature of bonding and attachment, and of the dangerous consequences when these are faulty; lack of understanding of the vulnerability of young children. There are also serious risks for the critical early development of children when delays occur in making important decisions for their care, either through indecisiveness or the procrastinations of administrative procedures. Three months in the life of a young child is very much more important than three months in the life of a busy social worker (Joyce Robertson, 1980).

In recent years, after tragedies involving young children, social services departments have been much criticized. Calls for more training, more supervision and more staff have been usual (DHSS, 1959, 1974). However, the hard fact is that the level of knowledge and experience of the subtleties of early development required to provide for the care of infants and young children is too comprehensive and specialized to be among the many skills expected of social workers.

223

We are of the opinion that *too* much is expected of them. When young children are involved, case loads need to be lessened and the expertise of another specialized discipline – that of child psychotherapist or similarly qualified person – needs to be readily available for consultation and supervision.

23

The Fallacy of 'Preparing' Healthy Young Children for Possible Hospitalization

Though deeply committed to the welfare of young children, voluntary agencies may be unaware of the limits to their knowledge of the emotional development and special vulnerabilities of the under-threes.

This chapter was written as one of a group of papers to alert the National Association for the Welfare of Children in Hospital to our concerns. NAWCH, a crusading organization founded and still led by parents, draws support and reassurance from progressive paediatricians and nurses whose common-sense guidance is nevertheless not, we feel, a source of the level of psychological knowledge of the under-threes that we advocate.

Although this common-sense approach does not interfere with the effectiveness of NAWCH's everyday work, we felt that when they unwittingly step outside their understanding, they do not realize that they have crossed a boundary implying the need to consult with those who have relevant psychological knowledge.

An example is that in 1981 NAWCH launched, without appropriate consultation, an ambitious national scheme to 'prepare' healthy young children for possible hospital experience. NAWCH members were visiting playgroups and nursery schools throughout Britain and giving talks about hospitals illustrated by books and toy instruments. Other members, well versed in early development reacted with concern about the possible dangers to the mental health of young children NAWCH wished to help, and after a special study day the project was abandoned. This paper was reprinted in several countries by groups with similar concerns for the welfare of young children in hospital.

DURING the past twenty years there have been increasing attempts to find ways of softening the experience of being in hospital for young children. Initially the main objective was to obtain unrestricted visiting to all children and to ensure that parents of under-fives could stay in hospital with them in order to help in their care and prevent the dangerous distress commonly seen in young children who go into hospital alone (Goldstein, Freud and Solnit, 1973).

But in recent years activity has extended beyond the sick child in the hospital ward to healthy children in the community. Attempts are being made to inform all young children about hospitals. The hope is that if a child thus 'prepared' goes into hospital he will be better able to cope.

Young children from playgroups and infant schools have been taken on tours of children's wards, told what happens there and shown some of the treatment procedures. Speakers from voluntary organizations visit playgroups and infant schools to talk to the children about hospitals, using books, slides, films and toy instruments to illustrate blood-taking, injections and other procedures.

These well-intentioned projects are misconceived, unnecessary and potentially harmful. They assume that the children will be reassured by what they are told. But this educational approach neglects the fact that in the early years children are coping with fantasies, labile emotions and limited comprehension; and that talks about hospitals with their undertones of separation and hurt may cause disturbance.

WHAT IS HOSPITAL TO A YOUNG PLAYGROUP CHILD?

It can mean seeing a hospital, visiting a hospital or being in hospital. It can mean being taken on a visit to a big building where strange things are seen and smelt and heard; or it may mean being ill, perhaps in pain in a strange place away from home where there are doctors and nurses who interfere with or hurt one's body; it can mean being frightened and confused.

Hospital is a subject which cannot be divorced from worrying feelings. This is true for adults or children; but for the child there is the added weight of possible separation from the people he is entirely dependent upon and a limited understanding of what is happening.

Adults and older children can understand the need for hospital and are glad of the help given. But very young children cannot possibly understand why they should be ill or in pain; they are additionally made specially anxious by the threat to their bodies.

But pain and illness and hospitals are not hidden from children. In the course of family life children gradually come to know about being ill, getting medicine, hurting themselves, getting a plaster, going to the clinic and seeing the nurse, and having the doctor visit them at home. They see hospital buildings, they see ambulances, and gradually learn their purposes – in the haphazard way of early childhood. The pace at which the picture is added to will depend upon the child's age, his personal experience, the family's experience (illness, accidents, birth and death) and what happens to the child's playmates.

For instance Sarah was not quite two years old when her father injured his back and went into the local hospital. During visits she saw that people were in bed and got their dinner there, that doctors and nurses looked at them and made them better. Then they went home, as her father did. That bit of learning was tied to immediate experience. Sarah's play reflected her anxieties and her limited understanding. Her mother helped her to work through them.

At three years she had an eye infection and was taken twice to out-patients. Her 'preparation' was simple. She was told by her mother that she was going to the hospital where a doctor and nurse would look at her eye. The mother explained and comforted as was needed. Sarah did not like the eye-drops or the patch over her eye, and said so. Afterwards there was much play about the visit, putting patches on her teddy-bear's eyes and telling her daddy about it. There was appropriate anxiety to be talked through such as why it had happened, what the doctor had done and how it would get better.

The return visit to the out-patient department a week later was unwelcome to Sarah but was accepted as necessary. More play and talk followed, about eyes and only about eyes, the subject of Sarah's anxiety.

Her other hospital experience was to visit a maternity ward to see a neighbour's new baby. This appeared to put no strain on her. Sarah's knowledge about hospitals had increased. But it was still limited to her experience and very much under the control of her parents.

Paul, the child next door, was three years old when he visited his mother in the maternity unit. This was his first experience of hospital. Some months later he saw Sarah's eye-patch and was told about her visit to the hospital where the doctors had made her better. He joined in the play with eye-patches. Both mothers were on hand to correct confusions and to cope with anxieties that arose out of the children's play and talk.

At four years old Paul cut his head and was taken to out-patients. He complained bitterly as he was held and stitched. Comforting at the time, and play and talk afterwards, increased Paul's understanding of what hospital is for. His knowledge about hospital is still limited but is reality-based and age-adequate. Unavoidably he is left with some anxiety.

Sarah and Paul sometimes play at doctors and nurses, but there is much that these two children do not know about hospitals. The parents avoid many of the illustrated books on hospitals since these open up anxiety-making issues which they feel their children need not know about yet. They do not want to overload them with more information than is necessary, but they are ready to support and protect them in the event of a hospital experience.

Learning about illness, accident and death, even in the safe setting of the family, inevitably causes anxiety. Parents do not tell a young child too much but keep most knowledge to themselves – giving out as much as they feel he needs to know and can understand. Young children differ from family to family, and from week to week, in their ability to take in anxiety-making knowledge.

A person visiting a playgroup to talk about hospitals will know little or nothing about individual children, and the playgroup leader herself is unlikely to know about them in detail. They would be unable to antici-pate the impact of a talk on any one of the following four children.

Mary, aged four years, has been ill a great deal and has already been to hospital twice, at six months and at eighteen months. She does not talk about hospitals and may not remember even the later stay. But as a result of illness and the hospital experiences she is more vulnerable to stress than other children in her playgroup. She gets worried when routines are changed or a strange person comes to the group. A visitor coming to talk about hospitals could not know this. Talk about hospitals and illness is likely to worry this child by reviving forgotten or repressed memories, then leaving her to cope with the memories unaided.

Peter, aged three years nine months, had an ear operation at two years six months. The experience was upsetting and his mother was not with him. Since then he has been specially anxious about ambulances and about any cut or bruise to his body. He has more minor accidents than most children. Peter was difficult to settle into the playgroup, stopping and starting twice before he eventually settled at three years six months.

How would he react to a talk about hospitals? He has been through an ear operation and he would be told of other things that might happen to him. Because of the emotional impact of such a talk, he may not listen properly; so to his basic anxiety might be added confusion and a further threat. Group 'preparation' could add to his problems.

Susan, aged four years six months, had difficulty in adjusting to playgroup. She started late but is now making efforts to be big and grown-up. Everyone, especially the mother who is pregnant, is heaving sighs of relief that Susan is settled in playgroup before the birth of the next baby which will take place in hospital.

The mother is in the process of preparing Susan for the new baby and for herself being away in hospital. If Susan's playgroup is told about hospitals, this already insecure girl could muddle who is going to hospital, she or the mother. It could unsettle her in the playgroup and thereby add to the family's problems.

Stephen, aged three years, is going into hospital shortly to have an abdominal investigation and perhaps an operation. His parents are about to tell him; they have not yet told the playgroup leader. If the children in his playgroup get a talk about hospitals, Stephen's parents may be forced to tell him about the impending hospital admission before they or he are ready. If this happens it is clear that Stephen and his parents will not have been helped.

The threat of an operation on their child will awaken anxieties in the parents themselves and will affect the way in which they prepare the child. It may be thought that the parents should have told him sooner or that a visitor to the playgroup would introduce the subject better because parents get anxious. Families differ in the way they cope with such situations and some may need help. But these differences should be respected.

What of those children in a playgroup who have not been patients in hospital, who are not specially disturbed, who have just the usual smattering of knowledge about hospital, and who play the usual 'doctor and nurse' games? Some of these children will not listen to the talk about hospitals; others will not remember what is said. They may not be affected one way or another.

Others will listen to part of what is said. These are the kind of children whose eyes glaze over at story-time, and whose thoughts wander off. These children still live a lot of time in their own world and join adults in theirs only fleetingly and not to order. They will go home with a very confused understanding of what they have been told about hospitals.

Some will sit rooted to the spot, seemingly fascinated by what they are told. It is sometimes thought that this confirms the value of what they are being told about hospitals. But this assumption has to be questioned.

Children can be fascinated by many a frightening thing which does them no good at all. For example, a child will sit fascinated by a frightening television programme until a parent turns it off. Then the child rushes about frantically or sits immobilized anxiously sucking his thumb.

Playgroup children can be looked at in another way. There are considerable differences between them in their levels of language, comprehension, memory structure and concentration. Some will not be able to differentiate between 'if' and 'when'. For example, one child was reported as asking after a hospital talk, 'Can I take my teddy?' He had probably understood that he was going to hospital.

The under-fives are living through a period of fast psychological growth, and they are from time to time troubled by fantasies, anxieties and conflicts. Parents know that, without warning, their moods change. They may become tense, or go off their food, or wet the bed, or become aggressive or anxious for some days or weeks.

Parents do not always know why, and do not have to know why. They tolerate the inexplicable behaviour, they support, comfort, and perhaps take the children to the doctor. Usually after a few days or weeks they return to an even keel. They have worked through some troublesome feelings – some aspect of psychological growth.

In any group there will be children who are working through something that is troubling them. To be told about hospital with its threat of illness, hurt and leaving home will add further anxieties to those they are already coping with in the course of normal development. This can only be disturbing to these children and their families.

When group talks are illustrated with instruments and books the emotional impact will be greatly increased. Children can shut their ears to some extent to protect themselves from what they do not want to hear. But visual material impresses more and is less easy to forget.

Group visits to hospital carry a further danger that the children see not only the planned exhibits but unplanned ones also which could confuse and frighten.

The examples given here have been of playgroup children, but much that has been said relates also to the five- to seven-year-olds. These infant school children, too, need protection from educational experiments. For experiments they are.

Studies are lacking on the emotional effect of group instruction or group hospital visits upon young children who do not become patients. There is no evidence that young children who go into hospital a month or six months after a group session have been helped by the 'preparation'. If a child goes to hospital, how much will he accurately remember of the 'preparation'? And how relevant to his actual experience will be the information he has retained?

It may be that adequate studies are impossible because of the great number of variables, their subtlety and complexity.

PREPARATION FOR AN IMMINENT HOSPITAL EXPERIENCE

If a young child is to be admitted to hospital, or is about to have treatment in the ward or out-patients department, it is usually the parents (given appropriate information by the hospital) who should prepare him – even if they do not do it perfectly. Parents know more about their current family experience (death, illness, accident, etc.). They are in the best position to undo misunderstandings, to modify fantasies and to boost reality, following the child's play and behaviour and answer his questions. The child will be more likely to express anxiety and to reveal confusions to his parents than to anyone else (Joyce Robertson, 1956).

Sometimes preparation for minor procedures which are soon over (such as injections and blood tests) if attempted too early can cause anticipatory anxiety which is more upsetting than the event itself. For such procedures parents could explain to the child just before the event, then handle the child's reactions as they occur. Play and talk afterwards will help the child work through his feelings.

If the child is facing a major event, play specialists and nurses may have to help parents to prepare him; or if the parents are not there they may have to take on the task of preparation. But without the intimate knowledge that the parents have, there is a risk that, however well intentioned, the nurse or play specialist may make bad mistakes. Preparing the child is much more than the giving of information. It is to understand and respond to the child's individual reaction to such preparation, and that means knowing the child's history (Joyce Robertson, 1956).

WHAT IS THE AIM OF PREPARATION?

It should not be the aim of preparation to make children submit without protest or anxiety to hospital admission or procedures. Submissiveness is not the measure of successful preparation. Anxiety and protest are often appropriate.

Anna Freud said (1952): 'When the body submits, the mind retreats.'

The true aim of preparation is to prevent children being overwhelmed by anxiety, so that in the longer term they can assimilate the experience and not be damaged by it. Allowing children to express feelings of anger and sadness, and to play and talk afterwards, are the safest and most effective ways of helping them to cope. These carry no risks and are always helpful. Appropriate books and play materials can aid 'working through' the experience of hospital and the feelings about it.

When young children do go to hospital they need to have their parents to stay to explain, to support, and to comfort. If a parent is not there, someone is needed who will take on these functions, ideally a substitute mother who will stay with him around the clock. A specially assigned nurse or play person who attends to him with some consistency can help to a degree (Joyce Robertson, 1956; James Robertson, 1958b; Robertson and Robertson, 1973a).

Adults are made anxious by the thought of young children going to hospital. But in contemplating the possibility it is important that we bear the anxiety within ourselves – as parents, doctors, nurses, playgroup leaders, play specialists, – instead of passing it on to children while they are too immature to bear that anxiety.

Bibliography

Place of publication is London unless otherwise specified.

Blom-Cooper, L. and Brent Council (1985) *A Child in Trust: The Report of the Panel of Enquiry into the Circumstances Surrounding the Death of Jasmine Beckford.* Brent Council.

Bowlby, J. (1946) *Forty-four Juvenile Thieves.* Baillière, Tindall.

———— (1960) 'Grief and mourning in infancy and early childhood', *Psychoanal. Study Child* 15:9–92.

———— (1951) *Maternal Care and Mental Health.* WHO Monograph Series 2 (UK: HMSO; USA: Columbia University Press) 1953 abridged version, *Child Care and the Growth of Love.* Harmondsworth: Pelican (1958).

———— (1969) *Attachment and Loss*, vol. 1, *Attachment.* Hogarth.

———— (1973) *Attachment and Loss*, vol. 2, *Separation, Anxiety and Anger.* Hogarth.

Burlingham, D. and Freud, A. (1942) *Young Children in War-time in a Residential War Nursery.* Allen & Unwin.

———— (1944) *Infants Without Families.* Allen & Unwin.

Coleman, R.W. and Provence, S. (1957) 'Environmental retardation (hospitalism) in infants living in families', *Paediatrics* 19.

DHSS (Central Health Services Council) (1959) *The Welfare of Children in Hospital: Report of the Committee* (Platt Report). HMSO.

———— (1974) *Care and Supervision Provided in Relation to Maria Colwell: Report of the Committee of Enquiry.* HMSO.

Edelston, H. (1943) 'Anxiety in young children: study of hospital cases', *Genet. Psychol. Monogr.* 28:3–95.

—— (1953) Letter: 'Visiting children in hospital', *Lancet*, 27 February.

Freud, A. (1952) 'The role of bodily illness in the mental life of children', *Psychoanal. Study Child* 7:69–81.

—— (1960) 'Discussion of Dr John Bowlby's paper (1960)', *Psychoanal. Study Child* 15:53–62.

—— (1974) *Infants Without Families and Reports of the Hampstead Nurseries, 1939–1945*. Hogarth.

Gesell, A. (1946) *How a Baby Grows*. Hamish Hamilton Medical.

Goldstein, J., Freud, A. and Solnit, A. (1973) *Beyond the Best Interests of the Child*. New York: Free Press.

Heinicke, C. and Westheimer, I. (1965) *Brief Separations*. New York: International Universities Press.

HMSO (1980) *Fourth Report of the Health Services Commissioner (Ombudsman)*. HMSO.

Home Office Children's Department Inspectorate (1969) *John*. Special edition bulletin, July. HMSO.

James, M. (1960) 'Premature ego development: some observations upon disturbances in the first three months of life', *Int. J. Psycho-Anal.* 41:288–94.

Jolly, J. (1974) 'The ward granny scheme', *Nursing Times*, 11 April.

Kris, E. (1962) 'Decline and recovery in the life of a three-year-old: or data in psychoanalytic perspective on the mother–child relationship', *Psychoanal. Study Child* 17: 175–215.

Kris, M. (1957) 'The use of prediction in a longitudinal study', *Psychoanal. Study Child*.

Lancet (1952) 'A young child in hospital' (report of film première at Royal Society of Medicine), 2 December.

—— (1970) 'John, 17 Months', 3 July.

MacCarthy, D. (1958) 'The children's unit at Amersham General Hospital', in James Robertson, *Guide to the Film: Going to Hospital with Mother*. Robertson Centre.

Micic, Z. (1962) 'Psychological stress on children in hospital', *Int. Nursing Review* 9.

Munro-Davies, H.G. (1949) 'Visits to children in hospital', *Spectator*, 18 March.

Nursing Times (editorial) (1948) 'The patient's guests', 17 January.

—— (1952a) 'Visits to children in hospital', 15 March.

—— (1952b) 'Sick children in hospital: daily visiting by parents', 15 March.

—— (1957) (editorial) 'The mind of a young child', 15 November.

—— (1957–8) Correspondence from 29 November 1957 to 17 January 1958 arising from Joyce Robertson (1956) 'A mother's observations on the tonsillectomy of her four-year-old daughter. With comments by Anna Freud', *Psychoanal. Study Child* 11:1295–300 reprinted in *Nursing Times*, 15 November 1957.

Parry, L.A. (1947) 'The urgent need for reforms in hospitals', *Lancet*, 13 December.

Prugh, D. *et al.* (1953) 'Study of emotional reactions of children and families to hospitalization and illness', *Amer. J. Orthopsychiat.* 23.

Robertson, James (1953a) 'Some responses of young children to loss of maternal care', *Nursing Times* 18 April, 382–6.

—— (1953b) *Film: A Two-year-old Goes to Hospital*. 16 mm, 40-minute and 30-minute versions, in English and French. Concord Video and Film Council. New York University Film Library.

—— (1958a) *Film: Going to Hospital with Mother*. 16 mm, 40 minutes, in English and French. Concord Video and Film Council.

—— (1958b) *Young Children in Hospital*. Tavistock.

—— (1960) 'The plight of small children in hospitals', *Parents Magazine*, June.

—— (1961) 'Children in hospital', *Observer*, 15, 22 and 29 January, 12 February.

—— (1962) *Hospitals and Children: A Parent's-eye View*. Gollancz.

—— (1971) *Young Children in Hospital*. 2nd revised edition with postscript, 1970. Tavistock.

Robertson, Joyce (1956) 'A mother's observations on the tonsillectomy of her four-year-old daughter. With comments by Anna Freud', *Psychoanal. Study Child* 11, reprinted in *Nursing Times*, 15 November 1957.

—— (1962) 'Mothering as an influence on early development', *Psychoanal. Study Child* 17:245–64. This vol., pp. 152–169.

—— (1965) 'Mother–infant interaction from birth to twelve months: two case studies', in B.M. Foss (ed.) *Determinants of Infant Behaviour*, vol. 3. Methuen. This vol., pp. 184–196.

—— (1980) 'A delayed infant adoption', *Adoption and Fostering* 101:9–11. See this vol., pp. 214–19.

—— (1983) *The Fallacy of 'Preparing' Young Healthy Children for Possible Hospitalisation. Paediatric Projects Incorporated*. Monograph No. 1. This vol., pp. 225–232.

Robertson, James and Robertson, Joyce (1967) *Film: Kate, Aged Two Years Five Months, in Foster Care for Twenty-seven Days*. 16 mm, 33 minutes, in English, French and Danish. Young Children in Brief Separation Film Series. Concord Video and Film Council. New York University Film Library.

—— (1968) *Film: Jane, Aged Seventeen Months, in Foster Care for Ten Days*. 16 mm, 39 minutes, in English, Danish, French, German and Swedish. Young Children in Brief Separation Film Series. Concord Video and Film Council. New York University Film Library.

—— (1969) *Film: John, Aged Seventeen Months, For Nine Days in a Residential Nursery*. 16 mm, 43 minutes, in English, Danish, French, German and Swedish. Young Children in Brief Separation Film Series. Concord Video and Film Council. New York University Film Library.

—— (1970) 'The problem of professional anxiety. Unpublished. This vol., pp. 1–4.

—— (1971) *Film: Thomas, Aged Two Years Four Months, in Foster Care for Ten Days*. 16 mm, 38 minutes, in English. Young Children in Brief Separation Film Series. Concord Video and Film Council. New York University Film Library.

—— (1973a) *Film: Lucy, Aged Twenty-one Months, in Foster Care for Nineteen Days*. 16 mm, 31 minutes, in English and French. Young Children in Brief Separation Film Series. Concord Video and Film Council. New York University Film Library.

—— (1973b) 'Substitute mothering for the unaccompanied child', *Nursing Times*, 29 November.

—— (1977) 'The psychological parent', *Adoption and Fostering* 87. See this vol., pp. 210–213.

—— (1982) *A Baby in the Family*. Harmondsworth: Penguin.

Sander, L.W. (1962) 'Issues in early mother–child interaction', *J. Child Psychiat*. 1.

Schaffer, R. and Callender, W. (1959) 'Psychological effects of hospitalisation in infancy', *Paediatrics* 24:528–39.

Spitz, R. (1945) 'Hospitalism', *Psychoanal. Study Child* 1:53–74.

Spitz, R. and Wolff, K.M. (1946) 'Anaclitic depression', *Psychoanal. Study Child* 2:313–42.

Thornes, R. (1983) 'Parental access and family facilities in children's wards in England', *B.M.J.*, 16 July.

—— (1988) 'Parents staying overnight with their children in hospital', Caring for Children in the Health Services Committee, NAWCH, RCN, BPA, NAHA.

Vaughan, G.F. (1957) 'Children in hospital', *Lancet*, June.

Winnicott, D.W. (1960) 'The theory of the parent–infant relationship', *Int. J. Psycho-Anal.* 41.

Yarrow, L. (1961) 'Maternal deprivation: towards an empirical and conceptual re-evaluation', *Psychol. Bull.* 58:459–90.

Index

This first edition of
Separation and the Very Young
was finished in August 1989.

It was typeset in $10\frac{1}{2}/13$ Erhardt
on a Linotron 202
and printed on a Miller TP41,
on 80g/m^2 vol. 18 Publishers Antique Wove.

The book was commissioned by Ann Scott,
edited by Ann Scott and Selina O'Grady,
copy-edited by Antonia Owen,
indexed by Jill Ford,
designed by Martin Klopstock
and produced by Simona Sideri
and Martin Klopstock for
Free Association Books.